For the Love of Golf

To Becky

For the Love of Golf

The Best of Dobereiner

Peter Dobereiner

Stanley Paul
London Melbourne Sydney Auckland Johannesburg

Stanley Paul & Co. Ltd

An imprint of the Hutchinson Publishing Group

17–21 Conway Street, London W1P 5HL

Hutchinson Group (Australia) Pty Ltd
30–32 Cremorne Street, Richmond South, Victoria 3121
PO Box 151, Broadway, New South Wales 2007

Hutchinson Group (NZ) Ltd
32–34 View Road PO Box 40-086, Glenfield, Auckland 10

Hutchinson Group (SA) Pty Ltd
PO Box 337, Bergvlei 2012, South Africa

First published 1981
Reprinted 1981
© Peter Dobereiner 1981

Set in VIP Century Schoolbook by
Computape (Pickering) Ltd

Printed in Great Britain by The Anchor Press Ltd
and bound by Wm Brendon & Son Ltd,
both of Tiptree, Essex

British Library Cataloguing in Publication Data

Dobereiner, Peter
    For the Love of Golf: Dobereiner, Peter
    1. Golf
    I. Title
    796.352′092′4   GV965

ISBN 0 09 145150 7

Contents

Foreword

We journalists like to think of ourselves as a raffish, Bohemian lot. We stand back from life, cynically observing the follies and foibles and ferocities of the world and then trying as objectively as we can to write about them in our newspapers. We cannot become involved in life because involvement must mean partiality. If the world brands us as outsiders, we take it as a compliment because that is what we are supposed to be. 'So you're from the *Daily Express*.' The words sound like an accusation. 'Yes, but please don't tell my mother. She thinks I play piano in a brothel.' The ultimate state for a journalist is to become dehumanized. 'Excuse me, Minister, but the press would like a word with you.' That's me, the press, tough and hard as a Heidelberg flat-bed.

Even so, I was touched and flattered to be asked to prepare an anthology of my best work. This meant recognition and respectability. After all, nobody uses a book to wrap up fish and chips, or light a fire, or stuff into the toes of wet golf shoes. There is a permanence about hard covers, a kind of immortality, which is most appealing in comparison with the ephemeral nature of newspapers.

The warm glow of satisfaction lasted right up to the minute I sat down and actually started assembling my material. Then, as I blew the dust from the files and began to read, my mood switched to despair, and finally to panic. Since I began writing professionally about golf in 1965 I have produced between two and three million words on the subject. Surely from such a monstrous slagheap of newspaper and magazine cuttings there must be enough nuggets worthy of salvage for a slim volume?

No. The critical habits I had developed over years of editing other people's work now turned against me. Every piece I picked up I rejected, as too dated, or too boring, or too ignorant, or too opinionated, or too badly written, or a combination of several defects. No man should ever be asked to compile his own anthology because it is like cataloguing your own weaknesses. Not a week goes by without my learning something new about golf. That means, of course, that I was ignorant of eight things about golf two months ago. Extend that process back nearly twenty years and the result is an impressive accumulation of ignorance. And ill-informed opinion.

Writing about golf is like golf itself, in that one is sustained by the dream that next time it will all come right. However, I make no apology for this selection. In the end, as the deadline bore down like an express train, I burst my bonds of despair and leaped from the track in the nick of time. I reappraised my criteria. Dated? Nonsense! Valuable insight into the attitudes of the day. Boring? They wouldn't have published it in the first place if it had been all that boring. Ignorant? By definition, ignorance is bliss. Opinionated? Excellent – people love taking issue with your ideas, as your daily postbag testifies. Badly written? Fie for such modesty; writing is simply communication and you get the message across most of the time. Victor Hugo had the right idea when he said that good writing was not the product of shutting oneself away in a remote cottage, free from interruption and accessible only to the promptings of the muse; it sprang from the hammering on the door by the baker wanting to get his bill paid.

So this much I can guarantee. The offerings in this book were all produced under the same literary stimulus which gave the world *Les Misérables*.

Peter Dobereiner

The illustrations of The Seven Ages of Golf were commissioned by the Fine Art Society in 1899 from my grandfather, John Hassall, and they were issued as a limited edition of colour prints. The golf backgrounds are from Royal St George's, Sandwich, where the family spent many summers.

Part One
What's It All About?
Diversions down some golfing byways

How It All Began

It would be pitching it a bit strong to say I lie awake at night pondering the origins of golf. I have better things to ponder during bouts of insomnia, but the subject is intriguing enough. Scholars have probed long and deep to discover how and where golf began. No one with any feeling for the game's past can examine the historical evidence without wondering where the credit for inventing golf rightly belongs.

There have been two main schools of thought on the subject. Some (mainly Scottish) historians maintain stoutly that golf was invented by the Scots. Other (mainly Dutch) historians claim with equal vigour that golf was invented in the Low Countries. The evidence is not conclusive either way.

It is quite certain, as we know from local authority records and paintings, that a golf-like game was played in Holland long before the first official record of golf in Scotland. The Dutch game of *Spel metten colve* (game played with a club) was well established in the thirteenth century, and over the years it developed into separate forms and the name evolved through *colf* to *kolf*. One version was miniaturized and played in a courtyard, or on ice, but mainstream *kolf* was a cross-country game, played in a series of separate 'holes' with implements remarkably similar to early golf clubs and with wooden balls of about two inches in diameter. The ball was even teed up on a small cone of sand exactly as we venerable codgers did in our youth.

All that evidence was purely circumstantial, or totally irrelevant, according to the Scottish school. After all, club and ball cross-country games of one kind or another had been played since Roman times. The point was that all the early Flemish paintings depicting *kolf* showed the participants playing to targets such as church doors, and golf's greatest distinction was that it involved a secondary game, the totally original concept of putting-out into a hole in the ground.

The argument thus revolved around the question: 'What is golf?' If it is accepted that the holing-out process makes golf unique, setting it apart from the Continental versions, then it is possible that a Scot invented this all-important refinement. There is not a shred of evidence to this effect, but at least it leaves the question open.

Mr S. J. H. Van Hengel, who is the foremost authority on the origins of *kolf*, has made some important discoveries. He managed to date an early beechwood ball, which was discovered driven deep into the earth under the pile of a dockside building, by delving into the records of the building.

The excavations for the new Amsterdam underground railway system turned up remnants of club heads which are similar to early golf clubs.

But the most significant discovery, in the context of the golf argument, was that *kolf* was eventually formalized to the extent of playing to a pole. Doors and the like had proved to be too easy as targets so the pole was introduced. These poles in their turn went through a process of evolution, becoming beautifully carved and ornamented artifacts. Indeed, they were so attractive that people started to steal them.

Now, what happens if a thief in the night walks off with a pole which has been stuck in the ground? Exactly, my dear Watson – a neat round hole is left on the exact spot where *kolf* players are accustomed to competing each phase of their cross-country club and ball game.

What would you do in those circumstances?

'My goodness, Hans, the pole is not there. How shall we finish?'

'There's nothing for it, Jan, old boy, but for us to knock our rollers into the hole.'

Thus, surely, was born the putt. And with it, golf. The evidence is presumptive but overwhelming. Here we have the missing link in the chain. It explains why later paintings of the Flemish school show *kolf* being played to a hole. (The idea that golf was re-exported from Scotland was never very convincing.)

Once we take the plunge and discard the Scottish theory – and it is an emotional wrench to abandon those fanciful ideas of shepherds putting acorns into rabbit holes on the linksland of Fife – then everything else falls into place.

Quite apart from Scottish military expeditions to the Continent, there was a flourishing trade link between Edinburgh and St Andrews and the Low Countries. It would be natural for the crews to pick up the game and bring it back to their homeland.

We already know that wooden balls were exported from Holland to Scotland, and that the Dutch switched to the sajet ball (uncombed wool stuffed into a leather cover) before the Scots began making their featheries.

St Andrews has had tremendous mileage out of calling itself the home of golf, but I suspect strongly that the noble city is an imposter. If I am right, the real home of golf is more likely to have been the village where a challenge match was played in the year 1296 and repeated annually for the next 430 years. That was the game which evolved into golf.

Move over, St Andrews – you are usurping the historic birthright of the village of Loenen on the Vecht.

Golf World, November 1975.

Out of the Barrel

It was an old driver, although well preserved and with a good pedigree. Like most golfers I am addicted to browsing in pro shops and, in particular, in the barrel of second-hand clubs which is, or ought to be, the most important display in the room.

After all, the novice's introduction to golf starts at the barrel, so the browser of today is likely to be tomorrow's customer for an expensive quiverful of shiny, matched clubs. Apart from being more fun, it is immensely valuable to start golf with an assortment of odd clubs because the learner gets to know which types of club and grip and shaft suit him, and by the time he is ready to splurge on a matched set he has the benefit of some experience.

I suspect that most people choose sets for the wrong reasons, seduced by appearances or by the selling power of the famous professional names on the back of the heads. But at least the novice who has started with a good mixture of old clubs will have some rational basis for making his selection. Anyway, I pulled this driver out of the barrel and waggled it the way pros do, making sure for this exercise, at least, that I was using the approved Vardon grip. You never know who is looking. Besides, there is always the slim chance of being mistaken for a pro and getting a discount.

The feedback which I received from my busily waggling hands was favourable, almost to the point of a guarantee that with this weapon I could carry the cross-bunker which stands as a mocking reminder of advancing years. Of course, it would be inconvenient to lug the thing around with me and then travel back to Britain with it, but surely the eventual triumph would make it worthwhile.

The proposition seemed on a par with traipsing off to Switzerland for a monkey-gland transplant, a minor inconvenience when set against the benefits. Besides, even if the thing did not work for me – the driver, not the monkey gland – I would not be seriously out of pocket with a second-hand club. A fiver maybe? I looked at the tag tied to the shaft: $135. Yes, one hundred and thirty-five dollars, or sixty-seven pounds fifty in what we in Britain used to call real money.

That experience set me off on a journey of exploration, in order to discover the minimum outlay possible for the beginner to equip himself for golf in America. That driver had been misleading, for although it was old it was aged in the sense that a 'black label' Bentley is old, and by no means typical of the market for second-hand equipment. I was not out for collectors' items but simply intent on picking up serviceable clubs – and these turned out to be surprisingly cheap.

American pros take old sets as trade-ins against new models, and these second-hand clubs mostly accumulate in storerooms, unwanted and unsold. Even so, the prices I was quoted were not irresistible, although doubtless I could have haggled them down a bit. Instead, I took myself off to the source of all bargains, to the temple of economical living, the local thrift store. To say that these emporia are like Oxfam shops is an injustice comparable to describing the Sahara desert as a pot bunker.

Imagine a warehouse crammed with a thousand jumble sales and you are nearer the mark. They are Aladdin's caves of mankind's unwanted, worn out, broken, obsolete trappings and they operate on the premise that one person's rubbish is another person's bargain. Usually this other person is on or below the poverty line, which is the posture I had adopted for this exercise.

Resolutely walking past an antique typewriter at £18 which I am sure the Science Museum would rank as an important historical relic, I immersed myself in a dusty heap of paraphernalia. First I sorted out a bag whose zip-fastener ran smoothly and wasn't torn or obviously disintegrating. That cost 50p and one pocket contained half a dozen golf balls which, while not exactly pristine, were good enough to cause me to hesitate to play one of them at a hole with a demanding water carry. Another 50p secured a 4-iron which I judge to be almost a virgin. The 8-iron, for another 50p, has seen service, although not enough to make it an object of scorn should I produce it at my home club. I'm not sure that I can say the same for a venerable 7-iron, but that cost only 25p.

Anyway, for the total outlay of £6 I equipped myself with a serviceable assortment of clubs, balls and bag. It would cost almost that much to hire a set for a day, more if you had to buy balls.

And so to golf. The two courses at Torrey Pines, La Jolla, are superb by municipal or any other standards and, but for a tournament, I could have played for a green fee of £2.50. A monthly ticket for an enthusiast would bring this cost down to 50p a round, with no nonsense about obligatory electric carts.

What's It All About?

So, all in all, while many people are concerned, and rightly, about the horrendous cost of golf in America, which is threatening to limit the game at the country-club level to a wealthy minority, at the other end of the social scale it is possible to enjoy golf, and good golf at that, at rates which would not bring a wince to the face even of an Aberdonian. The only trick is to live in an area, such as San Diego, where the local authority has an enlightened golf policy.

Observer, January 1979

Make Friends at Leisure ⚑

When life gets me down I am sustained by the warmth, kindness and essential goodness of my fellow man. Human nature is an unfailing source of inspiration. The other day, for example, a gentleman stopped me in the street and said, 'Pardon me, stranger, but I observe that you have a pimple on your nose which must be a considerable embarrassment and discomfort to you. This is indeed a fortunate meeting for I am able to help you and shall be privileged to do so.'

With that he let me have his very last bottle of snake oil for a giveaway $5, assuring me that it would also transform my sex life, eliminate my inferiority complex and do wonders for my bad breath. This transaction by no means exhausted his generosity. When we parted five minutes later with an effusive handshake, I had in my pocket the deed to the Brooklyn Bridge, which this philanthropist had practically given to me for a mere $50.

On arrival at my destination, inevitably a golf club, I walked into the professionals' shop and my eye was caught by an attractive set of new clubs. In an instant an enthusiastic young assistant was at my side.

'Aren't they beauties?'

They truly were, as I conceded. Shiny, immaculate and exuding an aura which suggested that with these weapons it would be downright difficult to play a bad shot. I said as much.

'You'd better believe it,' said the young man. 'Just look at this. These clubs are precision instruments.' He held up a club by the top of the grip between finger and thumb, with a plumb bob clamped under that selfsame thumb. 'Observe how the string falls exactly across the centre of the widest sweet spot in the business. And how about this?'

He put the club on a swingweight machine. 'Every one is exactly matched, D-1 swingweight, perfect for a fine figure of a man such as yourself. And just look at these new shafts, Supa-Dynamite-Flex, which accumulate kinetic energy and release a mule kick in the impact zone to give you an extra fifty yards every time – guaranteed.'

By now he was in full flood. 'Low profile, heel-toe balanced, contoured sole. These clubs represent a breakthrough in the latest scientific principles, the biggest advance in golf equipment since the invention of the rubber-wound ball. No wonder the pros are shooting the lights out these days with clubs of such ultimate perfection. Makes you feel sorry for the old-timers thirty-five years ago, hacking around with their primitive implements.'

The one thing you could never call me is gullible. I delivered a short lecture expounding on the theme that thirty-five years ago Byron Nelson wielded his primitive implements with greater effect than any man in history; that consummate shotmakers, such as Harry Vardon and Bobby Jones, played with clubs that were matched in neither length nor swingweight which, being a static measure, was a useless criterion for a moving object.

Further, the expression 'sweet spot', in so far as it referred to the centre of gravity, was a point so small that it could not be measured.

The young assistant was by now selling a shirt to a portly customer but he called across the shop: 'In that case, wise guy, why do all the pros play with precision-matched sets?'

Well, I have observed, as you may so observe for yourself, that very few tournament professionals do use matched sets. Look in the typical pro bag. You might well find a George Bayer driver, a Toney Penna 3-wood, a Ping 1-iron, a Wilson pitching wedge, a Hogan sand-iron, and a Ray Cook putter. The irons mainly belong to the same family . . . but what is this? Most of them have lead tape stuck on the back of the heads, casting serious doubts on the efficacy of swingweighting.

The fact is that most tournament stars tend to collect their clubs in much the same way as the players of the hickory era, searching for years to find individual clubs that look and feel just right. At this point I must add, since the advertising director is holding a Colt .45 to my temple, that if you are happy with factory-matched sets then stick with them. Buy more matched sets. Change your clubs frequently and support the industry. Preserve your faith in swingweighting and revel in the advantages of a sweet spot two inches wide.

However, may I make a suggestion to add interest to your golfing experience? Almost every professional's shop has a back room stacked with second-hand clubs, traded in against glittering new sets, and they can be bought for peanuts. Browse among them. Waggle them. Forget about collecting clubs with the same name on the back. Every once in a while you will pick up a club that feels exactly right. You will know at once that with this club, in spite of that rust mark on the hosel, you can play like a giant. It may take years but eventually you will acquire a full complement of true and faithful friends, each one with a personality to match your own.

After all, you do not go to a party and come away with a matched set of fourteen new friends. Find your clubs the same way, through happy encounters in the least expected places and circumstances. Trust your instincts and feelings.

My own clubs are now as much a part of me as my fingers, and this indissoluble union is all a result of my not being gullible. With that thought I must leave you because I have to attend to my friends. I keep their grips tacky by giving them a light smear of snake oil.

Golf Digest, December 1979

Let's Play with Ten Clubs

What is so special about the number fourteen anyway? In demonology the number seven was significant for its evil properties and fourteen, presumably, would be doubly so. It is certainly a hellish number in golf, either as the score for one hole or as the number of clubs in the bag. But why fourteen?

The number fourteen was chosen arbitrarily when the rule-makers decided to stop the absurd proliferation of clubs that the professionals were carrying. Correction: the clubs that their poor, groaning caddies were required to carry. Walter Hagen had as many as twenty-eight in his bag, and that was by no means the record. Hagen, who was paid by various clubmakers to display their wares, insisted that each club was vital for the proper playing of the game. 'Baloney,' said the rulers of golf, and in 1938 they set the limit at fourteen.

That limitation has now been in operation long enough for us to attempt a judgement on whether it has been a success. In my opinion fourteen clubs have proved to be excessive. The limit was too generous, and it has significantly failed to accomplish its purpose. One of the most important reforms the custodians of golf's essential spirit could introduce would be to lower the limit to ten clubs.

By permitting fourteen clubs the lawmakers have removed from golf one of its greatest challenges and, it follows, one of its major joys. In normal conditions a golfer armed with a quiver of fourteen specialist clubs is required to hit only one basic shot. He knows the distance and therefore the appropriate club. His only problem is to reproduce the standard stroke that he has perfected by endless repetition on the practice ground. That is modern professional golf, and it is one good reason why people are switching off their television sets by the millions.

Now, suppose the golfer did not have the appropriate club in his bag. Suppose the standard shot, using the limited equipment in his armoury, would either put him through the back of the green or leave him fifteen yards short. What would he do? Well, he would either starve or he would be forced to play the game like Harry Vardon or

Bobby Jones or Tommy Bolt or Christy O'Connor or Bobby Locke. In short, he would have to think about the shot (an element that has virtually disappeared from pro golf) and then he would have to contrive a stroke suitable for the distance and conditions.

Note well that I am not suggesting for a moment that the modern professionals are incapable of playing like this. Many of them can, and they do so from time to time when the wind blows or the ground is hard. I would just like to see them all doing it all the time, because I believe that golf is a game for artists rather than for artisans.

Of course, you and I would equally be limited to ten clubs and just think what that would mean. Many of the evils that have been spawned by the fourteen-club limit would be eliminated or reduced. There would be no need for mechanical golf carts and buggies (except for the old and infirm) because we could conveniently carry our clubs – in light bags instead of those gigantic hernia-busters. The cost of golf would be cut. Thousands of people could take up the game who are at present deterred by the expense. Play would be faster and, I insist, more enjoyable.

Aha, you say, baring your fangs and striking for my jugular, fourteen clubs is a maximum, not a minimum. There is nothing to stop anyone from using ten clubs, or fewer, and thereby bringing about this Utopia of brisk, bracing, brilliant golf. In theory that is a valid thrust, but, human nature being what it is, it would be impractical to seek a voluntary revolution along these lines.

So long as fourteen clubs are permitted, then golfers will feel that they are putting themselves at a disadvantage by carrying fewer. Results from limited-club competitions disprove the case, but that nagging doubt persists: 'Perhaps if I had been able to use fourteen clubs I could have scored even better.' No, the full force of golf legislation is needed to introduce this important reform.

Why ten? Why not nine or eleven? Well, the precise figure is negotiable. I happen to believe that ten should be the upper limit, if the full benefits of the change are to be enjoyed. To go much lower – down to seven, for instance – would be too fundamental a change and I suspect that such a limit would adversely affect the ability of the great players to reproduce their present standards of scoring.

Ten looks about right. A typical bag thus could contain a driver, fairway wood, putter, sand iron, wedge and five irons roughly equivalent to 1-3-5-7-9. Obviously some people would prefer to carry three wooden clubs and discard the 1-iron. The bag would also contain a full quota of dilemmas – whether to float a 5-iron into that short hole or hood the 7-iron and hit a forcing draw.

What's It All About?

An intriguing question is whether the great players of today would retain their lofty status under a ten club limit or whether new stars would arise. Nobody knows, but I for one would dearly love to watch all the reputations go into the melting pot and see who comes to the top.

Golf Digest, October 1979

Drive It 553 Yards

On my home course we have a killer hole, about 460 yards and sharply doglegged to the right around a stand of noble beech trees. The other day I was going through my regular routine in preparation to tackle the monster. This involves sucking in six deep breaths to load the system with oxygen, plus a mental wind-up based on yoga, self-hypnosis and a Zen exercise designed to persuade me that, sure, I can hit a power fade twenty yards around the corner. Just as I was about to unleash my double-hernia swing, a companion remarked, 'Remember how you always used to whip one straight over those trees with your 4-wood?'

It was a cruel reminder of advancing years. My game plan – to follow the drive with a blue-flamer fairway wood, then a middle iron and hope to chip in for my par – was shattered. That evening I slumped into a chair, tucked a vitamin pill under my tongue and sought solace from back numbers of American golf magazines from around the world. Since I had already read the articles, I concentrated on the advertisements and gradually my spirits revived. Gad, what a fool I had been. Here, under my very nose, lay the answer to declining physical powers.

A pair of socks with a miracle sole, guaranteed to add 10 yards to my drive. Shoes promising another 10 yards, thanks to a similar miracle of technology and long-lasting tungsten spikes to boot. What's a few measly bucks? I'd give my entire fortune, which consists of a few measly bucks incidentally, for an extra 20 yards.

That dream proved to be mere chicken feed. Now came the real stuff. A fancy grip promised to release the tremendous power in my legs, and drive the ball 300 yards or more. And only $6.95. Next comes a driver with an aerodynamic design to give me an extra 10 yards. If I get one of those and fit it with a graphite shaft (guaranteed 10 per cent more distance) and my new grip, that is 300 yards plus 10 plus 10 per cent. Wow, 341 yards!

For a mere $1.75 I can get a repair manual which will show me how to assemble this wonder club. Add my extra 20 yards for shoes and socks and I'm up to 361 yards. That is before I've even pulled on a

27

glove. What latent power lies in gloves! I never dreamed that a glove could make me hit a ball 10 yards farther – but here they are, complete with guarantee. Now, 371 yards!

Frankly, I'm not overimpressed by the promises of swing trainers, practice nets, standing on a mat marked with Sam Snead's footprints, muscle-builders and fast improvement plans, 'guaranteed to take fifteen strokes off your scores'.

The same goes for range-finders which will save me five strokes a round, or a book of putting hints which will produce instant rhythm, tempo and overspin for $18.95 and save me another seven to fifteen strokes a round. Right now I'm into power and I do not particularly want to take advantage of the promised forty strokes which I could save every round by using all these aids, some of them not legal. I would make Jack Nicklaus look a fool, and I have no wish to do that. I just want to outdrive him.

Here is a device which looks like an ankle shackle from the chain-gang days. It will stop my swaying and enable me to hit the ball farther, harder and straighter, a bargain at $14.95, even if the extra distance is not actually specified. And what of this loaded wrist strap whose 'miracle motion of weights develops real clubhead speed'? I'll take a chance and accept the offer to rush me one for only $4.95, although I'm worried about using it in conjunction with my wonder glove. Perhaps I could wear it on my other ankle to help release that tremendous power in my legs.

Between the two of them I should get an extra 10 yards at least. So far, all my calculations have been based on a regular golf ball and that has clearly been a mistake, for here we have an announcement headed: 'Golf hustler's secret revealed.' It goes on to make the confident assertion: 'Here's what it *must* mean to you – 30 yards on every drive.' Another brand also claims to outdistance all other balls by 30 yards, but adds, rather shamefacedly, that it is ever-so-slightly illegal. I'll have none of that malarkey, but stick with my original choice at three for $5.

My guaranteed drive is now approaching a satisfactory 411 yards but there is more to come, for a ball-heater ('Plugs into any standard electric outlet') promises me a 20 per cent increase in distance, boosting me to 493 yards.

I am disappointed in the golfer's belt, which makes no promises about extra distance but merely offers the assurance of keeping my stomach ventilated during wear. However, the marvels of science have not yet exhausted their beneficence, and one of the major sources of extra length is to be found in the unlikely shape of the tee peg. At a paltry $2 for eighteen, the Slant Tee's bellcrank action propels the ball and promises me 10 per cent more distance, giving me a guaranteed total of 542 yards.

But wait. The MighTee FlighTee not only will save me 75 cents but ensure me an extra 60 yards. And it is endorsed by Bob Toski, no less, giving me a grand total of 553 yards, every inch of it guaranteed by the advertisers. I must go with the MighTee FlighTee, especially as a later announcement adds: 'Redesigned to conform with USGA regulations.'

You may imagine you have detected a flaw in my dream. Armed with the full cornucopia of mail-order goodies, I will drive too far, flying every green – sometimes by 200 yards or more. I have thought of that and shall adjust my equipment on every tee, sometimes using a cold ball or discarding my ankle shackle, so that I reduce my potential to suit the length of the hole. But there is one gadget I will use faithfully on every tee. If I understand the illustration and description properly, it resembles a small handgun into which you load your tee peg. You then hold it against the surface of the ground and press a button which releases a pneumatic hammer to drive your peg into the earth. What a labour-saving device. The good ideas are always the simple ones.

Golf Digest, March 1979

Back to Basics, Please

In the American idiom, America is 'something else'. During the course of a turbulent love affair with the country over the last half-century I have often had cause to wish that America really was something else.

At the moment I have the tight-lipped moodies with America over its crazy adherence to the democratic principle. Public opinion is all very well in reasonable doses, but here it carries the force of an autocratic monster. Once America makes up its mind that something is best, then that favoured something gets star treatment and its rivals are eliminated.

Take the lettuce. American public opinion decided that the lettuce must have the quality of crispness. Pretty soon there was only one variety of lettuce available. It happens to be colourless, tasteless and, for all I know, devoid of nutrition, but it is the 'in' lettuce and all the other lettuces are out.

This frightening and arbitrary process is the stimulus for the advertising industry which goes to absurd lengths to enslave public opinion. A current example is a TV campaign in which an attractive girl appears wearing a nylon dress which clings alluringly to her contours. She then squirts an aerosol spray at her thighs and the material collapses in dull, straight folds. 'Eliminate static cling,' she squeals in delight. In Britain, I like to believe, such an exhibition would immediately prompt the formation of a Society to Preserve Static Cling, but in America the thing could easily snowball and turn static cling into a social disaster, like dandruff.

This awesome power of public taste has not left golf untouched, alas. Palm Springs, in the Californian desert, would, by normal demographic standards, support three golf courses. In reality it has thirty-eight, a fact which causes the civic publicists to boast that this is the golf capital of America or, alternatively, the winter golf capital of the world.

I do not complain of golfing overkill, but I do regret that public opinion has decreed a certain uniformity of style for each of these thirty-eight courses. As with the lettuce, so the American public has fixed an ideal for golf. Above all, the course must be lush and green, even if nature must sometimes be helped with a spray of latex grass paint. The course must be manicured, with blue lakes and dazzling white sand in the bunkers.

Now if there are two natural features which are totally alien to a desert, they are green grass and lakes. The only concessions to the desert environment are the trees, mainly date palm and tamarisk. For the rest, the golf courses ring false, and to a Kentish mud-dweller it is a sad disappointment to escape into a desert only to find thirty-eight counterfeit Royal Mid-Surreys.

The other major example of how public opinion has harmed golf – and this applies right across the continent – is the commonly accepted notion that it is infra dig to walk around a course. This is the one aspect of professional golf which the American club member refuses to copy, despite constant exposure to tournament golf on TV.

The idea has gained the force of holy writ that the best way to play golf is to ride on an electric cart, and many courses do not allow pedestrian golf. Of course, it is good for business and golf these days is important business. Too important, some might think.

There is a danger of American golf becoming the preserve of the rich. Which would be the greatest of pities because it is so unnecessary – or would be if it were not for this accursed parody of the democratic principle, which first decrees what is 'best' and then insists that only the best is good enough.

Far be it from me to argue with *vox populi*. If America says that dart-board courses are best, and that sedentary golf is best, then so be it. I just wish that, by those terms, there would emerge in America a powerful apostle of the second rate. The country needs a champion of mediocrity to promote the cause of cheap golf. Cheap and nasty, if you like, but golf played by people hiking briskly around unkempt, unlush, ungreen courses with a few clubs rattling around in a shoulder bag and getting round in two and a half hours.

Without a solid base of coarse, basic golf the game is surely doomed to evolve into a kind of electro-mechanical polo as a diversion to speed overweight millionaires to their graves. The game and America deserve better than that.

Observer, January 1979

Start the Day Right

The common generalization that the standard of professional golf is higher in America than anywhere in the world is only partially true, at best. Over the past season there have been plenty of occasions where the finest golf on any one day, or even over one entire tournament, was played in Europe, or Japan, or Australia, by one of us foreigners. That is a simple matter of record.

Even so, I accept the basic premise that the best golf is mostly American and I am often called upon in my travels to explain, in print or in conversation, why this should be so. Well, it is a matter of statistical fact that there are more good players operating on the American circuit. In addition, America is the most highly competitive society in the world and so its golfers tend to be more dedicated, more industrious and better competitors. However, over the years I have become convinced that there is another overwhelming factor to explain American golf supremacy – and that is the American breakfast.

Breakfast is the key to human behaviour. Breakfast programs the day. And, as the computer men say: garbage in, garbage out. Show me a man who, by choice or by unfortunate circumstance, starts the day on a piece of dry toast and a cup of coffee and I will show you a man whose judgement is not to be trusted.

The American breakfast is the nation's finest expression of civilized living. For myself, I have never proved equal to the challenge of a pile of hotcakes garnished with butter, bacon, sausages and maple syrup, but there is such a rich variety of choice that every man's taste can be satisfied at any drugstore counter.

It does not matter to me that scientists can prove that there is less nourishment in breakfast cereals than in the box which contains them. Nor am I unduly put out by medical claims that coffee disturbs the sense of balance and should never be drunk before golf. One of the certainties in this life is that, whenever an expert makes such a statement, another equally eminent scientist will proclaim that his colleague is talking through his hat.

My only regret is that the scrambling of eggs is a lost art in America.

For the rest, the American breakfast has my unstinted approval and admiration. And the important point, so far as golf is concerned, is that the players can enjoy the breakfast of their choice every day of the year, wherever they happen to be.

That, regrettably, is not the case on the European circuit. Europe has half a dozen different breakfast traditions. Take the French, who commonly start the day with a tiny cup of viscous fluid which resembles the drainings from your car sump on its 20,000-mile service. They call it coffee, and it is so vile that it has to be chased down with a glass of neat cognac and a piece of bread. When an entire nation subjects its system to a shock like that every morning it is hardly surprising that it produces tiresome people like Napoleon, or that Van Gogh should have become sufficiently enraged to cut off his own ear. The French have bred only one great professional golfer, Arnaud Massy, and he was a Basque. He probably ate a Spanish policeman, raw, for breakfast every morning.

The Portuguese rise to bread and jam, the Germans to spicy cold sausage, the Italians to cheese, and the Dutch to an obligatory hard-boiled egg. The world regards the Dutch as being stolid, serious and inflexible people. Could it be that they are victims of their hard-boiled egg diet and in reality are permanently constipated?

Anyway, just imagine the devastating effect of such diverse breakfasts on the golfing tourists as they move from one country to another every week. Take the Australians, who form a significant part of the European circuit. They have been brought up on a breakfast regimen of steak and beer, and having to play golf on a croissant smeared with raspberry jam is often just too much for them. Or too little.

The South Africans and the South Americans suffer terrible torments over the inadequacies of the Continental breakfast. However, the most plaintive cries in hotel breakfast rooms from Sardinia to Stockholm come from the British, for whom bacon and eggs are a sacred tradition.

The surest bet in the history of golf was a French Open some years ago when Peter Oosterhuis was invited to stay at the residence of the British Ambassador in Paris. That was probably the only place in France where a proper English breakfast was available in the grand style, with silver dishes of devilled kidneys and kippers, in addition to bacon and eggs, to supplement the fresh toast and Cooper's chunky Oxford marmalade. Peter was surely awakened, furthermore, in the only manner fit for a civilized man, which is to say with a light feminine touch on the shoulder and the announcement that a steaming cup of tea is waiting on the bedside table. Oosterhuis won that championship by a mile.

In time, my pioneering efforts to educate Continental Europe to the beneficial habits of early morning tea and cooked breakfasts may bear fruit – with a dramatic rise in golfing standards as a result.

For the moment, though, the American breakfast, which put the first man on the moon, will surely keep American golf in the highest orbit. But do not be complacent, America. Already Europe has produced a golfer in Severiano Ballesteros who can operate efficiently on a bread roll and a cup of coffee. We may yet find one who can rip off birdies on garlic sausage. And if porridge were to catch on in Europe, a Scotsman might even emerge as a fearsome competitor.

Golf Digest, December 1978

Days of Liberation

Let us examine the proposition, at least for the sake of argument, that women golfers are people. It requires an effort to adjust to this idea, for ever since the beheading of the first woman golfer, Mary Queen of Scots, the golf world has openly regretted that the practice didn't start a trend.

Today the conservative element in the game successfully maintains the pretence that women do not exist, and the advanced thinkers regard them as a subspecies to be barely tolerated as long as they keep their place.

But suppose for a moment that all this was to change. Imagine, say, a blitzkrieg in the sex war, a Lysistrata movement which smashed down the male barriers of prejudice and intolerance and ended in unconditional acceptance of the principle that women are human beings and entitled to the same privileges as men.

One effect of such a change – I hesitate to use the word 'reform' in this context – would be to turn golf clubs into places where members would go primarily to play golf rather than male sanctuaries, drinking parlours, or annexes to business offices with golf as an incidental benefit. They would become, in fact, like tennis clubs. The membership would not, in the happy phrase of that famous official circular, be broken down by age and sex, but everyone would be simply a player.

One can see difficulties, of course. But women's golf is here to stay and this is an age in which intolerance can no longer be tolerated. And once the battle was over, after the last major general (ret.) had fallen at the gate and the hordes of women overrun the citadels from Royal St George's to Muirfield, there would be certain advantages in the new situation.

For a start, we might see a British victory in the Curtis Cup. At least it would put the British Isles team on even terms before the match started instead of psychologically two down. To be a woman golfer in Britain is to be subjected to a hundred and one snubs and subtle insults, such as separate and inferior quarters, special tees, which, more often than not, are just mown areas of uneven fairway, restricted hours of play, and no voice in the running of the club.

At one Midlands club there is a flight of five steps down from the verandah which women are not permitted to use. A visiting female journalist who innocently transgressed was brusquely ordered to go back up and descend by the 'mixed' steps a few yards farther along. Another club does not allow women to walk in front of the clubhouse in trousers.

My absolutely favourite story concerns the Royal and Ancient Golf Club of St Andrews when there was a cloudburst during a tournament. A group of women was huddled against the leeward side of the sacred precincts, getting thoroughly drenched, when a club flunkey approached with stately tread.

'At last,' sighed the crowd as one woman, in much the way the Ladysmith Garrison must have sighed on sighting the relief column, 'they have taken pity on us. Chivalry has proved stronger than prejudice and they are going to invite us to take shelter, even if it is only in the trolley shed.'

'Ladies,' said the club servant, beaming benevolently, 'I have a message from the members. Would you mind putting down your umbrellas, because they are obscuring the view of the course from the smoking-room windows.'

Admittedly these women were not even members of the club, but the incident demonstrates the attitude, the official policy indeed, of golf towards the female sex. Men golfers, who are doubtless quite kind to their wives and daughters, rationalize this apartheid and defend it with vigour and a sort of logic. But so could Dr Verwoerd.

Women don't like their lesser station, of course, but, oppressed and outnumbered as they are, they haven't been able to do much about it. And their sporadic revolutionary activities are mostly misdirected. Just before the 1968 Curtis Cup match, for instance, Vivien Saunders lobbed a verbal Molotov cocktail, in the form of a letter to a golf magazine in which she pleaded for a square deal for the British team.

Miss Saunders deserves to be heard, since she is a very considerable golfer with a great deal of international experience. Her letter reveals a deep sense of grievance, and is to be welcomed since until now her public utterances have been confined to muttered cries of 'Knickers' on the occasion of her rare fluffed shots.

She pointed out that scoring in women's events must naturally be proportionately higher since they play on courses of 74–78 Standard Scratch, and not 69–71 as the men do, and may haye to take wood for as many as a dozen of their second shots in a round.

Most people, I imagine, appreciate this and adjust their reflexes to the fact that women are not quite such long hitters as men. Of course, physique must be taken into consideration in comparing golfers. Gary Player, for example, has to be a better golfer than Jack Nicklaus in order to be as good. The same goes for comparisons between women and men.

Observer, June 1968

Lightning Reflections

What do the following golfers have in common: Bobby Nichols, Lee Trevino, Jerry Heard and Gary Player?

The answer is that they have all been struck by lightning and, happily, survived with no apparent lasting damage.

These four were the lucky ones. Hundreds of people have been killed by lightning on golf courses. The American National Fire Protection Association lists golf courses in its lightning protection code as the most hazardous location (along with open fields and athletic grounds) during thunderstorms.

The risk to a golfer is much increased if he is sitting in a golf cart or pulling a trolley, if he is near a wire fence or overhead wires, if he is on a hilltop, if he is near an isolated tree, and if he is holding a raised umbrella.

The threat of lightning provides one of the two reasons (serious illness is the other) which permit a golfer under the rules to stop play, but he does not have to wait for official suspension before he makes a prudent dash for cover. But where to?

Everybody's first idea is the best one. The clubhouse is the safest place on the golf course during a storm, as well as the most comfortable. But one of the natural laws of golf decrees that storms never break out until you and I are at least two miles from the clubhouse, at the far extremity of the course.

If there is no building fitted with a lightning conductor within reach, the next best bet is a large building without one. For preference it should be metal framed, such as many clubs use as an implement shed. If you do opt for the implement shed, the worst possible thing to do is to cadge a ride on the greenkeeper's tractor. Walk to the shelter – and persuade him to do the same.

Incidentally, many people are confused about just how safe it is to be in a motor car during a storm. Is it better to get out and stand well clear of the car? The dilemma seldom arises on a golf course, but the expert advice is to stay in the car. It does afford good protection.

That natural law of golf which I mentioned usually guarantees that none of these desirable sanctuaries is available to the stranded player. In that case there are certain rules which should be followed.

Go for a dense clump of trees in preference to a solitary tree. Single trees present a serious lightning risk, especially if they are on high ground. The second rule is always move downhill rather than up. Low-lying ground is much safer.

Many golf clubs provide small shelters, usually of a rustic variety, for the convenience of members. If the shelter is on high ground in an exposed position, then it will carry a high lightning risk. Your best bet would be to put your clubs in the shelter and find a safer place for yourself, even if it means standing out in the storm. If the shelter is in a low-lying area, then the balance of advantage swings your way, and, in the absence of dense woods, you will be better off inside.

The thing to remember is that the lightning is going to search out the shortest route to earth, via the best conductor, and in the case of trees that means down the trunk. So stand clear, under the outspread branches, and if you are in a small shelter keep away from the walls and supports.

Some golfers get nervous during thunderstorms about the metal spikes in their shoes. Should you go barefoot through the tempest? Well, the experts say that spikes do not increase the danger to any significant degree, so you might as well keep your shoes on. The alternative probably carries a greater risk – from pneumonia.

Observer, December 1976

'Like, I'm Not in the Disco Scene, Man!'

I must congratulate the secretary of Basingstoke Golf Club on his perspicacity. Commenting on a recent article of mine, he drew a vivid picture of how he saw the author in his imagination. 'Wad some Pow'r the giftie gie us, To see oursels as others see us!' wrote Rabbie Burns, and now, praise be, some power has done exactly that in my case.

One single person who combines all the sins and omissions of present-day young golfers ... an expensively but tastelessly dressed young man ... wearing golf shoes, leaning over the bar talking on Christian name matey terms with some long-suffering steward ... he has just come off the course, not changing his clothes, of course ... not having replaced a single (large) divot ... having dropped the flagstick heavily on every green ... having missed a number of short putts ... is loud in his condemnation of the greens committee... desires a hell-on-earth golf club with deafening disco music ... Grumbling, but ask him to take on a job to help the club and you can't see him for dust.

The secretary scores a number of direct hits, but perhaps I may be permitted to take his points one by one.

One single person etc.: My wife had a good old chuckle with my probation officer over this bit, and they felt it was about right. I thought it a bit steep. Taking the Old Testament view of sin, there are a couple of Commandments I haven't even attempted to break. On the other hand, on the more modest seven-sin scale of Dr Johann Faustus, which so absorbed Christopher Marlowe and Goethe, I suppose there is no point in trying to deny my pride, covetousness, wrath, envy, gluttony, sloth and lust.

Expensive but tasteless dress: Oh, come on! Only the other week I finally had to face the fact that either I must replace my demob suit or risk arrest. In the bargain basement of the cheapest department store in Augusta, Georgia, I selected an (admittedly tasteless) jacket and engaged the saleswoman in negotiations. She said: 'Ah jerst lurve ta heah y'all tawk.' 'In that case,' said I, 'let us talk some more and haggle over the price.' She trilled with laughter and said, 'Have y'all seen the ticket? This heah has been marked down fahve tayums alriddy.' The price was $4.75, or just over a couple of pounds.

Matey talk with steward: It is true that during Christmas week I did remark to the steward: 'Same again all around, please, Charlie.' There is a widespread feeling within the club that I do not engage in this form of social contact with the bar staff often enough.

Not changing clothes after play: Bang on. See above remarks on snappy dressing.

Large divots: I consider the size of a man's divots to be an intensely personal matter and not a fit subject for public debate.

Dropping flagstick on green: Wide of the mark, alas. My golf consists almost exclusively of four-ball play. My role in the proceedings normally consists of pockcting my ball after taking four hacks at the thing in a bunker and saying to my partner, 'I'm afraid this hole is up to you, mate,' and walking directly to the next tee. Would that I had the chance to drop the flagstick more often.

Missing short putts: You have been spying on me.

And loudly complaining about the greens committee: That *proves* you *must* have been spying.

Desires disco music hell: Like I am not into the disco scene, man. I don't dig even such an inoffensive trio as Olivia, Newt and John. Pop music, in short, I find decidedly un-heavy, trip-wise. My musical bag is strictly squaresville. For me, Freddy Chopin is out of sight. The modern stuff is best out of earshot.

Grumbling and running for cover when asked to help: This is rather a sore point. The inference that I could make a valuable contribution to the deliberations of the various committees is well made. With my distinguished background in agronomy, catering, management and a lifelong study of the liquor trade (a real labour of love in this last case, my researches frequently leaving me exhausted and red-eyed the following morning), I would be a perfect selection for any committee.

By some extraordinary aberration of the democratic process I never seem to get nominated, much less elected. However, there is always the possibility of being coopted, and one drops hints in subtle little ways. The other day I kissed the hem of the captain's rain-jacket and all he did was rebuke me for ruining the water-proofing. The chairman of the house committee has let it be known that he does not care to have me lick the polish off his spiked shoes. Short of making a formal

41

complaint to the Race Relations Board on the grounds of discrimination – there is no representation on any of our committees by a member with Black Foot Indian origins – I cannot see what more I can do. Lord knows, I am willing, but whenever I broach the subject you cannot see the committees for dust.

Well, it is their loss. Just because I am away for ten months in the year is no reason for not asking me, is it? I'll bet Basingstoke Golf Club would have me on all the committees.

But I do not complain. I am not one to kick against the pricks – except that I do wish that when I write an article seeking to guarantee a supply of trained and dedicated stewards and greenkeepers for this great game, those who disagree with me would stick more or less to the point.

However, Mr Secretary, as one who was almost (accidentally) shot in the Prohibition gang warfare of New York and whose sixpence pocket-money used to purchase half a pint of beer, five Woodbines and a packet of crisps, I forgive you everything for those constantly repeated references to my youth.

Golf Illustrated, May 1974

Natural Laws of Golf

The poor golfer has rules enough to learn, plus exhortations as to his behaviour on the course, and as often as not he must make himself familiar with special club rules and possibly special local rules as well. In the light of such a weight of legalistic ballast one hesitates before adding to the golfer's legal cargo, but there is another set of rules which apply to golf and, so far as we can discover, they have never been properly codified. Actually, rule is perhaps not the word. It would be more accurate to describe these additional requirements as golf's natural laws.

The best way to introduce them is, perhaps, by example. During a recent Continental tournament Tony Jacklin hit his drive into a copse of young trees. As with most such new plantations, the club had rather overdone the planting, clearly with the idea that if some of the saplings did not take there would be no need for replacements. In fact, they had all grown and the copse was a positive thicket of maturing conifers, standing about twenty feet high. This writer was among the first on the scene, in itself something of a novelty, but we need not pursue that subject. Our hero duly came crashing through the undergrowth, and asked: 'Have you teed it up nicely for me?' 'No need,' we replied, 'Rule 2.'

'Rule 2?' asked Jacklin in some perplexity, his bantering manner vanished. 'Yes,' we replied. 'In golf the second law of nature states that professionals always find a gap.' It is no less than the truth, and this incident bore it out to the limit. Jacklin's ball had come to rest in the one part of the thicket where he could not only take an unimpeded backswing, but could fire the ball out between the trees in the required direction. 'If that had been me,' we further stated, 'the ball would surely have finished right behind a tree.'

This sort of thing happens far too often for coincidence. When Billy Casper was playing off against Gene Littler for the US Masters, he hooked deep into the jungle at the second hole. The area where his ball came to rest was swampy, with a creek running through a valley entirely surrounded by Georgia pines as thick and tall as Nelson's column and completely blocking out the sky. You or I, having hit such a shot, would have been in the creek for sure. And even after dropping out under penalty we would have had no shot. A Panzer tank could not have fired a 100-millimetre shell out of that place through the trunks of those massive pines. Casper's ball had stopped short of the creek and lay not too badly. He could swing, but where could he hit to? He looked around and then gazed upwards. There, about a hundred feet above, was a patch of blue sky about the size of a handkerchief. He took his 9-iron and lofted a shot through the gap back onto the fairway. That one blow alone was worth the Masters title, which he duly collected. But the point is: *there was a gap*.

Again at Augusta, playing the tenth hole, Jack Nicklaus faded his drive into similar woods near where this observer happened to be standing. As he walked down the fairway we had ample opportunity to inspect the lie and noticed, with great excitement, that Nicklaus was stymied dead behind a massive pine. 'Aha,' we thought, 'the law of nature has failed for once. Here is a pro and he has no gap.' Nicklaus took one look at the ball and then addressed it. With his feet planted solidly for the shot he raised one hand and beckoned an official. It was then that we noticed the codicil to the law of nature. Nicklaus's left heel just bisected a white line drawn around an area of slushy mud. The official nodded. Nicklaus picked up his ball, dropped it at the nearest point of relief not nearer the hole, *and now he had a gap*.

It was these incidents which first set us off on a preliminary draft of golf's natural laws. Much research remains to be done into these mysterious forces but, just to set the ball rolling, we would like to advance a few tentative findings:

Rule 1: Whenever a spectator seeks out a really good vantage point, and settles down on shooting stick or canvas chair, the tallest and fattest golf watcher on the course will take up station directly in front.

Rule 2: As already outlined, pros always get a gap.

Rule 3: Whenever a golfer is late arriving for an important match he breaks a shoelace.

Rule 3A: In the wake of Rule 3, the professional's shop is either shut or has run out of laces.

There must be other unwritten laws of golf of this ilk. One was indeed submitted along the lines that every time one leaves a golf umbrella in the boot of the car to lighten the load, the heavens open when the golfer is out at the farthest end of the course.

Another promising-looking law, namely that when a long handi-capper selects an old ball to play a water hole he loses it in the rough on the *opposite* side of the fairway, proved unreliable.

So the arena is thrown open for public debate and submission of prospective laws. Each suggestion will be given a thorough testing, and if it passes the validating committee, will be dignified with the appellation of A Natural Law.

At the present moment the committee is examining the hypothesis that every time a greens committee creates a new bunker, not one member of that committee is able to give a satisfactory golfing reason for the addition. That one looks as if it might achieve the status of A Natural Law and any evidence, for or against, will be welcomed.

Golf World, December 1975

A Man after My Own Heart _____⌐

I thought I had heard everything when I received a letter from a student in the Far East enlisting my help in researching for his doctorate's thesis on the subject of 'The Forward Press in Golf'.

Now, however, the *Golf Journal*, the official magazine of the United States Golf Association, reports that Charles Sager graduated from the University of Puerto Rico on the strength of his dissertation on the need for an 8-inch hole. *Summa cum laude!* This Sager is a man after my own heart.

It may be presumptuous, but I feel confident in adding the congratulations of Peter Alliss and Tony Jacklin to my own.

The University of Puerto Rico does not bestow degrees lightly, and I long to put some supplementary questions. How long did it take him? Three years? Four years? Did he use a putting machine or were his conclusions reached entirely as the result of putting on the carpet in his hostel? All we are told is that he finally came up with the conclusion that, by almost doubling the size of the hole, a greater premium would be placed on accuracy to the green.

Here we have the crucial point about the bigger-hole argument. Traditionalists always respond by saying, 'You only want a larger hole because you are such a bad putter.' I admit to being a rotten putter, but that has nothing to do with the argument. The bigger-hole reformers are concerned with justice. They want to reward the man who approaches accurately and penalize the golfer who misses the green.

Putting cannot be isolated as a separate branch of golf. As we all know, putting bears heavily on every stroke in the game. It is the *coup de grâce*, the final thrust towards which all the preliminary cape work and picador blows have been directed. By this analogy, putting to a 4½-inch hole is like finishing off the bull with a machine gun.

Thanks to the work of Jack Reddy, the USGA scoring analyst, we have a composite picture of the potential golf champion. On average he drives 250 yards and hits a 35-yard-wide fairway eight times out of ten. (Missing the fairway will cost him half a stroke.)

He hits his long irons just over 200 yards to within 40 feet of his target. With a medium iron he will get inside 30 feet. As a general rule, on mid- and short-iron play the accuracy of the champion will be less than 7 per cent of the distance of the shot. Thus from 100 yards he will normally finish inside 7 yards from the hole.

Now for the kill. On the green a 75-foot putt will finish 4½ feet from the hole, progressing to 2½ feet from 40 feet, and 1.8 feet from 30 feet. He will be 'dead' up to 2½ feet, have a 50–50 success rate from 7 feet, and hole about one in seven tries from 20 feet.

And here comes the statistical case for the larger hole: the champion will chip from the fairway with the same standard of accuracy as he shows with his approach putting. Therefore, provided he is not in the rough, he is not penalized at all for missing the green.

The man who is 75 feet from the hole, and off the green, is likely to get down in two. The man who is on the green 8 feet from the hole is likely to get down in two. The proposition, as Euclid would most certainly have observed if he had taken up the game, is absurd.

This is the situation which demolishes the case of the preservationists who argue that enlarging the hole would be nothing more than an exercise in relativity. Instead of twitching on the 7-footers, they say, the golfer would simply get the same heeby jeebies from 10 feet and the better putters would still prevail. That would indeed be so if we were playing a game of putting. But we are actually playing golf, to a green whose proportions remain the same.

Go back to our example and the man 75 feet away and off the green would still need two strokes to get down. But our virtuoso who hit his approach to 8 feet would now get his due reward with a single putt into the larger hole. (Actually, I believe Mr Sager is overdoing things with his advocacy of an 8-inch hole; my experiments suggest that 5½–6 inches would do the trick. I would combine that reform with a general move towards smaller greens and more fringe or semi-rough around them.)

Dai Rees puts up a strong, or at least spirited, argument in favour of a smaller hole, of 3 inches. This, he says, would really reward the man who knocks his approaches close. Possibly. But what it would not do is reduce the emphasis on putting, which is partly the object of the exercise. Nothing you do in the way of altering the size of the hole will diminish the advantage enjoyed by the superior putter, which is as it should be.

But no one, I think, can seriously argue against the proposition that with every other club the golfer gets out of the shot a result in exact proportion to the amount of skill he puts into its execution. In putting there must always be an element of chance because, with the rarest of exceptions, the course of the putt is subject to deviations due to irregularities in the surface.

A far more telling case is put up by the traditionalists when they support the status quo by falling back on emotional arguments. Here is how the USGA puts it:

'We have to put up with more than enough change in the other parts of our lives. We are entitled to have the game left as it has been without the infernal meddling of those who never fail to perceive themselves as having superior perceptions; we are entitled to sit back in our rockers on lazy summer afternoons and argue the relative merits of John Miller's 63 at Oakmont v. Hogan's 67 at Oakland Hills and, for that matter, Jones's 66–68 at Sunningdale. We lose that part of the game's charm once the size of the hole is changed.'

Granted. But at the risk of being accused of imagining myself to enjoy superior perceptions, I would diffidently suggest that in a changing world some things may have to be changed in order to keep them the way they were. I don't think you can make a valid comparison between Miller's 63 and Jones's 66 anyway, let alone get a decent argument brewing.

What can be asserted is that golf for our forefathers was the best of all possible games. Could it not be that for the new generation of players, with their changed attitudes, a larger hole is necessary to maintain golf as the best of all possible games? If so, that is reason enough.

One puzzle remains. What does a man do with a degree as a qualified bigger-hole evangelist? Who employs him? If Charles Sager is really stuck, I shall be happy to recommend him for the greens staff at my club.

Observer, October 1973

Sheer Self-Denial

There was no collusion, I promise, although it would not have made any difference. As a veteran of a thousand editorial conferences I am all too familiar with the way a bad idea can germinate and flourish on a thin news day:

'As chroniclers and devotees of sport we ought to be setting an example in the ongoing *mens sana in corpore sano* situation. I think it would make a deeply meaningful exercise if we sent one man swanning off to a health farm for a week. At this time of year they are mostly filled with strippers toning up for the cabaret season. McIlvanney would be perfect. Then we could send Brasher to run up and down Scandinavia. Now all we need is someone to go on a bread and water diet.'

It could have happened like that but it didn't. It was purely by coincidence that I decided my too, too solid flesh must be made to melt. 'Terrific,' they said, 'write five hundred words about how you did it.' Very well, here goes.

I have not eaten for forty-eight days.

That's seven words and that is about all there was to it. Actually, it started on the golf course. There is a steep rise between the second green and third tee at my club and, while I did not deliberately lose that second hole, I found myself grateful not to have the honour on the third because that gave me a chance to catch my breath.

My weight had never bothered me much before. What is 16½ stone, after all? 'You've got the height to carry it,' friends assured me. Fat people have a remarkable capacity for finding virtues in fatness. Physical solidarity is equated with moral dependability. What rot. Yon Cassius has a lean and hungry look. Give me men around me who have a low cholesterol level in their blood.

I made a number of firm decisions. I would not go on a diet. I would not become a Weight-Watcher. I would not slim. That would be antisocial, for there is no bore quite so boring as a slimming bore, lest it be a fitness freak, than whom no other variety of bore can bore your tits off more rapidly. Much as I wished to lose my own pendulous paps,

What's It All About?

I would not eliminate them at the expense of other people's. I began by shaving off my beard and moustache; an important psychological step this, for it instantly transformed me into a different person, which was the object of the exercise. Then I stopped eating. It was not total self-denial, you understand. But where I would have taken ten mouthfuls before, I cut my consumption down to one. By the time the novelty of a shaven chin had worn off so had a gratifying stone or so of excess blubber.

I took to not wearing a hat, since 60 per cent of the body's heat loss is through the head (or so I had read somewhere), and I thought that my metabolism would have to dig deeply into the reserve supplies of fat in order to maintain normal body temperature. It does not work out like that. Just as women's thighs grew thicker in the mini skirt era, so my scalp seemed to develop a protective layer of lard. End of experiment.

The crisis in every weight-reducing regime is the moment when the bathroom scales seem to stick. You are still not eating, but you are not losing any more fat. Some days you actually go up a bit. Up till now I had not thought about calories but I fell into slimming-bore ways to counter my depression. As a result the daily half bottle of claret was struck off the programme, to be replaced for social purposes by slim-line tonic with a dash of lime. The odd slice of bread, I discovered, was not too high calorically. The real poison is the butter and the cheese. By converting my boilers to black tea and coffee, with sweeteners instead of sugar, and to hell with the scare about cyclamates, I got the weighing machine needle on the move again.

After a bit my appetite began to shrink in direct ratio to my diminishing waistline, and that is half the battle. Losing weight is all very well but unless you stay slim – and that means changing your eating habits – then the exercise is a waste of time and willpower.

Numerous benefits flowed from my weeks of self-denial, such as a ten-year-old suit which not only fits again but is almost back in fashion. I cannot say that I ever suffered greatly from flatulence (truth to tell I rather enjoyed it), but there has been a dramatic drop in turbulence. My golf has improved by a good six shots a round.

Was it worth it? Certainly, both physically and mentally I am a different person. Of course, I am still a slob, but a thin slob, and there is a world of difference between the two.

Observer, December 1978

So You Want to Be a Pro

From time to time young golfers ask my advice on whether they should turn professional. There was a time when I took my responsibilities very seriously in giving my answer. In several instances I walked eighteen holes with one of these aspirants to observe his swing and general approach to the game, and then I agonized over whether to encourage him to take the plunge.

After spending much of my adult life among professional golfers, I have come to the conclusion that if a youngster has to ask whether he should try his luck on the tournament circuit then he is not a suitable candidate.

In order to save much heartache and disappointment I have devised a simple test so that young golfers who are contemplating a life on the tour can immediately revise their views and switch to useful careers as tinkers, tailors, soldiers or sailors.

1. Which of the following is the most important issue in the world today?
   (a) The possibility that the world may be destroyed in a nuclear holocaust?
   (b) The fact that two thirds of the world's population is suffering from malnutrition or is downright starving?
   (c) Your three-foot putt, which will make the difference between a score of 77 and 76?

2. Your first wedding anniversary falls on the third day of a tournament in which you are competing. Do you:
   (a) Deliberately miss the cut so that you can get home for a surprise celebration?
   (b) Wire her flowers and call her before you leave the motel for the golf course?
   (c) Do nothing because you have forgotten the date anyway?

3. As you drive into your hotel car park late at night a mugger jumps from the shadows with a gun and demands that you hand over your clubs. Do you:

    (a) Hand them over?

    (b) Try to resist the robbery by force?

    (c) Say: 'Listen, buddy, you can take the clubs and car and a thousand bucks besides, provided you will just leave me the driver and the putter'?

4. You are playing a tournament and observe one of your fellow competitors cheating. Do you:
    (a) Challenge him there and then?
    (b) Report the facts to a referee?
    (c) Do nothing, on the grounds that any unpleasantness might upset your mental equilibrium?

5. You are off form and badly need to practise before a tournament when the mother superior of your local orphanage asks you to do a fund-raising clinic. Do you:
    (a) Agree?
    (b) Say: 'Talk to my manager'?
    (c) Decline on the grounds that you do not have the time just now?

6. In the same mail you receive two invitations, one to compete in the Masters and the other to play an exhibition match for a million dollars in Iran that same week. Do you:
    (a) Accept the exhibition offer?
    (b) Refer the invitations to your manager for his advice?
    (c) Throw away the exhibition offer without a second thought?

7. Can you bring yourself to believe it possible to pack the Empire State Building into a matchbox for:
    (a) One second?
    (b) Five seconds?
    (c) A full minute, or whatever time it takes you to plan and execute a full 1-iron shot from a cuppy lie through a two-inch gap twenty yards away?

8. The President calls you and offers you a job, with full ambassadorial status, to travel the world investigating where the best food, the finest wine and the most gorgeous and accommodating women are to be found – you know, the assignment Henry Kissinger used to have. The only proviso is that you may not play golf. Do you:
    (a) Accept on the spot?
    (b) Ask if the prohibition on golf might be negotiable?
    (c) Reject the offer out of hand?

9. You have a two-stroke lead in the Masters in the last round when

your approach to the thirteenth screws back off the green and rolls into the creek. The ball is lying not too badly on a mud bar, but as you arrive on the scene ambulance men are removing the prostrate form of a golfer who has just tried a similar shot and has been bitten by a water moccasin. Do you:

(a) Take a drop under penalty?

(b) Take off your shoes and socks, wade in and play the shot?

(c) Call a referee and point out the Rule that says a golfer is not required to put himself in physical danger, insist that the creek be checked for any other snakes, and then wade in to play the shot?

10. You have finished with the low score in the Open and are standing beside the eighteenth green with the chief referee watching your last rival line up the ten-foot putt that will beat you by a stroke. You notice that his caddie is standing directly behind him on the line of the putt. Do you:

(a) Nudge your neighbour and point out the potential infringement in time for him to do something about it?

(b) Call out: 'Hey, Jack, that's two shots unless you get your caddie to move'?

(c) Do or say nothing while the stroke is played?

Now, if you have unhesitatingly answered 'c' to each of those ten questions, then you, my son, have every chance of becoming a great champion.

Golf Digest, September 1980

Old Persimmon Returns

A *cause célèbre* for Sodding Chipbury?

In the long history of the Sodding Chipbury Golf Club there have been few incidents to disturb the tranquil pace of life. Of course, as in any club, conversation is fuelled by a constant succession of gossip-worthy trivia. In the last month, for instance, the mysterious affair of the captain's left shoe provided the main topic for speculation for three days.

The shoe had been discovered by the pro, Old Persimmon, early one morning on the putting green, soaked with dew. How had it got there? The captain had left his shoes, as usual, with the Apprentice Sex Maniac to be cleaned, but overnight this left shoe had been spirited from the locked pro's shop (whose locks had not been tampered with) and had rematerialized on the green. Odd. Extremely rum. Or, so went the consensus of gullible opinion.

Then there was the sequel to the monthly dinner dance, when the lady captain reversed from the car park with unusual panache. The front bumper of her car had hooked into the back bumper of a neighbouring Volkswagen during this manoeuvre, with the result that the VW ended up on its back, like a floundering cockroach, on the first tee. The members got five days' worth of malicious chat out of that.

The hero of the monthly medal, a market gardener named Higgins, was widely suspected of having nursed his handicap in much the same way that he husbanded his cucumbers, but this was too regular a subject to provide much conversational mileage.

Such items are the regular diet of golf clubs and hardly the stuff of a *cause célèbre*. In a hundred odd years, Sodding Chipbury had enjoyed few really devastating incidents.

There was the case of the vanishing assistant professional before the war (the First World War, that is). He had gone out to play a round by himself and never returned. The fact that his clubs were discovered by the seventh green gave rise to a vast amount of scandalized speculation. The seventh hole runs past the kitchen garden of Sodding Chipbury Hall, which was owned – and still is – by a charity devoted to the elevation of fallen women from their sadly horizontal state.

Generations of assistants and young bloods among the membership have joked about going down to the seventh to look for lost balls, and when this particular assistant vanished it was widely assumed that he climbed the wall, probably at the invitation of some beguiling siren among the inmates, and was being held a willing prisoner behind the drab Victorian brickwork.

Golfers who played the seventh hole at this time heard – or thought they heard – shrieks of female laughter. After a week of lurid discussion the club sent a small deputation round to the hall to make formal inquiries. They were met by the matron, who so far forgot herself as to send the deputation packing with their ears crimson with embarrassment, but for the rest of his life the leader, a retired missionary, cut across from the fifth green directly to the eighth tee to avoid that unsavoury seventh.

That scandal reverberated through the club for six months until one of the members, on holiday in Blackpool, recognized the missing assistant working in a fairground. The prosaic truth was that he had planted his clubs on the seventh, knowing that this clue would thoroughly confuse the issue, and simply skipped out on an impressive string of tradesmen's debts.

Another issue which turned father against son, and split the club into two warring factions, occurred in 1938 and arose from an innocuous entry in the suggestions book. It read simply: 'That the cross bunker at the fifth be filled in.' It was signed by three influential members and it raised fundamental issues of golf course architecture. For a lowish handicap golfer the cross bunker represented a stern challenge. A good drive followed by a spanking wood was needed to get home and, such is the frailty of human nature, nearly everyone tried to play it that way.

But, as we all know, the handicaps of most golfers are highish rather than lowish, and accordingly that vast chasm of sand gathered in a high proportion of second shots. And once trapped within that gaping maw, many a golfer required two or three strokes to recover. One celebrated member expended no fewer than twenty-seven strokes, to the accompaniment of a solemn liturgy: 'Twenty bloody one, twenty bloody two, twenty bloody three ... ' which became something of a catch phrase for a while.

On medal days that bunker looked as if it had been used for a wedding, with torn-up score cards scattered like confetti throughout its length. Special general meetings were called to thrash out the future of the bunker, but the war came along before any decision could be reached.

The war did not mean suspension of hostilities by any means. Letters arrived at the club from Malaya and Africa and Italy with cryptic notations such as: 'Hope that bunker is still OK' or 'Trust you have filled in that damn pit and put it to useful service like growing spuds for the war effort.'

Clearly, peace would bring a renewal of the club's civil war – and then fate took a hand. A Heinkel 111, bound for the factories of Coventry, was intercepted and separated from its formation. With a Hurricane in close pursuit, the German pilot prudently lightened his load by dropping his 500-kilo penetration bomb and scored a direct hit on the bunker guarding the fifth.

And so it was, when the surviving members returned to Sodding Chipbury, they found in place of that notorious bunker a splendid pond, much enhanced by the water lilies which Old Persimmon had stolen from the ornamental gardens of the Hall. Furthermore, the drainage problem that had made the fifth green the soggiest on the course was cured. Honour was satisfied all round. The bunker had gone but the hazard remained, and life at Sodding Chipbury returned to its normal bickering.

Until five months ago. Then it was that the latest great division split the members into opposing factions. Like many great conflicts, it began with a small incident. And the assassination of the Grand Duke which was to plunge the club into turmoil was the arrival of a solicitor's letter, addressed to the secretary. It read: 'As trustee of the late Arnold Rumbold, it is my duty to inform you of his testimentary request that his ashes be scattered on his beloved Sodding Chipbury golf course where he spent so many happy hours. Accordingly, the ashes are being dispatched under separate cover, and the trustees hope that you will make the necessary arrangements for the scattering in a place which would satisfy the last wishes of our late client.'

A simple enough request, and not an unusual one – or so you might think. The letter was put to the general committee. In life Rumbold had not been popular. He was a retired schoolmaster, and had a reputation as the meanest man in the club. His reluctance to stand his wack at the bar was a byword and his tee peg, to which he had attached a piece of wire and a ball of wool, had long since lost every vestige of paint in years of service.

But human nature has reserves of richness which are only tapped in the presence of death. Men who had referred privately to Rumbold as 'Scrooge' for years suddenly saw his parsimony as loveable eccentricity. *Nil nisi bonum.* Now they must do the right thing by him.

The question was: what was the right thing? Or, what was the right place? Some opted for the last hole, so often the scene of Rumbold popping two shots onto the green and holing a winning putt. Some thought the sixth should be his spiritual home, since his hickory-shafted 4-wood had covered its 130 yards with unerring accuracy for a certain three almost as a matter of routine.

Finally, with the subject seemingly at complete deadlock, the captain put a proposal to the committee. 'Gentlemen, we are getting nowhere. In our endeavours to do the right thing by Rumbold we are doing nothing. And that is surely failing him in his last request. In this great game of ours there is a convention, I might almost say a tradition, that for all disputes there is one final arbiter, a source of all wisdom. I refer, of course, to the time-honoured solution: Ask the pro.'

The old pro did not hesitate. 'Gentlemen, I have given much thought to this question which has vexed the membership for so long. I have not spoken out because it is not my place to do so. But now that you have sought my advice I give it willingly. In my mind there is absolutely no doubt that only one place on this course is suitable for the purpose – the seventeenth green.'

Old Persimmon drew a handkerchief from his pocket and passed it across his eyes. 'You will not embarrass me by asking my reasons. A man's memories of a fine gentleman are private but I assure you all that there is only one spot – the seventeenth.'

The room was silent. After a minute the captain said in a solemn voice: 'So be it.' The entire committee, led by the captain and with Old Persimmon carrying the urn, moved in procession to the seventeenth. The captain took the urn and thought for a moment. 'I have been contemplating whether this act should be accompanied by a few words. But I think that we have all spoken enough. The rest is silence.' He tipped the ashes onto the green and they returned, like men who have put down a heavy burden, to the club house.

Old Persimmon retired to the back recesses of his shop. On the bench was a sheaf of papers. Six months previously the zealous chairman of the greens committee had asked the technical representative of a horticultural firm to advise on the upkeep of the course, and this was his report. All the recommendations were neatly tabulated. 'First hole: rake-harrow in spring, dress sulphate of lime. Second hole: selective weed-killer required to eliminate plantains. Third hole: French drain front of green could eliminate fusarium.'

Old Persimmon flipped over the page and read: 'Seventeenth green: potash deficient.' He smiled a secret smile and put the report in a cupboard. Old Rumbold, he reflected, would have appreciated this final act of economy.

Golf Illustrated, May 1973

Then The Schoolboy With His Satchel   And Shining Morning Face.

Part Two

Around the World

A globetrotter's view of the game

No Place for Mugs

Not to put too fine a point on it, Carnoustie is a pretty good place to emigrate *from*. The little township on the east coast of Scotland, which is to be host to this year's (1975) British Open championship, has few pretensions to charm. It is just a few streets, with the little stone houses huddled together for warmth, straggling along the railway line from Edinburgh to Aberdeen. By some freak of geography this stretch of coast has its own peculiar climate. Most people who know Carnoustie only from reading about its past Opens have the idea that the place is continuously lashed by gales and/or stinging rain. That is not quite fair. It can be calm here but then, even in mid-summer, it is liable to be visited by a phenomenon known locally as 'haaaaar.' Purists of the Scottish dialect may complain that there are one or two surplus 'a's' in that rendering, but that is the phonetic form of the word, a teeth-chattering exclamation to describe the sea mist which strikes icy daggers into your very bones, regardless of how many precautionary layers of cashmere you may have adopted, and which mercifully obscures the view.

Twenty miles inland the sun may beat down warmly on some of the most magnificent country to be found within the British Isles, but in Carnoustie, when the haar rolls in from the North Sea, you know exactly how a bottle of champagne feels as it is plunged into an ice bucket. Haaaaar! How, you may ask, can life be supported in such a place? For many of us that is a fairly moot proposition, but the inhabitants have evolved a unique survival technique. It is based on the finest flowering of the Scottish culinary arts, an object resembling nothing so much in texture and taste and appearance (except for being yellow) as an ice-hockey puck. This is the infamous mutton pie. Human digestive juices can make no impression on it and, left to itself, it would simply remain in the system like an outsize gallstone.

However, generous measures of whisky will break down the mutton pie provided the mixture is well agitated. Hence the inhabitants of Carnoustie make a daily pilgrimage to the foreshore and play golf, regardless of the weather. Now a wonderful chemical process takes place. On reaction with the whisky, the mutton pie dissolves and spreads to the epidermis, forming an insulating layer akin to thermoplastic. The people of Carnoustie are thus double-glazed, as it were; or vulcanized, if you prefer. They go about their business with the minimum of clothing, remarking cheerfully to each other on what a bonny day it is.

The men of Carnoustie are fortified against all natural hardships and it was this quality which gave Carnoustie its special place in the history of golf, notably American golf. For towards the end of the last century, when golf in the United States was gathering momentum as a social craze of epidemic proportions, there was a chronic shortage of teachers and clubmakers to service the game.

Scotland, home of golf and economically depressed at the time, was the obvious source of golfing missionaries. The Atlantic steam packets were laden to the plimsoll line with migrant professionals. The village of Carnoustie (for such it was) sent some 150 of its sons to spread the gospel of golf in the New World.

How could a village produce so many pros? Well, in truth they were probably not all professional golfers in the sense we have come to understand the term. But for a Carnoustie boy, playing golf was as natural as breathing. It was something everyone did in the normal course of life.

The most famous of the Carnoustie immigrants were the Smith brothers, Alex and Willie, who both won US Open Championships in due course, and Macdonald, reputedly a better but unluckier player than the lot of them.

One Carnoustie man did not make it. Legend has it that he decided to emigrate to South America, although in all probability that meant the southern states of America rather than the subcontinent. His friends gave him a lavish send-off party and, at a late hour, having downed a generous measure of mutton-pie-dissolving-fluid and with many a slurred promise to send the lads a card when he arrived, he staggered off into the night in the general direction of Dundee. The next thing he knew he was awaking, in an alcoholic haze, looking about him and remarking, 'So this is South America, I'd better build myself somewhere to live.' We do not know how far he progressed with his house-building before he realized his mistake, but one thing is certain. Far from being in South America he was, in fact, only a mile away from Carnoustie, on the site of what is now the tenth hole, which is known as 'South America' to this day.

At a rather later date, another Carnoustie man successfully made the trip to America and caused a bigger stir than even the Smith brothers. That was Tommy Armour, who was blinded in one eye during the First World War and who once climbed out of his tank to strangle a German with his bare hands. He brought some of that same directness of approach to his teaching of golf after his playing triumphs were over. Actually, it is cheating to call Armour a Carnoustie man, for he was born in Edinburgh, but when he returned to Scotland to win the Open at Carnoustie in 1931 it was too tempting a local-boy-makes-good story to quibble about a few miles.

At least, Armour brings us to the Open and to the links of Carnoustie. It is impossible to trace the origins of these old Scottish courses because in the beginning, in the fifteenth and sixteenth centuries, there was no formality about the layout of courses. You simply tucked your clubs (all wooden, of course) under your arm, put some balls in your pocket (featheries for the rich, boxwood for the poor) and went off to play over any promising golfing ground.

The land at Carnoustie was wild and bleak, and it still retains enough of an unkempt quality to justify Gary Player's horrified description of the course as 'a good swamp, spoiled'.

He should have seen it in 1527, when we have the first written record of golf at Carnoustie. A certain Sir Robert Maule was described as a devotee of hunting and hawking and 'he exersisit the gowf, and oft times to Barry Lynks quhan the wadsie was for drink.' For anyone not too well up in medieval Scottish, that means that he frequently played golf for a whisky-sour nassau.

Even so, the finish was thought to be weak. In preparation for its inaugural Open, Carnoustie remodelled the closing holes to make a run-in of unrivalled severity.

Many clubs boast tough finishes. Merion, Pebble Beach and St Andrews are often cited as rugged examples. They are tame compared to Carnoustie, and especially in a teasing wind. Let us mentally play them together. The sixteenth is a par-3, satirically speaking, at 243 yards, as often as not needing a button-popping smash with a driver to a hog's-back green. The Barry Burn, which winds as insidiously as a tapeworm across the links, waits to swallow a hook or pull. On the right a tangle of heather threatens a fate scarcely less painful. The sensible way to play this hole is to lay up with a 3-iron or so and hope to get down in a chip and a putt. But what golfer was ever that sensible?

Seventeen is worse. They call it the Island hole, a typical case of pawky Scottish wit because that Barry Burn snakes across the fairway four times, producing five possible islands on which you may choose to land your drive. On the tee you work out a complicated equation, involving your bicep size, courage rating and wind strength, and come up with a suggested target area. It was here that Jack Nicklaus once came tragically to grief. In the 1968 Open he had been playing his usual calculating, cautious game and he went into the fourth round trailing Gary Player. On the long sixth, Nicklaus hooked out of bounds, turned and kicked the bag out of his caddie's hands. Old Nicklaus watchers thrilled to the sight of this outburst. Now Jack would forget all about safety and turn it on. He had to. And so he did, producing an exhibition of matchless shotmaking. By the seventeenth he had Player in his sights and groggy. On the tee Nicklaus wound himself up and slugged the ball as hard as he could. The ball, flying all the convolutions of the burn, carried enough of the hole's 485 yards to leave him no more than a wedge to the flag. Player, laying up, had a 4-iron second shot.

It would be possible to draw up a list of fifty golfers almost guaranteed to birdie the hole after such a drive, but Nicklaus, with that toy wedge of his, would not get many votes as a pitcher of the ball even from his own family. He duly made a hash of the shot, barely bobbling the ball to the front edge of the green. That gave Player the safety margin he needed.

Memory plays one false – and, anyway, you can look it up in the reference books if you are really interested – but the impression is that Player played the eighteenth in a series of nervous hops with his 7-iron. It was a par-5 then, with out of bounds all the way down the left, the infamous burn intersecting the fairway three times with the final twist just in front of the green to make you sweat, and rough up to your knees just for good measure.

That, then, is just one glimpse of Carnoustie. There are really 365 Carnousties, different golf courses with the varying weather each day of the year. Yesterday's clubbing is meaningless as a guide for today. Physically, it is the longest championship course in Britain at well over 7000 yards, but it can play as the shortest. The 1975 Open will be the fifth to be played over this capricious, unpredictable links. After Armour in 1931, Henry Cotton took the 1937 championship with a last-day 71 in a downpour. He played the finest golf of his life for that round of one under par. Then in 1953 Ben Hogan entered for his one and only British Open. He won with descending rounds of 73, 71, 70, 68 in what many people hold to be the finest four rounds of competitive golf ever played in Britain. Lastly, as we have seen, Player took the title in 1968 after that heroic duel with Nicklaus.

Perhaps that roll of honour tells more about Carnoustie than any hole-by-hole description of the course. No one can anticipate what the

1975 Open will bring. Only one prediction is safe – that the winner will be a great player.* Carnoustie is no place for mugs.

Golf World, July 1975

* It was, in the event, Tom Watson.

Obsession with Length

They are not worried about vampires at Golf House. As for ghosties and ghoulies and things that go bump in the night, the members of the United States Golf Association are terribly brave and do not even sleep with the light on, or so I believe. Nevertheless, they are gripped by a neurotic, superstitious fear of the supernatural, in the form of a golf ball that will need only a gentle tap to make it soar off a quarter of a mile down the fairway.

They have visions of a mad scientist stirring polysyllabic plastics in a cauldron and producing a ball that will render every golf course in the world obsolete overnight. To counter this unseen menace, the USGA invokes spell-breaking incantations, such as: 'Under the Overall Distance Standard the ball shall not cover an average distance in carry and roll exceeding 280 yards, plus a tolerance of 8 per cent.'

So what, you may ask? They are harmless. Let them hang up sprigs of garlic for all we care. The natural laws of physics make it impossible to add significantly to the distances a golf ball can be hit. The only way to get increased length is to breed more powerful golfers who can swing the clubhead faster.

But the hysteria over the limitation of distance has created an unhealthy climate of opinion in golf, especially among architects who tend to believe these days that anything under 7000 yards is a pitch-and-putt course. This obsession with length and power has led to a decline in one of the glories of golf, the short par-4, from 251 yards to about 360 yards. You still find them in new courses, but they are nondescript holes calling for a routine drive and pitch. Pros regard them as easy game for a birdie. The vanishing short par-4 that I have in mind is a rare jewel, the embodiment of the dictum that small is beautiful.

Good architects of the strategic school chortle with malicious glee as they draw their plans. 'Every shot must challenge the mind and skill and the nerve of the golfer,' the architect reasons. 'There must be a straightforward way to play the hole but I will deny the robot golfer his birdie with this little stratagem. I will entice him to drive over here

66

into this broad expanse of fairway and then cut off his line to the green with an obtruding stand of trees.

'Now, for the man who thinks and can play all the shots I will disguise his options, and even if he detects the optimum placement I will make him play a superb shot to get there. If he falters I will grab him and punish him with this pond or this ravine. He must tread dangerously to follow this way, but if he has the guts and the finesse and the power to find the promised land then I will offer him the reward of a likely birdie, always assuming that he can repeat the entire process for his approach shot.'

That is the philosophy behind the greatest of the short par-4s. On both shots through the green the player should be assailed by a barrage of emotions from fear, to greed, to puzzlement, and he should be forced to assess his own capabilities with complete honesty. Power and bravado should never be enough to conquer a great short par-4. Oddly, Augusta National does not have one. Both the third and seventh, which qualify by length, are difficult without being devious. The same goes for the eighth at Baltusrol and the tenth at Merion. I would qualify them as penal holes.

We are getting closer with the seventeenth at Pine Valley, a little brute of a hole at 344 yards where you drive over a daunting desert to a deceptively generous oasis of fairway, tempting you to swing all out. What does it matter if the ball fades or hooks slightly? It matters. There is an area about the size of a tennis court that offers the golfer a chance to play a birdie-winning approach shot with confidence. That is the reward, if he is smart enough to recognize it and good enough to find it. For the others, they must concern themselves with getting the ball up over trees, or bending it around them, or carrying a bunker, and with such considerations in mind the chances of getting the ball close to the hole are reduced.

The finest short par-4 in the United States that I have seen exists only in my warped imagination. Everyone is familiar with the six-teenth at Cypress Point, the most photographed hole in the world – and rightly so. Clamber up the hillside with me in a journey of conjecture and let us build a tee seventy yards behind the real tee. We now have a hole of 303 yards, well within range of two shots by the most modest of hitters. But what shots they would have to be, absolutely precise and played under the most nerve-jangling stress. Yet, as you observe if you can achieve a moment of lucidity, the fairway is broad and the green generous. Draw the outlines of such a hole on a flat field, and a 24-handicapper would have no problem. Put it on its natural site and you have, for my money, the very essence of golf and a great short par-4.

The only drawback is that in the process you would destroy the most splendid par-3, possibly, there is.

Golf Digest, April 1980

Land of the Rising Golf Ball ___

The odd man out was a character with a flight bag bearing the printed inscription 'Kinki Nippon Tourist'.

Every other spectator of the Japan v. America golf match had a paper carrier bag, and with each puff of wind they set off a rustling flutter, like Oriental chimes. These bags, containing a periscope, programme and draw sheets, were given to each paying customer and were just one of the novelties which made Japanese golf such a fascinating experience for this Nippon tourist, kinky or otherwise.

In the first place, this match was sponsored by a religious order, the Church of Perfect Liberty, or PL, the twentieth-century offshoot of Shinto and Zen, whose main precept is that life is art. Under the philosophy that life consists of a succession of acts of self-expression, recreation has a natural place in PL thinking, both for its own sake and as a means of creating international goodwill.

Hence this match was played at PL's own country club. The trophy was a gold cup presented by the Supreme Patriarch, Tokuchika Miki, plus cash prizes which made this the richest golf tournament ever held in Japan. And, hence, PL is reputedly paying a million dollars to bring Pele and the Santos team for a Japanese soccer tour.

Apart from a profusion of carved wooden ornaments, the clubhouse is unexceptional, rich and comfortable in a style you might find anywhere. Outside, however, the course presents a scene as unmistakably Oriental as a willow-pattern plate.

The land around Osaka is extravagantly contoured, with small but very steep hills and precipitous ravines. The amount of earth-work which is needed to bulldoze this unpromising golfing landscape into rolling fairways is staggering, as I saw at a nearby course under construction. And that is just the start.

Having, as it were, moulded the pot, the Japanese now take infinite pains with the decoration. Every tree is shaped. Formal flower beds (chrysanths, of course) are planted around the teeing areas. And as for the ponds, one hesitates to use such a prosaic term as 'water hazard' for the ornamental lily ponds stocked with fat goldfish.

Some of these fish, as fat as a Sumo wrestler's forearm, are extremely valuable. While I was at Osaka one of the members suffered a sad bereavement when the prize of his private collection, a venerable monster worth $4000, died of old age. The grieving owner shed a tear and then, making the best of the situation, had his pet baked and served with caper sauce for supper. *De mortuis nihil nisi*: bone 'em.

For the tournament a certain amount of temporary structures were needed – grandstands, TV towers and scoreboards – and here again no expense was spared to make them attractive. Every inch of scaffolding was bandaged in red and white cloth, like barbers' poles, and a red carpet was laid for the entire length of a fifty-yard path from the clubhouse to the eighteenth green.

While all this gave the place an air of novelty, it was still recognizably a golf course. What made it entirely unreal to Western eyes were the people. PL has a number of schools, so manpower, or more properly girl power, was no problem. Some 400 of these doll-like creatures, all rehearsed in their duties for months, were drafted for the week.

One group of about company strength (yellow jackets, grey slacks, green caps) carried plastic buckets and paraded by the practice tee, and on another command they broke ranks and scampered across the field, filling their buckets with practice balls.

Another larger party (white jackets, blue slacks, blue caps) were the field force, acting as gallery stewards, and, very efficiently, as scorers and fore-caddies. Then there were a number of English-speaking dolls in blue suits, wearing badges labelled 'Your Companion'. They performed the more ceremonial functions, such as presenting bouquets, carrying national flags. In the press room it seemed that there were about a dozen of them charged with the sole responsibility of seeing that I was never without a dish of green tea, a liquid which I cannot trust myself to describe either as to taste or appearance.

And, oh, yes, they bowed. My goodness, how they bowed! They were all over the place, so everywhere you went you created a ripple of bobbing black heads. When I took out a cigarette by the first tee no fewer than three lighters snapped into flame.

The opening ceremony, on a dais under the main scoreboard, was like a Japanese meal, a mixture of little bits which were vaguely familiar although you couldn't quite place them. It started with a morsel of Mansion House pomp (fanfare of trumpets), followed by a touch of TV spectacular (formation posturing by a girls' percussion band). Then came a hint of Armistice Day parade (flag raising to national anthems played by what appeared to be a band of cinema commissionaires), and a short address by Patriarch Miki. Echoes of a mass wedding (teams marching to dais followed by hostesses with bouquets) brought us back to a show business atmosphere with a Japanese equivalent of Jimmy Tarbuck relying heavily on the joke: 'We wish you luck but hope you lose.'

In the event, the Americans won. The format of the three-day match was that teams of nine played medal rounds each day, and at the end the best seven scores from each side were compared. It was not a method designed exactly to promote maximum excitement, but the crowds seemed to love every minute.

The Japanese golf spectator is unique. Where the English cheer from behind the nose ('Oh, well played, Jeremy') and the Americans root from the throat ('Great shaat, Jack, baby'), the Japanese cheer comes from the stomach, half growl of approval and half sigh of envy.

Anyway, at the end of it all the Americans won by nine strokes, with a total of 504, and Billy Casper sank a thirty footer on the last green to tie for the individual prize with Masashi Ozaki, an ex-baseball player whose golf still has about it something of the slugging of a home run into the bleachers. I suspect we shall hear more of the powerful Ozaki in the coming years.

This, then, is the world of Japanese golf which exercises such a powerful influence on the life of the country. Form is every bit as important as substance in Japan, and the progress of a Japanese businessman is charted in ritual symbols. First comes the Mont Blanc fountain pen, then the Burberry raincoat, then the Rolex watch, the Italian shoes, the Dunhill lighter.

Eventually the pinnacle is achieved; membership of one of the 500 private golf clubs. The cost is immense, but a legitimate business expense. In one respect the tycoon golfers of Japan do not emulate their American counterparts. Instead of playing $50 nassaus, or more, the Japanese are content to play for no more than a five-cent chocolate bar. The playing is triumph enough.

For the golf spectator there are some fifty professional tournaments a year to watch between March and November,* another circuit of some ten tournaments for the country's sixty women professionals,* and a daily dose of golf in some form on TV. The ubiquitous Dunlop Company is a power in the land, and the pintable parlours, which are on every street, pay off the winners in golf balls. Golf terms are rendered in English and when a Japanese says 'player', it comes out as

*More now in both cases.

71

'prayer'. That is all too fitting. In a country where the game is a religion, the terms are virtually synonymous.

Observer, November 1971

Deer, Deer – Oh Dear!

When the late Tony Lema played an exhibition match in Denmark in 1963 they hired extras so that he would not feel deflated by a meagre gallery.

A mark of the enormous progress which golf has made in Scandinavia is that last weekend (June 1967) a fair-sized crowd actually paid to watch me tee off in the Danish Open championship. A more extreme example of golf fanaticism it is impossible to imagine.

The purpose of entering this £2500 tournament was to see something of the progress of the game in Denmark and, if possible, to get an insight into the life of a professional by living as a tournament player for a week.

Most of the Scandinavian pros and hot-shot amateurs were already there by the time I arrived. In the locker room, apart from a faintly disconcerting moment on confronting a pretty blonde girl mopping out the loo, it might have been anywhere before any big tournament. The atmosphere is universal – bantering chat, a faint smell of shoe polish and wintergreen, and a preoccupation with feet.

A young pro was kneading grease into his shoes, another clipping his toe nails as if he was doing a hole-in-the-heart operation. Yet another took ten minutes to put his shoes and socks on, what with powdering his feet and bandaging his calves and ankles. The foot fetishism seemed rather overdone, even by the hypochondriac standards of professional golfers.

(I revised my opinion about this the next day, when the combination of rain seeping into my shoes and shrinkage of my socks produced two agonizing blisters.)

And so to work. First, a couple of hours hitting balls on the practice fairway, then a quick snack, and off for a round to explore the course.

Copenhagen Golf Club is in the Royal Deer Park, thirty square miles of wood and heathland, and the deer – some 3000 of them – do not let the golfers forget that they are the intruders. At this time of year the stags are getting into practice for their big match-play event, and our golf was played to the accompaniment of crashing antlers.

By the next morning I was decidedly nervous, and began to experience some of the tension which affects most of the pros. True, mine was of a different order. My reputation was not at risk, for I had none. But I was naturally very anxious not to embarrass the sponsors who had so kindly welcomed a rabbit to their tournament, although one well outside the handicap limit for such events.

And the sense of occasion was growing as the preparations advanced. Danish Army signallers were setting up their walkie-talkie posts to relay the hole-by-hole results back to the scoreboard on which the name of 'amatorer' Dobereiner, Peter, England, appeared to my stage-frightened eyes to be twice as prominent as anyone else's.

So it was with a measure of relief that I learned that my partner for the preliminary pro–am tournament, John Cockin, wasn't going to be able to get to Copenhagen after all. That meant I could go out as a marker, playing a carefree round and picking up my ball if I got into trouble.

The club gave a lunch for the press and television and, in an astute stroke of public relations, invited a number of mayors. Golf in Denmark is still considered an eccentricity of the wealthy minority and unsuitable for the man in the socially democratic street. Only recently the Elsinore club was deprived of nine holes to make way for football pitches.

The attitude which prompted this municipal barbarity is all the more unfortunate because Danish golf is, in fact, entirely free of any insidious distinction of money or class. Women golfers have complete parity with men.

I was fortunate in my neighbour at lunch, Mr Frederik Dreyer, a lawyer of freewheeling charm who edits the magazine of the Danish Golf Union as a hobby. He, as much as anyone, has given practical expression to the surge in popularity of the game in Denmark. As a golf architect he has had a hand in nearly every one of the courses built in recent years, including the new one in Jutland which promises to be of the highest championship standard.

In 1947, Denmark had ten courses and 1500 players. Today there are twenty courses in use or under construction, and the playing population has almost quadrupled. The expansion in Sweden has been a deal more spectacular (eighty-four new courses in the past twenty years) with, I am told, gratifying side effects on tourism. Rain threatened as we changed for the afternoon pro–am, and I remarked on the disagreeable prospect of having to play in waterproof clothing. There is as yet no form of golf rainwear which keeps the water out without generating an excessive amount of heat. The result is that a golfer generates an individual warm front: hot air is cooled as it strikes the cold outer skin of waterproofing, condenses, and it rains inside his clothing as well as outside. The result over any length of time can lead to acute discomfort.

I was marking for the host professional at Copenhagen, Henning Kristensen, an ebullient extrovert with the refreshing golf philosophy of 'Give it a go'. We duly did so.

There are some very useful performers among the British golf writers, and when they play in amateur tournaments there is a convention that their reports end with a modest sentence along the lines: 'Your correspondent contrived to discover every trouble spot on the course with some thoroughly execrable golf,' or words to that effect. And then you look in the results and see that this disaster was in fact a respectable 73.

Well, in this round your correspondent played rather well except for one patch when Henning Kristensen gave him the excellent advice: 'Finish with your hands high. At least you'll look like a golfer and that's halfway to being one.'

The group of spectators out on the course who kindly applauded our progress contained a high proportion of extremely pretty girls, and the thought crossed my mind that they might have been planted in the crowd by the organizers for aesthetic reasons, much as one puts flowers in a guest room.

At the end of thirty-six holes of the championship proper I had hit five good shots and nearly 200 bad ones. On the thirty-first I sliced into a group of deer and they retaliated, I swear, by eating my ball. No matter how badly I play, I always enjoy my golf and these two rounds were no exception, but when I flopped down on a bench in the locker room I was angry, ashamed and depressed. And when I took my shoes and socks off I was astonished as well, for I had somehow acquired somebody else's feet – great puffy, glowing excrescences that obstinately refused to fit into my walking shoes. It was relief to realize that I wouldn't have to play two more rounds the next day, and I didn't have to wait to hear the qualifying score to know that mine would be one of the fifty names on the scoreboard with the word *udgang* chalked against it after the second round.

Two of the players who had qualified invited me to join them for the evening. During tournaments an efficient grapevine operates in the locker room to tell players where the action is and, although different players have individual preferences for unwinding after the tensions of the day, it is common knowledge that membership of the PGA does not involve vows of temperance or chastity. And I needed a lift to my morale.

The recommended temple of wickedness was a standard international night spot with pretty hostesses, waiters in cream dinner jackets cut slightly too full across the shoulders, and a four-piece band trying to set some sort of decibel record. My playboy companions ordered gin and tonics and, believe it or not, made them spin out for two hours while they talked about golf. At midnight they went back to their hotel to turn in, sated by the evening's excesses.

And that just about wound up my experiment as a tournament golfer. I went out to the club in the morning to collect my bag. Guy Wolstenholme was winning with a comfortable four-shot margin, clapped all the way by a large and enthusiastic gallery.

It had been a splendid tournament. Every year the Danish Open grows in stature and the way things are going it will soon be too important for the sponsors to permit such frivolities as accepting entries from middle-handicap golf writers. That won't worry me a bit. For, if I can't go as a player, I shall return in my other capacity, described in one of the Danish papers as *golfekspert*.

Observer, June 1967

Golf in Ireland

I worry about Ireland. Every time I go there I am like a puppy having its first encounter with a hedgehog. The experience is at once fascinating and perplexing and frustrating. You cannot move in Ireland without running your nose onto the sharp spike of paradox.

The saddest paradox is still to come. The country's main asset is its haunting and timeless beauty. And in order to survive, Ireland must attract tourists in such numbers as to destroy the very quality that makes it attractive. Who wants to visit a silent valley echoing with the blare of motor horns? Or march across a Connemara bespattered with caravans?

The Irish know it is happening, and they recoil from the prospect of their land becoming no more than a view from a hotel window and themselves picturesque figures to animate this landscape. They know they are eating their seed corn. Except in this case, being Irish, they are distilling it into their peculiar brand of anaesthetic. As a result, they live in a mood of haphazard gusto and strictly day to day.

When I go to Ireland I normally order a hire car in advance, so that it is waiting for me on arrival. In theory, that is. In practice, I have lost count of the number of times I have been told: 'Sorry, sir, we have no reservation in that name.' On the other hand, whenever this has happened, I have invariably and without compunction been given a car reserved for someone else.

Experiences like this are inescapable. The Irish like to tell the story of the German industrialist who set up a factory in Ireland. He set out with Teutonic efficiency to establish his business, and was soon at the brink of insanity. Whenever there was a wedding or a funeral or a coming-of-age party in the neighbourhood, the entire factory staff simply took the day off, mostly being distantly related to each other and joined by an even stronger bond if they weren't: free booze is thicker than blood.

Faced with the choice of losing his mind, or his factory, or both, the German sensibly decided that if he couldn't beat them he must join them. He became an Irishman by association, a sort of honorary second

77

cousin, and joined in the festivities at every opportunity. He went to all the wakes and cried and drank and called for another chorus of 'Molly Malone und her veelbarrow mit'. And the odd thing was that, despite all the unscheduled stoppages, the productivity per head was higher than in any of his other factories in Europe.

There must be a moral there somewhere. About four times a year my golfing work requires me to visit Ireland, and on every occasion, as the date approaches, the prospect produces an irrational excitement. Part of it is a foreboding amounting to a racing certainty that such plans as I have been foolish enough to make are going to be irreparably wrecked. Partly it is the realization that many of the most memorable experiences in my life have been in the company of Irishmen – and many of the near-disasters, for that matter, in the company of Irish women.

Before each trip I give myself a lecture. Ireland is a fully paid-up member of the twentieth-century community of nations. Its technology is as advanced as anybody's. I tell myself firmly that Ireland is no different from any other civilized country. All that Pat and Mike rubbish is just the comic patter of professional entertainers and has absolutely no relevance to the Ireland of the seventies.

Thus, freed of all preconceived misconceptions about the place, I arrive, briefcase in hand, ready to do business. And so it is that I am always caught off balance by the sheer Irishness of the place.

It happens suddenly. Once, within fifteen minutes of landing, I was driving into the interior with my resistance getting lower by the minute from the bliss of driving on roads virtually free of other traffic. Thanks to what I take to be a national pastime of breaking off signposts so that only a stump remains containing one or two letters, I became lost. Nothing unusual in that.

The only living creatures I could see were an elderly man and a pig. The man was standing in the middle of the road and trying to stuff the struggling creature into a sack. (Don't ask me – I haven't the slightest idea.) I asked if he could direct me. 'Let me see, now,' he said, repeating my destination two or three times. 'Lisburn ... Lisburn now.' He screwed his face into a frenzy of concentration. At last he seemed to get it straight in his mind and drew a deep breath in preparation for what were obviously going to be pretty complicated instructions. He fixed me with a look which implied that if I hoped to grasp the Theory of Relativity in one gulp, I'd better keep my wits about me. I responded with due attention.

'You carry along on this road.'

'Along this road.'

'And then you come to a town.'

'A town. Got it.'

'And when you get into the town, you turn ... '

'Yes?'

'Nowhere!'

And so it was. Absolutely straight ahead. For a while I turned over the theory that he was a plant, paid by the Irish Tourist Board to give local colour to susceptible visitors. But it happens too often.

The same day another stranger directed me to carry on until I came to a fork and then go straight ahead. You'd need an army of unemployed actors to work such a scheme. It has to be geniune.

Irishness flourishes in many forms. No doubt it still drives creative men like Shaw to emigrate in gloomy frustration. In small, well-rationed doses I find it engaging.

You may be wondering what all this has to do with golf. It is simply this: whereas Irishness can be tiresome in the extreme to a visiting dynamic businessman anxious to get on with the job, it is perfectly attuned to golf. The game is leisurely, paradoxical and depends for enjoyment on social contact. So is Ireland. It is a perfect mix. The people, the climate and the lifestyle all conspire to improve the golf and give it a unique flavour.

At this point a small personal confession is necessary. When the Irish talk about their own whimsicalities it may be mawkish but at least they have every right to pull their own legs. For a foreigner to do so can all too easily sound patronizing or superior. I am aware of the danger and so must quickly point out that when it comes to what the efficiency experts call Organization and Method, I am a complete non-starter.

The clerks in the booking office of my local railway station are no longer surprised when I put a pound on the counter and ask for a packet of cigarettes. And, like others before me, I have been known, on arrival in London in my Sunday-go-to-meeting suit, to telephone home to ask where I am supposed to be going. So if I make gentle fun of Ireland I can assure you that Ireland, in the form of my many friends there, takes ample and justified revenge.

With that preamble out of the way I can progress with my story, which began with a kindly editor ordering me to go and play a round at Portmarnock with Harry Bradshaw. I had two projected trips to Ireland coming up, the first to Belfast and then later to Dublin. Obviously it would be much more convenient to visit Portmarnock while I was in the neighbourhood on the Dublin visit.

Needless to say, when I got to Belfast I telephoned Harry and said that I believed we were supposed to play golf, and how about Thursday. It says much for him that not by so much as a tremor in his voice did he betray any surprise at a lunatic calling him up to keep an appointment six weeks early. 'Sure, that will be grand,' he said. It was months later that I discovered that I'd got it all wrong.

Those who have never seen The Brad hit a golf ball have missed a unique experience. The Irish do not take kindly to regimentation. They are too individualistic. So, while the English and Scots, and to a large extent the Americans, work to mould their golf into a classic style, the Irish pay little attention to correctness of form. They are not concerned with how they look so much as how they score, and while it is true that they do not have correct golf coached into them, it is equally true that they don't have natural ability coached out of them.

As a result, most of the Irish professionals have 'faulty' techniques. Christy O'Connor commits the cardinal sin of flicking at the ball instead of keeping arms and club in one solid entity through the ball. Wristy Christy has never lost a moment's sleep over this fault from the time he became the first man to win a four-figure cheque on the British circuit to the time he won a record £31,532 in the 1970 season. Jimmy Kinsella uses a driver with two shafts, one hammered down inside the other, thus putting superfluous weight in all the wrong places. He wields this absurdly unsuitable weapon with an action which led me to describe him as the only man who plays golf without a backswing. His method is a compromise between a convulsion and a lunge. It is a hopeless parody of a golf swing, and the only redeeming feature about it is that he hits the ball farther and straighter than most professionals.

Paddy Skerritt, by comparison, is almost orthodox except in his temperament, which is totally unconventional. Concentration, as we are constantly being reminded by the experts, is half of golf. You can tell that the great players are concentrating by the way they prowl around, scowling and cursing. They toss bits of grass into the air to test the wind, and pace off distances, and ask the galleries to keep quiet and swear at photographers, and make dozens of practice swings. Skerritt seems to imagine that you can play golf without any of these preliminaries. He never scowls. Even when his ball goes into a bunker he just gives a wry smile and hits it out. Otherwise, he simply looks at the target and makes his shot. Just like that. Dammit, he makes golf look like a game.

But none of them are quite so eccentric as Bradshaw. Possibly someone once told him that it cost two penalty strokes if you raised the club above waist level. (It would be just like the Irish to get confused with the rules of hockey.) Anyway, that's the way he plays it, and his attitude on the course is, if possible, even more casual than Skerritt's.

In appearance, Bradshaw looks like a country butcher, portly and ruddy faced and with a cap pulled in the manner of a guardsman so far over his nose that he has to tilt his head back to see out, peering from under his cheese-cutter. Even when he walks onto the tee and hits off, you do not immediately suspect that here is a vastly accomplished professional golfer. For a start, it all happens so quickly. He stoops to tee his ball, takes one glance up the fairway and it has gone, dispatched with a flick from massive hands, straight but not long enough to suggest that he will give you much trouble.

On that perfect day, hot and with hardly a breath of wind, the first hole at Portmarnock looked easy meat. I felt confident that I could sail my drive way past my opponent's ball. I took out my spoon. I did not want to humiliate a great player whose best years were past. A suspicion of a hook took my ball into the rough. Bradshaw trundled his onto the front of the green. As luck would have it, my ball tucked itself into a bank from which I could only hack it back onto the fairway, and so it was just as well that the pitch finished close to the flag. Harry took one glance at the line of his putt and stroked the ball straight into the hole.

I consoled myself that you can't play against flukes. All you can do is plug away and wait for the luck to change. Harry chatted amiably all the while. We talked about the time when he should have won the Open. It was at Sandwich in 1949 and Harry's ball, by a million-to-one chance, had rolled right into a broken bottle. Would a referee have allowed him to drop clear?

The question is academic because Bradshaw did not ask for a ruling. He smashed the ball out of the bottle with his wedge, a venerable instrument with a brown enamelled shaft and the thinnest of grips. It had not brought him fortune at Sandwich, because he had lost the play-off against Bobby Locke, but today it was enchanted. He was getting up and down from everywhere. Eventually it penetrated my thick skull that it was not luck at all. It looked like magic all right, but that superannuated wedge and an even older putter were murdering me.

The greens at Portmarnock are, quite simply, the best in the world and on that day they were superb. Even I holed putts from long distances, but I could not live against this man. From a hundred yards out he was guaranteed to get down in two. I blushed at the memory of having entertained a hope that with my handicap shots and a bit of luck I might give him a game. A little while previously Harry had been engaged to play a filmed TV match at Portmarnock against the redoubtable Billy Casper. As the day approached the members were torn between loyalty and the seductive odds offered by the local bookies. Harry was having back trouble. And, even without that disability, he was not as long as he had been in his prime.

Casper, on the other hand, was right at the top of his powers and arguably the most accomplished golfer in the world. One of the members put the agonizing problem to Harry. Of course they all wanted him to win and they would be out there pulling for him. They honoured and respected him, and wanted him to understand that nothing would ever change that situation, but the time was fast approaching when the serious matter of putting down the bets had to be faced. The ties of friendship and loyalty were placing an intolerable strain on their consciences. 'Don't worry about that at all,' said Harry. 'So far as I am concerned it won't make a scrap of difference if you bet on Casper.' These generous words were as comforting as a papal absolution. 'But,' added Harry, 'I can tell you one thing. I will win.' There are sportsmen from whom such words would be meaningless, nothing more than a braggadocio attempt at self-reassurance. Coming from Bradshaw, the statement meant exactly what it said. And, of course, he did win, much to the profit of the faithful, who duly celebrated in fitting style.

Not that the Irish need much encouragement in such matters. After Bernard Hunt won the inaugural Carroll's tournament, the tiles on the clubhouse roof were popping under the strain of the merry-making. In the early hours of the morning a policeman arrived to investigate what sounded like a revolution, and the following exchange transpired:

'What's going on here?'

'We're celebrating a famous Irish victory.'

'But Bernard Hunt is English.'

'Ssssssh!'

Although incidents like this enliven the life of a golf correspondent, it is not Irish tournament golf which attracts me to Ireland. Tournaments, after all, are still work, even though they may be spiced with a certain element of novelty. My delight, and it is shared by everyone who has experienced it, is to play golf in Ireland. It is probably the last country in the world which can offer the type of golfing experience which used to be enjoyed by the wealthy and privileged in prewar England and Scotland.

As I have already mentioned, driving a motorcar in Ireland still retains an element of recreation. Motoring is a pleasure rather than a chore, and this in itself is a bonus for the golfer. He can put his clubs into the car and be off, on the whim of the moment.

Unless you happen to choose a fashionable Dublin course on a summer weekend, there is no need for preliminary phone calls or formal letters of introduction from the secretary of your own club. You just arrive, pay a tiny green fee, and the course is yours. To those who come from countries where golf clubs treat casual visitors as if they were suffering from infectious and fatal diseases, the mere fact of being made to feel welcome is a refreshing change.

But the real change is the courses themselves. A wealthy and well-connected golfer in London can play some wonderful golf courses, but they are basically of two types, heathland or parkland. Edinburgh is rich in golf, but again the choice is limited to links or parkland. Glasgow is the same. From Dublin, however, you are within half an hour's drive of all manner of golf. There are the majestic championship links of Portmarnock and Royal Dublin. There is dunes golf over the Island, lush parkland at Castle. You can play in the clouds among the mountaintops at Howth. Or, if your legs and lungs aren't up to such exertions, you can stroll over the flat clifftop fairways at Woodbrook. There are thirty clubs in and around Dublin and all of them of a different nature. Not all of them are great courses, or even good ones, mind. But they are different certainly.

My own preference, however, is to get right away from cities whenever possible and to ponder on the larger spiritual issues, such as which is the greatest golf course in all the universe. I have narrowed it down to two: Royal County Down on the east coast and Ballybunion on the west. One day, after many more field trials, I trust, I shall arrive at a firm conclusion.

These two are, of course, big and magnificent links. Killarney is magnificent also. But, at the risk of sounding like a travelogue, I would urge that the itinerant golfer in Ireland should on no account neglect the small and out-of-the-way courses. Some of them are ludicrous, and I remember one, which shall be nameless, where the men who built the greens were clearly working from the plans for tees. All the greens are exactly rectangular, like up-turned cake tins.

Others are gems. If you drive through County Kerry and take the right turning off the coast road down a cart track and then again turn down the right track from the previous track, you will, if you are lucky, discover Dooks. I found it by accident, and since there was no one but sheep to whom I could pay a green fee, I slipped what I considered a suitable offering through the letter box of a hut which does duty as a clubhouse and went out to play. Even at the time, it was a dreamlike experience, playing over the rolling hills and guessing, often wrongly, which hollow would harbour a green. I did not see another human all day.

Not that human contact is unrewarding on Irish golf courses. Quite the contrary, as my friend Mark Wilson discovered. He is, if I may say so, without offence, one of those players to whom half the glory of golf is belting the life out of the ball. And being a powerful man, he can belt it with stunning effect.

He went out to play one evening and engaged a caddie, a bright lad with flaming red hair and a keen interest in his master's golfing welfare. They came to a hole with the tee elevated high on a mountainside. The fairway, hard and fast, sloped away below and the fresh breeze blew directly from behind – exactly the circumstances to quicken the pulse of a belter. Mark caught the ball with one of his Sunday specials, right off the screws.

'Boy!' exclaimed the lad, 'that was some drive.' As they walked down the fairway the caddie kept emitting expressions of astonishment and admiration. 'You certainly gave that one the business, mister.' 'That was a real beauty,' and so on. As they came nearer the ball the lad's chatter became more and more excited. At last he burst out in excitement, 'You've done it. I've seen them all play this hole – O'Connor and Joe Carr and all them big hitters. They none of them ever got it this far. That must be the world record.' He looked at Mark with hero-worshipping awe and added, 'I never did see the like of that drive all my life.' And for the rest of the round he kept up the reference to that Herculean drive. 'Just give her one like you did back there.' All of which was highly agreeable to Mark's ego, and he tipped the lad liberally when they finished.

Later, Mark was talking to the club secretary in the bar and the conversation went like this:
'Good round?'
'Very pleasant, thank you.'
'Enjoy the course?'
'Very much.'
'Caddie all right?'
'Excellent.'
'Which one did you have?'
'Ginger-haired lad, a boy of excellent judgement.'
'Did you tip him well?'
'Yes, I did actually. Why do you ask?'
'At what hole did he tell you that you'd hit the longest drive he'd ever seen in his life?'
'Twelfth ... You mean?'

'Everybody. Never fails. It's pretty hard not to get a long way off that twelfth tee. That boy will be a millionaire before he's twenty.'

Finally, if anything I have written should persuade you to try Irish golf for yourself, please don't all rush at once. That would ruin everything. Pick a companion, or two or three. And take care to choose men whose drinking rate corresponds with your own. Then sneak across quietly in twos or threes and sample the game as it should be played. As it was in the beginning – world without end (if we are lucky).

The Golfer's Bedside Book (Batsford), 1971

Golf in the Sky

The lift of the Eiffel Tower lurches suddenly as great winding wheels, reminiscent of a coal mine, take up the slack of steel wires. The lift makes an oblique ascent up one leg of the monstrous tower, a curious sensation much like a dressage rider must experience doing an *épaule en dedans*. Just as horses are designed to move in the direction they are aimed at, so lifts ought to go straight up, and this deviation from nature's way is faintly unnerving. From the first stage upwards all is well. Back to the normality of the vertical, to the second stage. Below, the lunacy of the day's rush hour traffic does not look nearly so serious because the cars have been reduced to Dinky Toys.

The guests at breakfast are a mixed bunch. Press and TV men and fulltime celebrities, rich and poor, famous and anonymous, all brought down to croissants and coffee, if brought down is the phrase for a meal to which we have been elevated 300 feet into the air.

Inevitably there are speeches. My neighbour from *L'Equipe* offers to translate. 'We are gathered here in the brotherhood of a great sport....' A look of distaste crosses his face and he ceases the translation with a shrug. Public relations waffle is public relations waffle in any language.

Another speaker takes over the microphone. He, at least, is delighted by his interminable discourse. The arrival of Arnold Palmer brings merciful release. 'Ah, Palmaire!'

The golfer goes outside the restaurant and mounts a platform. He poses patiently, shoulders hunched and his weathered face screwed up against the rain, as a hundred flashbulbs pop. 'Just one more. Can you hold the club up? This way, please, Monsieur Palmaire.' Palmer's grizzled hair is now plastered flat against his scalp as he grinds his spiked shoes into the rubber mat and sets up a golf ball.

He cautiously raises his club, and notes that his backswing just clears a steel stanchion by a few inches. He peers out over the edge of the platform towards his target, an impossibly narrow strip of formal grass in the Champ de Mars. Not inappropriate that. Palmer, a kind of god of a kind of war, tries another slow motion swing to test that he can get the clubhead back without cracking a photographer's shin.

He addresses the ball, goes back in a cramped parody of the Palmer swing, and hits, truncating his characteristic twiddle on the follow-through. The ball disappears from human view, lost against the grey sky. Scurrying figures below detect the ball's descent and indicate that it has fallen wide of that narrow fairway somewhere in the symmetry of trees and bushes of the eighteenth-century park. Another attempt, equally cramped and crabbed in the execution.

That one, and the next also, go wide as the ball is grabbed by the buffeting headwind. Palmer moves the mat forward to the edge of the platform. Now, with a bit more room to move – enough to swing a cat if not a golf club – he makes good contact. Excited figures in plastic raincoats calculate by trigonometry of triangulation, or some such mathematical wizardry, that he has driven the ball 254 metres and 14 centimetres. Call it 280 yards. Not a world record but certainly the longest drive ever hit from the biggest tee peg in the world. It must be a record of sorts, although it means nothing to Palmer. The only record he relishes is his 57 hours 25 minutes and 18 seconds flying his own jet around the world earlier this year (1976), breaking the previous record by no less than twenty-nine hours.

The only thing this morning's business meant to him was that it cost him a favourite driver. On the last smack the shaft caught the handrail on the follow-through. He is philosophical about it. He is accustomed to stunts and this one was not much dafter than most. It was designed to promote a perfume company and that was too apt. As an exercise it was £5 worth of bottle and 10p worth of content, but the pictures made the evening papers. As an amateur, Palmer once hit a drive 450 yards, so you could hardly call 280 yards a huge success. But in the publicity game there is success and success.

Observer, October 1976

Oasis in Israel

The late Baron Edmond de Rothschild had his priorities about right when he endowed the infant Israel with a parliament building, an educational television service, and a golf club.

He thus guaranteed a source of wisdom, tolerance, honest self-appraisal and good health for the new nation. Who knows but in time the Knesset and the TV may eventually prove to be valuable gifts as well?

Caesarea remains the only golf club in Israel. Driving to it north from Tel Aviv along the coast road, the visiting golfer passes mile upon mile of virgin sand dunes, perfect raw material for a string of magnificent links to rival the best that the Fylde coast of England or the Lothians of Scotland can offer.

The temptation to get at it with a bulldozer and a packet of Bermuda grass seed is overwhelming, although a few conditions must obviously be satisfied before the golf virus can multiply in Israel to anything like epidemic proportions.

The leisure which only a permanent peace can provide, and a change from dearth to surplus of fresh water to pour onto the thirsty sand, are two requirements. They will surely come in time.

Then there is the slight inconvenience that any excavation more ambitious than a healthy divot with a pitching wedge is almost certain to disclose precious archeological finds from Roman, Crusader or Byzantine times, and work has to stop. By the time the scholars have dug 200 feet with teaspoons and toothbrushes and removed the historical treasure, the golf developer would be liable to have lost patience and departed.

However, there is something in the air of the Holy Land which encourages prophesy: Israel will rise as a golfing power and the game will coexist happily with other religions.

So far as sport is concerned, Israelis are emotionally linked with Europe even though they find themselves the victims of Asiatic geography. As such they have little chance of escaping the golfing plague which has attacked the rest of us.

That is looking well ahead, and for the moment the germ is kept isolated in Caesarea. The British visitor, whose ideas about Israel have been conditioned by headlines and newsreels, soon has his pre-conceptions about the country turned upside down.

Every pretty girl does not carry an automatic rifle, and the sight of the locals sitting at pavement tables, sipping coffee at midnight and analysing how Liverpool Football Club failed to win the championship, dispels the notion of a beleaguered fortress.

The golf course provides another surprise for those who are accustomed to the lavish splendour of English Jewish clubs. The clubhouse is unpretentious to the point of modesty, although the course itself is a beauty, as it could hardly fail to be on such ground.

Take a decent Scottish links, remove the hurricane, bring to a gentle simmer in the Mediterranean sun and decorate the fairways with edgings of olive trees, eucalyptus and cedars of Lebanon, and you get some idea of the place.

Observer, April 1975

'You Don't Need to Be a Giant to Play My Courses' –

Jack Nicklaus

Jack Nicklaus marched across the land, typical undulating country-side of northern Ohio, lightly wooded, with streams trickling through the valleys. Suddenly he stopped. His bright, calculating eyes softened as he stood admiring a magnificent poplar. He pointed to this vener-able specimen and turned to an associate: 'The first thing we do, the very first, is put a lightning conductor on that tree.'

The incident, trivial enough in itself, occurred during a preliminary site inspection by Nicklaus in his role as golf course designer. It gives a clue to a side of his character which, to my shame, I had never suspected. I knew Nicklaus the man who had never flinched or complained when the cruel crowds taunted him with insults in the days when he was toppling the demigod, Arnold Palmer, from his pinnacle. I knew Nicklaus the golfer who planned his campaigns with the cold, mathematical approach of a Montgomery – the man who analysed the risks and the scores and who sometimes lost tournaments because of his reluctance to take a chance. I knew also, and preferred, the Nicklaus who was forced by desperation to abandon such careful strategy and who then produced rare bursts of golf such as no mortal has ever played before. And I knew Nicklaus the social companion whose lively intelligence made him a stimulating and provocative talker.

His friends had always said that once Nicklaus had achieved his goals in golf he would quit tournament play and devote himself to the good life of fishing and collecting fine wines for his cellar. He would not linger on in golf as one of those sad, ageing heroes who are always hoping for a comeback. I accepted that judgement since I had detected nothing in Nicklaus's character to contradict it.

Well, Nicklaus is far from finished with playing ambitions. That Grand Slam still looms as a spectre to taunt him. He does not speak of it. Indeed, he consciously tries to ignore it. But it is there, and he is not yet ready to concede that the challenge is beyond him.

But more and more, in these last few years, he has become obsessed by golf course design. His playing programme is strictly limited while his life as a designer expands each year.

Nicklaus says, 'I've always wanted to be a designer. I suppose it comes from the way I play. In planning my approach to any hole I have always started by asking myself what the architect had in mind. I would try to redesign any hole that did not make sense to me. It helped me in my golf, and all I needed to make designing a career was the opportunity.'

I believe that Nicklaus was born with a creative streak in his character which golf cannot satisfy. Creativity is compulsive. It demands an outlet. Painters have to paint and writers have to write, regardless of whether anyone is interested in their work. A professional golfer has no release for this consuming virus of creativity – except by designing courses.

The evidence to support this theory becomes overwhelming as you talk with Nicklaus about his new passion. Frankly, I had expected him to reveal himself as an analytical designer, plotting angles and distances with the soulless efficiency of a computer, and superimposing his strategic ideas on the landscape with ruthless efficiency. In fact, as I was surprised and delighted to discover, that side of his character is almost totally sublimated to his instincts. He operates by eye and feel, by balance and counterpoint, the way an artist works.

As he learned from the experienced designers he hired, Nicklaus's press conferences began to reflect his growing confidence in the technicalities of the trade. Where another golfer would say he had hit out of the rough, Nicklaus would explain that he played from a clump of hybrid-bent, or drop an aside that rye grasses cut down backspin. When a coarse grass infested the greens at Augusta, he really came into his own. By the time he had finished explaining what it was like to putt across a patch of *poa annua*, there wasn't a dry eye in the house.

Against all the trends in American designing, Nicklaus-designed courses are relatively short. 'Power in golf,' he says, 'has become totally out of proportion. This is a game of precision, not strength, and that aspect has become so important to me that I plan my playing programme accordingly. I just do not want to play those long, dull, wide-open turf-nursery courses any more. Where is the challenge in just beating at the ball? Any idiot can do that. Length is only one factor, and if everyone is to enjoy golf the course must be within his capabilities. Golf should make you think, and use your eyes, your intelligence and your imagination. Then, if you hit your best shots, you should be rewarded. To me, variety and precision are more important than power and length.'

There we have one fundamental precept in the design philosophy of

Nicklaus. A preference for modestly sized greens is another. But he insists that nature is the best architect and that there are no Jack Nicklaus trademarks. 'I would hate golfers to recognize a "typical" Nicklaus design. What I want is for them to say, "This is a fine course," without knowing, or caring, who designed it.'

What, then, of strategy? Even if one could not recognize physical idiosyncracies, would it not be possible to detect the Nicklaus touch in the type of challenge presented to the golfer? 'I hate strategic golf courses,' said Nicklaus, revealing that unsuspected artistic side of his personality. 'You can always see where an architect has deliberately set out to force you to play a hole in one particular way. Often I will put in a bunker, or a lake, or trees, which have no possible bearing on the play, just because they improve the appearance of the hole.'

Finally, Nicklaus felt himself ready to go solo as a designer, which brings us back to that poplar and the lightning conductor. The place is named Muirfield Village (no prizes for guessing why he chose the first name), 1600 acres near his old hometown of Columbus, Ohio. This is Nicklaus's Augusta National, an inevitable association, although he does not particularly relish being held up and compared alongside the legendary Bobby Jones, like matching specimen fish.

Muirfield Village is Nicklaus's baby, the culmination of that long apprenticeship and the realization of a dream. It is indeed a village development, with houses and roads, because in America this is the way that most golf courses today are financed. Hard economics, that vulgar villain of golf development, with its ugly attendants, urbanization, land-utilization and infrastructure, invariably grab the choicest parts of the site. The poor architect is left to fit in the course as best he may, compromising at every turn with the greedy demands of the money-making bricks and mortar.

Nicklaus, as developer, designer and builder, reversed the process. The course came first, with absolute priority. The homes would have to be fitted in where they could afterwards. And not just an ordinary course. This was to be the first golf course designed specifically to cater for vast crowds (up to 80,000) for tournament golf. Yes, yes, there will surely be a Nicklaus tournament, which will inevitably add another dimension to the fish-matching game with the Masters of Bobby Jones.*

Natural amphitheatres overlook each hole at Muirfield Village, which, like most of his other efforts, is less than 7000 yards. Water, in

*And, indeed, it began in 1976 – The Memorial Tournament.

some form, is present on fifteen holes but, as with the seventy-one bunkers, in some cases the purpose is purely visual. The greens are small to medium, the fairways generously wide, and in most cases the land falls away in front of the tees. 'Golf is a better game played downhill,' says Nicklaus. 'It is more visual and more fun.' No one who has experienced the exhilaration of standing on Old Sunningdale's tenth tee, with the fairway swooping majestically below, will be disposed to argue with that thesis.

One innovation at Muirfield Village is pure Nicklaus, stamping his signature on the place as surely as the autograph on the back of his irons. It is the practice ground, usually the last item to receive consideration in planning a new layout. In most cases the practice ground turns out to be any bit of land that happens to be left over.

This one is circular, 300 yards across, with five target greens in the centre. From the raised tees on the perimeter a golfer can practise into the wind, whichever way it happens to be blowing. Two more practice greens on the circumference are reserved for chipping and bunker play.

Muirfield Village is the first course to be planned right from the drawing board as a tournament site, although Nicklaus believes that others will follow to cater for the sophisticated demands of television and live galleries.*

What next for Nicklaus in his new role? He reckons he should be able to design about five courses a year until he retires from tournament play. After that, the sky's the limit, he says with relish. 'Then I will be into golf architecture fulltime.' His secretary comments wryly, 'It's fulltime now; playing golf is the sideline. He took more plane rides last year to look at golf course sites than he did to play in tournaments.'

Golf World, June 1974

---

*The new Tournament Players Club in Florida, permanent site of the US Tournament Players' Championship, is such a course.

Playing against Loaded Dice ___⚑

Mr Podgorny is a sociable chap, by all accounts, but intense. At the end of the Russian leader's three-day state visit to Zambia (April 1979), President Kenneth Kaunda was up to here with exchanges of fraternal greetings, the exploring of avenues of mutual interest, bilateral discussions, joint statements of goodwill, and talks both full and frank, not to mention a threat of indigestion from all that banqueting.

No sooner had the guard of honour ordered arms after the last salute as the Russian jet took off from Lusaka, than President Kaunda climbed into his helicopter and ordered simply: 'Golf.' He landed in the grounds of State House, and within minutes appeared in slacks and sports shirt to greet his guests.

These were rather different guests from the newly departed Russians – a dozen professional golfers, the British Caledonian Golfing Lions team. Rumour had it that Mr Kaunda had been trying to put the bite on Podgorny for a loan. Now suspicions grew that he might be about to redress the nation's unfavourable foreign exchange balance with a few side bets on the coming match.

A notice was distributed outlining the conditions: 'The match will be played over eighteen holes medal. Should the visiting team have any doubts about the rules, a member of the home team will give an unbiased ruling which will be final. Therefore all members of the home team will act as Tournament Referees. S. Kazunge (Secretary to the Cabinet) will, as always, compute the score, and his reading of the result is final. Many visiting teams have made favourable comments about his fair play. As always you are most welcome to Zambia and to State House Golf Club. May the better team win – State House.'

The special local rules for the occasion carried the same message of jaunty confidence:

1. Birds and animals. Peacocks, guinea-fowl, duck, dicker, impala, etc., have unquestioned right not to be disturbed, and anyone who causes injury or death to any of these birds and animals (including the 'etc.') will suffer the following penalties: (a) immediate and ignominious suspension from State House Golf Course; (b) The Minister of Home Affairs, who is a member of State

94

House team, will be alerted as the case may be classified as illegal hunting, i.e., poaching. Poaching carries a heavy penalty in Zambia.

2. *Preferred lies*. Depending on the weather, the Captain of State House Golf Club (His Excellency the President) in consultation with members of his team will take a decision on the day whether we should prefer lies on the fairways. Note: *On the fairways*. Fairways are demarcated by the home team. The home team is known for its fairness.

3. *Stones*. Free drop at player's option is allowed. Do not carry stones in your pockets as a means of getting a free drop from a bad lie.

4. *Lost ball*. To speed up play, another ball should be dropped near the point where the original ball was lost. *Penalty*: N.B. The word 'near' as used here is given as liberal and generous interpretation as is consistent with the spirit of good sportsmanship. Only one penalty shot.

5. *Newly constructed lakes*. No fishing is allowed, and players are not allowed to pursue any ball that may drop in the lakes. The golf balls in the lakes will be 'raked' out once a week and remain the property of State House Golf Club. The Captain will, at his discretion, dish out the 'loot' to his team mates at an appropriate time. Only one penalty shot for losing a ball in the lakes.

Before play began, His Excellency led us into lunch and commanded that the guests be plied with copious draughts of wine but that his team should abstain. I swear that one High Court judge took him seriously for a minute and froze with glass half-raised.

In an international league table of golfing heads of state I suppose President Kaunda would rate as a contender for the championship, just below King Hassan II of Morocco and President Marcus of the Philippines. Kaunda took up golf six years ago as a relaxation from the cares of office but quickly became absorbed by the new challenge the game offered. He plays nine holes after work whenever possible, taking with him as many ministers and government officials as are available. Sometimes there are fifteen of them playing together. Those close to him swear that his interest in golf has been of enormous benefit to him.

He plays a 14 handicap, even a few shots better, as on this occasion when his net 67 was good enough to halve his match with Brian Barnes. Zambian handicaps are regulated by a bank computer and, frankly, I would not care to keep my overdraft in a bank which can give former Oxford Blue, David Phiri, a handicap of 11.

To nobody's surprise, the full professional strength of the golfing Lions proved no match for the wiles of assorted ministers, generals and chief justices. It is widely believed in Lusaka that on these occasions the handicaps of the State House team are not allotted until after the match, when the opponents' scores can be duly considered.

In fact, there is no need for any such duplicity. The aforementioned S. Kazunga has forces at his disposal to overwhelm any team of mere professionals. There has been only one slip up in the history of the State House Golf Team, a shock defeat at the hands of the Combined Forces. That was some years back, and I have no doubt they are still doing time to this day, brass hats or no.

Observer, April 1977　　　　　—

The World's Best Fifty Courses Outside America

Anyone who sets out to compile merit lists, be they of the world's ten most beautiful women, the seven deadliest sins, the twenty finest works of art, or the fifty best golf courses outside the United States of America, lays himself open to charges of prejudice, ignorance, folly and corruption. So be it. Let the accusations fly. The defendant pleads guilty on all counts except that of bribery, all opportunities for which were sadly absent from the exercise.

If personal preferences mean prejudice, then the list is prejudiced. If something less than an intimate knowledge of every golf course in the world means ignorance, then the list is ignorant. And if undue emphasis on an especially delightful feature of an otherwise ordinary course means folly, then the rankings in some places are foolish.

The courses are listed in order of preference from one to fifty, along with a capsule description of each and the name of the architect if known.

Perhaps it would be best to present the rankings badly, without explanation or justification, but that would be both cowardly and arrogant. Some kind of rationale must be offered for what is essentially an irrational project, for it is impossible to apply precise, scientific standards to courses. Presumably it's possible to devise equipment and techniques to measure the trueness of a putting surface, but they would be useless in assessing whether it was a good green. How can you calibrate the feelings of a golfer as he settles over a long, downhill putt with the hole cut on a brow and a water hazard waiting to swallow an overbold stroke?

Most of the values of a golf course register only in the golfer's mind, or his gut, or his subconscious, and even then they must be treated with suspicion. No two golfers react the same way. Ask three club members to nominate the best hole on their course, and you are likely to receive three different answers.

Sometimes a consensus is achieved, especially in the case of an individual hole that by general agreement is bad, or weak. It may well be a 'nothing' hole, with no obvious merit, but often enough an architect will introduce such a hole deliberately into his design, for tactical purposes.

After a run of difficult holes, the respite of an easy 'nothing' hole can play havoc with the golfer's state of mind. He mentally drops his guard and relaxes, falling victim to one of the most dangerous thoughts in golf, namely that it is an easy game. Then, if the architect is a real master of the black arts, he will follow this hole with one that looks easy but is in fact diabolically difficult. The fairway may stretch in generous expanse, with never a hazard in view, and the golfer, who has been lulled into complacency, will fail to recognize that only one third of the fairway offers a direct approach to the green. By such chicanery the architect springs the trap he has set on the previous hole – and who now can call that a 'nothing' hole?

I used three basic guidelines in selecting the top fifty courses around the world outside the USA: aesthetics, golfing quality and condition. Subject always to the ultimate veto of personal bias, a course in order to qualify must score at least six points, on a scale of one to ten, in each department. There is a school of thought which holds that the measure of a course's greatness depends on whether it would be suitable for a great championship. Here we enter the realms of controversy, for quite a large proportion of the courses in the list are not of championship quality, mainly because they lack the length to provide the ultimate test considered essential for a championship.

No apologies are offered for numbering shorter courses among the greats. The expression 'championship course' has become thoroughly debased in recent years. At best it means very little in the strictly golfing sense, for championships tend to go to courses where there are hotel facilities and parking and easy access.

'Championship course' is a catch-penny label used by resort developers, and signifies only that the course in question is a dreary slog of over 7000 yards for anyone foolish enough to play it off the back tees. Championships are a highly specialized form of golf which bear little relation to the pastime that ordinary golfers enjoy, and one of the criteria for greatness must be a course that every category of golfer, from rabbit to tiger, can play with supreme satisfaction. So let us consider those three elements of greatness – aesthetics, golfing quality and condition – in further detail.

Aesthetics

On the whole, golfers are not poetic types who drool about the beauty of nature, or stand transfixed at the intoxicating sound of a birdsong, or go into rhapsodies as sunbeams piercing the delicate tracery of a weeping willow's branches dapple a green with light and shade. More likely they growl, 'A man can't hear himself think for the din from that damned bird?' or 'How can you read a putt with all these shadows on the line?'

Golfers tend, in short, to be earthy types who are more interested in the view presented by a succession of fours and threes on their scorecards.

It can be asserted with total confidence that one of the most important reasons why we golfers believe golf to be the finest of all games is that it is played in beautiful surroundings. Golf represents an escape from our concrete jungles and invoices and telephones and income taxes and mechanical contrivances – an escape from all the paraphernalia of modern life back to the natural life. It is an instinctive, primitive appeal to get out into the country, to feel grass underfoot.

Doubtless there are people who will argue that natural beauty adds nothing to their golf. It is easy enough to conjure up a picture of such a person – a bad-tempered little man with a face like a weasel and a soul withered from years of repossessing old ladies' TV sets. Now hear him say, 'Take a big, flat field and mark out the outline of the sixteenth at Cypress point and it will play exactly the same as the real one.'

Of course it would do no such thing. The rocky coastline and the crashing waves and the view across Carmel Bay all contribute to the shot which must be played. In theory the shots may be identical, but in practice there is a world of difference between them because of the golfer's reaction to his surroundings, as the weasel-faced little man would be forced to admit if he were put to the test.

At Royal County Down in Northern Ireland the mountains of Mourne sweep down to the sea. Though several miles away, they dominate the scene as you play the inward holes. In prosaic fact, they ought not to affect the way you play, and yet they do, for they affect the way you feel. Golf, after all, is a game played against one's inner self.

It is self-evident that anyone with the physique to knock the head off a daisy with a walking stick can hit an excellent golf shot. All of us have hit superb shots from time to time. Why can't we hit them all the time, one after another? The ball sits still, waiting to be hit. No opponent tries to obstruct us. The answer is that the inner self fouls us up. He is the real opponent and he is the one who appreciates beautiful surroundings. Put him in a lovely place and he may – just may – soften in his vicious efforts to sabotage our swing. That, essentially, is why beauty is requisite to greatness in a golf course.

Golfing quality

My first requirement of any golf course is playability: that is to say that everyone, including the very shortest hitters, must be able to get around in reasonable fashion. This is so basic as hardly to need stating, but it is possible to find individual holes that are quite beyond the capacity of some players, who fire away at an impossible carry until they run out of ammunition and then have to walk in.

The second requirement is that the course should provide scope for the proper playing of the game, and here we move into the area that separates good courses from bad ones. Golf architecture has always been an imprecise mongrel of a profession, calling for rather more than a smattering of civil engineering, agronomy and cost accountancy, plus an inspiration and vision which can only come from a profound understanding of the game and which is a gift given to very few men.

There are far more bad architects than good ones, and always have been, and not a few charlatans have been attracted into the ranks. The good architect sees golf as two exercises. First comes the problem, laid out in front of the golfer as he stands on the tee. On great courses this mental challenge is every bit as important as the execution of the shot. Unless the golfer selects the correct solution, the finest shots will not bring their reward.

Let us take an extreme example. You hit your best drive straight down the middle. Then you appraise the second shot, carefully select your club and hit the ball exactly as you planned. Now, if your ball should fall twenty yards short, into a water hazard, then you know that you have been outsmarted in the battle of wits between you and the architect. You did everything right and he conned you. At this point, instead of slamming your club into the ground and swearing that the yardage marker must be incorrect, you should respectfully doff your cap to the genius who tricked you and analyse how he did it.

Most of the trickery of the great architects is much more subtle than that. It involves a probing of the golfer's character to exploit his weaknesses. A diagonal hazard at driving distance, for instance, tempts the greedy player to try to bite off more than he can handle.

The good architect also maintains a fair balance between reward and punishment. He arranges his hazards so that the man going for the jackpot, say a full wood second shot into a par-5 green, must flirt with the potential disaster of running up a seven if he falters in the execution of the stroke. However, the cautious player who attacks the hole as a three-shotter has a relatively trouble-free passage to the green.

Likewise, the great architect uses optical illusions to confuse the golfer and nowhere more so than on the green, where it is possible to make a left-to-right putt look like a right-to-left swing. All this knavery is acceptable – indeed, it is the very soul of golf – provided that the problem is presented fairly, which brings us to the question of blind shots. Can they be tolerated in a great course? Here the world of golf is divided, and the two opposing views must be offered with strict impartiality.

The traditionalists, poor misguided boobs that they are, claim that golf is a game of luck and that blind shots are just another example of the lottery of the game. They might as well campaign for greens as rough as possible, making putting even more chancy, for all the sense they make. Anyway, that is their opinion and they are entitled to an unbiased presentation.

Enlightened moderns concede that luck can never be eliminated entirely from golf but hold that everything possible should be done to reduce it to the very minimum, making golf more a game of skill than chance. That means true greens, fairways that offer a decent lie and no blind approaches. Some courses with great reputations have been omitted from the list because of their blind shots. True, there are blind holes to be found on some of the selected fifty, but only in cases where other virtues are overwhelming.

Condition

So far we have covered the factors that delight the eye, elevate the spirit, challenge the mind and examine the golfer's capacity to make strokes. Now we come to the final element, the one that introduces pure pleasure into golf. The most perfectly conceived hole, in the most delightful surroundings, can be a misery if it is built on heavy, undrained clay. Hitting a golf ball from a sloppy lie robs the game of control and pleasure.

By the same token, courses that are badly maintained cannot be stamped with the imprint of greatness. Sand-based courses enjoy a huge advantage in this respect, which is the only valid reason (although not the one the traditionalists cite) for the opinion that links golf is the only true expression of the game. As drainage and maintenance standards rise, so courses based on different subsoils offer conditions underfoot that are in no way inferior, although nothing can quite match the sensation of a crisp shot struck from the fine turf of a course with a sand base.

Finally, the great dilemma. No matter how painstakingly we approach the task of placing courses in an order of merit, there remains one problem that defies logic. How can you compare a links with a forest course, or a parkland course to a mountain course or a jungle course? For better or for worse, personal preference must make the arbitration and no rational explanations can be offered, any more than a man can say why he prefers whisky to gin.

1. *Royal County Down, Newcastle, Northern Ireland*
In the year 1889 the club was formed and the secretary was instructed to commission Tom Morris to lay out and construct a course at a cost not to exceed £4. Magnificent links on Dundrum Bay with the mountains of Mourne sweeping down to the sea.

2. *Royal Melbourne, Australia*
All the natural forces of weather, topography, vegetation and subsoil combine to make the Melbourne sand belt perfect golfing country, and Royal Melbourne, shaped by a genius of an architect, is the best of an outstanding bunch. Smoothest greens anywhere. Architect: Alister Mackenzie.

3. *Durban Country Club, Natal, South Africa*
Rolling sand hills, lush tropical vegetation, cooling sea breezes and an exceptional layout that has stood the test of time since 1920 give Durban its pre-eminence on the African continent. Architect: Laurie Waters.

4. *Cajuiles, La Romana, Dominican Republic*
Surely the most visionary of contemporary architects, Pete Dye, took on the challenge of creating a course from the unpromising Caribbean coastal terrain and was stimulated to build one of the few masterpieces of modern golf.

5. *El Saler, Valencia, Spain*
The late Javier Arana has never received the international recognition that his genius deserved, mainly because he worked exclusively in his native Spain. Seaside golf at its best, combined with a very special Spanish flavour.

6. *Muirfield, East Lothian, Scotland*
The home of the Honourable Company of Edinburgh Golfers, possibly
the oldest golf club in the world, Muirfield is a traditional links and the
fairest of them all, with hazards clearly visible and splendid views
across the Firth of Forth. Architect: unknown.

7. *Hirono, Kobe, Japan*
Hirono predates the great Japanese golfing explosion, having been
built in 1932, and it therefore served as a model and an inspiration for
those that followed. Classic parkland course. Architect: C. H. Alison.

8. *Lagunita, Caracas, Venezuela*
Another park course, Lagunita is relatively short by championship
standards at less than 7000 yards, but its superb design by a master of
the craft makes it a tough proposition for the best. Architect: Dick
Wilson.

9. *Royal Birkdale, Southport, England*
In fact, as with so many links courses, nature is the true architect of
Birkdale, with huge sand hills dictating the character of the holes. A
tenacious variety of willow scrub makes a unique rough which can
break your heart if not your club. Architect: Fred Hawtree.

10. *Dorado Beach, Puerto Rico*
If the developer has enough cash and the architect has enough
imagination, anything is possible, as Dorado Beach proves. Once a
mosquito-infested swamp, it is now a millionaire-infested golfing
playground. Architect: Robert Trent Jones.

11. *Royal Montreal, Canada*
Another unpromising site transformed into a glorious course on
which the designer unashamedly invites the golfer to pause and
admire the views during his progress along the fairways. Architect:
Dick Wilson.

12. *Kasumigaseki, Tokyo, Japan*
With not a blade of grass out of place, it seems almost profane to play
golf on such lovingly and lavishly manicured terrain. But well worth
it, for this is Japanese golf at its very best. Architects: Kinya Fujita
and C. H. Alison.

13. *Ballybunion, County Kerry, Ireland*
You cannot get farther away from it all than this wild and glorious stretch of Atlantic duneland, nearly always to be played in a spanking wind with the tang of peat smoke in your nostrils, and always in gratitude at being alive. Architect: unknown.

14. *Nchanga, Chingola, Zambia*
You have never heard of it? Sadly, few can ever see it, for this jungle course built by copper miners is rated by Bobby Locke as the finest course south of the equator. Great Golf, plus botanical garden, plus safari park. Architect: unknown.

15. *Walton Heath, Surrey, England*
Although the majestic design has been slightly modified by tampering committees and intrusive roadbuilding, Walton Heath remains one of Britain's glories of inland golf. Architect: Herbert Fowler.

16. *Club zur Vahr, Bremen, Germany*
Carved through a forest of massive conifers, Vahr combines a superb strategic layout, demanding the widest variety of shots. Architect: Bernard von Limburger.

17. *New South Wales GC, Matraville, Australia*
Very tough, very attractive and mostly very windy, the golf here is enhanced by the bonus of sea views over the Pacific and Botany Bay. Architect: Alister Mackenzie.

18. *Penina, Algarve, Portugal*
Henry Cotton took an unlikely area of paddy fields and created a botanical extravaganza. A monster off the back tees, but swallow your pride and move forward and the course becomes a delight.

19. *Club de Golf Mexico, Mexico City*
Definitely one for tree lovers. Club de Golf Mexico cuts its majestic way through groves of cypress, eucalyptus, pine and cedar. Architects: Percy J. Clifford and Laurence Hughes.

20. *Den Haag, Netherlands*
Justly proud of its reputation as the best links course in Continental Europe. The Hague has switchback fairways and some of the most undulating greens to be found anywhere, making golf a sometimes frustrating but always rewarding experience. Architect: Sir Guy Campbell.

21. *Great Harbour Cay, Bahamas*
Unashamedly a resort course, it is an outstanding example of the genre in the idyllic surroundings of a tiny Caribbean island with golf muted to a holiday mood. Architect: Joe Lee.

22. *Pevero, Sardinia, Italy*
A resort for wealthy holiday-makers, but what a tiger of a course for the poor, tired businessman. Blasted out of the boulders and scrub of the Macchia country, where brigands once hid from the law, a stray shot spells a lost ball. Magnificent golf. Architect: Robert Trent Jones.

23. *Wack Wack, Manila, Philippines*
A decent, honest course with a well-deserved international reputation. Wack Wack was named after the cry of the crows which formerly nested there, not (as many assume) from a caddie's description of his master's efforts. Architect: Jim Black.

24. *Banaff Springs, Alberta, Canada*
Surely the most spectacular course in the world, set among the Rockies and positively defying the golfer to keep his eye on the ball. The scenery often obscures the fact that the course is superb in its own right. Architect: Stanley Thompson.

25. *Royal Johannesburg, South Africa*
This is flattering golf, for the ball flies vast distances in the thin atmosphere of the High Rand, but it is also frustrating golf, save for the trusty few, because the vicious nap makes putts break uphill. Glorious African parkland. Architect: R. G. Grimsdell.

26. *Portmarnock, Dublin, Ireland*
Built on a peninsula of rolling sand dunes piercing into Dublin Bay, Portmarnock is possibly the finest expression of links golf to be found anywhere. It is fair golf, both in the sense of being honest and in the biblical terminology of behold, she is fair. Architect: unknown.

27. *La Gavas, Rio de Janeiro, Brazil*
Except for the intersecting highway, this lovely course in a valley between mountains and sea would surely rate a higher place on the golfing totem pole. Accuracy is the watchword and for full appreciation the course must be played several times. Architect: unknown.

28. *Sotogrande (Old), Spain*
Artificial lakes, undulating greens of terrifying speed, bunkers of eccentric shapes – these are the Trent Jones trademarks. But here he was in a relatively benign mood and his course is a joy to play and look at. Architect: Robert Trent Jones.

29. *Falkenstein, Hamburg, Germany*
Hilly country with trees and heather provide faint echoes of Scotland. Architect Harry Colt, who learned his golf at St Andrews, added to this impression by building large greens. High premium on driving and putting.

30. *Quinta do Lago, Algarve, Portugal*
Glorious survivor of an ambitious development that went west during the revolution, Quinta is built through wild country of pine and cork oak and is surely destined to become the centre piece of a fashionable resort. Architect: William Mitchell.

31. *Lake Karrinyup, Western Australia*
Dominated by the lake from which it gets its name, Lake Karrinyup offers a rich variety of wildlife as a bonus to the excellence of its golfing quality. Sand, under the turf rather than in the bunkers, is the secret of its playing virtues. Architect: Alex Russell.

32. *Carnoustie, Scotland*
A stern test when the wind blows, as it often does, Carnoustie has the most inland nature of any of the British championship links. The convolutions of the Barry Burn create one of the toughest finishes in Britain. Architect: Tom Morris; revised by James Braid.

33. *Mount Irvine Bay, Tobago*
Probably the best of the architect's prolific output, Mount Irvine Bay winds through palm groves over hilly ground, making it hardish work in the tropical heat. Planter's punch is a great restorative, though. Architect: John Harris.

34. *Royal Salisbury, Rhodesia*
Rhodesia, or Zimbabwe as we must learn to call it, has many fine courses. Royal Salisbury, set in attractive parkland, takes pride in its maintenance. Architect: L. B. Waters.

35. *Falsterbo, Sweden*
Except for the wealth of fine links courses in the British Isles, Falsterbo would surely rank high in European golf for it has a special charm and remoteness which is enhanced by the birdlife and Baltic Sea Views. Architect: unknown.

36. *Royal Dar es Salam, Rabat, Morocco*
A typical Trent Jones course in a Moroccan setting, with flamingos striding disdainfully beside the artificial lakes. But what sets this one apart is the standard of upkeep. Nothing is spared to groom the course, for it literally has to be fit for a king. Architect: Robert Trent Jones.

37. *Noordwijk, Netherlands*
This is a rare type of course, for it is a modern links, designed and built since the Second World War, following damage to the original Noordwijksche Club's premises. Pine trees add greatly to the links scenery. Architect: Frank Pennink.

38. *Royal Selangor, Malaysia*
After a long and checkered history, including Japanese occupation during the war when the course reverted to jungle, Royal Selangor has been restored to championship standard. Massive trees and numerous water hazards are the features of this former swamp. Architect: unknown.

39. *Wairakei, New Zealand*
Here is golf with a difference, a course built on pumice stone with the steam of geothermal hot springs drifting across the fairways. A sound rather than an inspired layout, Wairakei is a government project and a fine test of golf. Architects: John Harris and Michael Wolveridge.

40. *Ravenstein, Belgium*
Properly the Royal Golf Club de Belgique, this is a mature course in a noble forest where royal personages once hunted wild boar. Superb chateau clubhouse. Belgians may complain that fortieth is too low. Architect: George Pannall.

41. *St Andrews, Scotland*
Scots will certainly complain of this ranking. However, the Old Course is too old-fashioned for the swinging seventies, although its historical associations and its influence on the game force it into the rankings. Architect: Evolution.

42. *Mid-Ocean, Bermuda*

This one really gets in on the strength of two holes, the first and last. You play from No. 2 to No. 9 trying to calm your nerves after the opening hole, and from 10 to 17 worrying about the eighteenth, where the Atlantic strikes like the ocean at Pebble Beach. Architect: Charles Blair Macdonald.

43. *Caesarea, Israel*

This is the only golf course in Israel to date – the new country has had little inclination or resources for such frivolous development. However, it is a pleasant, links-type course with a refreshing, pioneer spirit among the membership. Architect: unknown.

44. *Le Touquet, France*

Here we have an agreeable blend of links country with some wooded inland holes over undulating ground. It is an excellent test of golf, and for a change the subsidiary forest course is foolish but fun. Architect: unknown.

45. *Singapore Island*

For urban Westerners there is always something exotic about playing a jungle course, no matter how heavily the overlay of civilization has tamed the area. The imprint of architect James Braid ensures golfing quality.

46. *Capilano, Vancouver, Canada*

This is golf at its most exhilarating, for Capilano is set on a shelf high above Vancouver, and unless clouds intervene below – creating a weird illusion of playing in paradise – the views are breathtaking. So are some of the climbs. Architect: Stanley Thompson.

47. *Gleneagles, Auchterarder, Scotland*

Less than championship standard and old-fashioned, but the golfer who strikes a spell of good weather can enjoy idyllic golf here amid some of the country's most majestic scenery. Architect: James Braid.

48. *Fujioka, Japan*

This one could make progress up the charts as it matures and acquires the patina of a reputation. Gentle slopes and tree-lined fairways and a wealth of imagination and innovation in the design. Architect: Tameshi Yamada.

49. *Morfontaine, Senlis, France*
Superb sandy subsoil provides the perfect golfing flora of pine and heather for a tight and tricky masterpiece of a course that lacks only length to bring it the accolade of a championship layout. Architect: Tom Simpson.

50. *Killarney, Ireland*
Almost hypnotic in the beauty of the lakes and mountains, it hardly matters to the visiting golfer that some of the holes are undistinguished. A must for the serious collector of rich golfing memories. Architect: Sir Guy Campbell.

Golf Digest, August 1978

A Dream out of This World _____ ⚑

In rare moments of mellow charity I have been moved to remark that it was the greatest of pities that Scotland, the land which wet-nursed the Dutch game of golf to maturity, was not blessed with a single good course.

My views were not shaken by meetings from time to time with wild-eyed travellers who croaked through frost-bitten lips: 'But there is a good course in Scotland, far to the north on the east coast where the sea is alive with eels as thick as a man's thigh and with heads like wolves. They call this place Dornoch, and the golf is out of this world.'

Quite. A glance at the map proves that Dornoch is very nearly out of this world. So the rumours could be discounted. After all, we have all met men who claim to have seen mermaids or pink elephants, and I ran across one deranged creature who claimed that Sam Snead once bought him a drink.

I checked with Gerald Micklem, whose knowledge and experience of golf is matched only by his constant kindness in pointing out my errors. 'Dornoch?' he said in shocked surprise, as if I had asked about the country club at Atlantis. 'Never seen it.' That was enough for me, or would have been but for the indomitable stamina and enthusiasm of the American Society of Golf Course Architects. A party of these mystics has paused briefly in the labour of laying down sources of man's enjoyment to visit Scotland.

Not content with playing Gleneagles, worshipping at the shrine of the Old Course, paying respects to North Berwick and approving Muirfield, they were adamant that a pilgrimage must be made to Dornoch, home of Donald Ross, who built 500 courses in America and who is to architects what Brunel was to railways. Perforce I had to follow them.

Now, if you will not take *my* word for it, you must respect the opinions of experts. In a word, they drooled. 'Easily the best we've seen.' 'Gorgeous.' 'Mind-blowing.' For myself, I blushed to think that I had once been persuaded to list my fifty best golf courses outside America and had omitted Dornoch. Ask me to explain that lapse and I can only answer with Dr Johnson: 'Sheer ignorance.'

The first reference to golf on the links of Dornoch occurs in 1616, and pretty informal it must have been because the records tell of Old Tom Morris being commissioned to lay out 'a proper nine holes' towards the end of the nineteenth century. You do not get a proper nine holes for peanuts, and the members had to pay subscriptions of two shillings and sixpence a year, giving the club an annual income of £3 18s 6d. J. H. Taylor made some additions and changes, as did George Duncan.

The course was finally restored to its present form, after wartime depredations, in 1948. It really is rather special. A curving bay with a broad beach (blessedly free of shouting children, one bonus of Arctic Circle golf) is backed by a narrow strip of softly contoured duneland rising in two distinct steps, providing just enough width for parallel fairways. You play out along the upper level and then retrace your route at beach level.

At this time of year (May) you are almost dazzled by vast splashes of yellow gorse and broomflowers which outline the fairways. Set against the green of the grass, with no sound except the sibilant hiss of the surf and the occasional lark doing its stuff, the effect is sensational.

Mind you, if you allow all this to go to your head – and the backdrop of seascape and distant Tarbat Ness do not help total concentration on golf – then it is all too easy to fire your ball into those vivid sweeps of gorse, at which times you are likely to become less lyrical.

As for the golfing qualities of Dornoch, links turf never felt more sympathetic underfoot, nor more inviting to a crisp iron shot. At just over 6500 yards the par of 70 is a severe target, with a high proportion of long par-4s.

Of course, the wind is often a factor. Thank heavens it was calm for my visit and I was able to do the course justice, as I usually do when I have the sense to leave my clubs at home and play in the mind's eye. In a brisk off-shore wind I doubt if even my fertile imagination would have permitted me to break 100.

Once the initial euphoria wears off, I suspect that those architects may reactivate their critical faculties and realize that this paradise is not entirely without blemish. You have to play the course twice before you know what you are supposed to do, a clear breach of the design axiom that the golfer should be able to see the problem he is asked to solve. There are a couple of blind drives, and for the second shot to the sixteenth, one of the few places on the course rich in potential for disaster, the green is set in an angle of tumbling cliffs, which danger is not visible to the golfer innocently letting fly over the skyline.

The other drawback is the difficulty of getting there, although that remoteness has its advantages once you have made the effort. One of the American architects was adamant about the stature of Royal Dornoch: 'Forget Cypress Point and the others. This is easily the finest course in the world, the absolute number one. I am glad it is difficult to get here and I am not going to tell anyone about Dornoch. I want to keep it for myself, the way it is, and come back every year until I die.'

Observer, May 1980

Then The Lover Sighing Like A Furnace ..
With A Woful Ballad.

Part Three

Inside the Ropes

Some stirring events on the course

Before the Open

Ever since the Royal and Ancient Golf Club announced that the 1977 British Open championship was to be played at Turnberry, I have had a vision of a district nurse in an old Morris pulling onto the A77 near Maybole at about six in the morning after attending an all-night confinement.

It is the same nurse whose ill-judged manoeuvrings at Blairgowrie a few years ago contrived to hook all the press tent telephone cables onto her rear bumper and rip them from their moorings five minutes before edition time.

On this occasion, muggy from chloroform fumes and the even more potent vapours of the Glenlivet used to wet the baby's head, she fails to observe an approaching tanker. The tanker jack-knifes and overturns, completely blocking the road.

Four hours later, at Turnberry, the starter for the Open championship is hoarse from calling in vain the names of competitors. Traffic by now is backed up solid all the way north to Stirling. Glasgow is paralysed. Not one golfer can get to the course. But wait, what's this? An unknown assistant who has slept in the car park steps forward as his name is called. He is the only competitor not disqualified and wins with scores of 79, 82, 91, 107, playing with a marker.

Despite reassurances from the local police, I cannot entirely erase that vision from my mind, and will confine conjecture about possible winners to players whom I know to be staying within easy walking distance of the first tee.

If golf were a game which invariably rewarded the best man, there would be no problem. We could have the presentation ceremony first, hand the cup to Jack Nicklaus and then play four rounds to determine the runner-up. But you can never be sure. The last time I stayed at Turnberry my bedroom window was torn out by the wind, and hailstones the size of golf balls tore horizontally across the room like cannon balls.

Nicklaus could get frostbite, or he might get hungry during a practice round and innocently expose himself to the Scottish outside

117

catering industry. Not even Nicklaus can play golf with stomach cramp, or coffee poisoning. Cold mutton pies have cost many a good man an Open. Or he might just go broody, the way he can at times.

We must consider other possibles. Hubert Green? On a Scottish links, yardages do not mean very much. You have to be able to judge a shot by eye and, frankly, Green's eyes are too close together to give accurate depth perception. Ask any optician, or maker of range-finders. You need the optics well spaced for triangulation.

Tom Watson has most of the credentials, good current form and a satisfactory spread between the eyes. I am not sure that his driving is certain enough for Turnberry. The winner will have to be long and inordinately straight off the tee because the rough is the special tungsten grass peculiar to the district. I am told that the local sheep get through two or three sets of teeth a year.

Mention of sheep naturally raises the question of Tom Weiskopf. He has the game for Turnberry, but I fear the sight of distant flocks might distract him. You cannot concentrate on golf if you are itching to reach for a gun.

Ben Crenshaw? Now there's a likely candidate. He has managed to convince himself that he likes links golf – and there's a neat psychological trick if you can pull it, rather like developing a taste for dining with the Borgias. My only reservation is that he has shown an unhealthy respect for the traditions of golf. He reads Bernard Darwin, and it would not surprise me to learn that he knows how to spell Auchterlonie and even pronounce it. I fear that playing in Scotland he may succumb to all that 'cradle of the game' rubbish and will therefore lack the essential contempt for bumble and bounce golf.

So far as I am aware there is absolutely nothing wrong with Gary Player. The last time I saw him he had discovered the secret of golf, and of putting, and was at peace with the world. He therefore faces a crisis and, unless his fertile imagination can conjure up an insuperable barrier to overcome, he is a goner. There must be some challenge left for him to conquer. He might try an imaginary broken leg, for instance, have himself put in plaster from hip to ankle, and become the first man to win an Open on crutches. Well, it is just a suggestion, Gary.

Severiano Ballesteros has already used the bad back ploy, in winning the Uniroyal, and I doubt if there is enough cortisone in the world to straighten out his driving sufficiently to tackle Turnberry. He is going to win the Open sometime, but not this year.

Graham Marsh is also going to win the Open in due course, although at the moment he is so thoroughly overgolfed that I fear even his iron constitution and implacable will cannot sustain four good rounds.

That leaves the British challenge. There is feeling abroad that, having been voted Pipeman of the Year (without ever actually lighting his pipe, so far as I am aware), Brian Barnes is now going for the Most Idiotic Headgear title. Do not be deceived by all this window dressing. Barnes has the game, and the golfing brain, and the will to win the Open, although his current form is not absolutely sharp.

And so to Tony Jacklin. He has been a soul in torment for so long that many people have written him off for good. At the risk of sparking off the usual spate of hate mail which always happens these days when I mention Jacklin, I must reiterate my faith in him. For months he has been wrestling with his private demons and lately he has shown signs of getting a head lock on some of them.

A decline in success usually means a loss of confidence, but Jacklin has too much of the stuff. He knows as a matter of objective fact that he is the best player when he goes to a British tournament. He therefore goes along having mentally picked up the trophy before play even begins.

That attitude, he rationalizes, has been the root of his problem. He has allowed his mind to race ahead of events, even to the extent of preparing to pick the ball out of the cup before he has hit the putt. Therefore he misses the putt. Therefore he loses the tournament.

Now he has been practising hard to get his mind synchronized with events. Take things step by step. Think about the putt. Hit the putt. Think about retrieving the ball. Retrieve the ball. Think about the shot to be played next and dismiss those insistent visions of the presentation ceremony.

That, Jacklin believes, is what stress is all about. The hardest thing is to keep your mind on what you are supposed to be doing at the time, which is what Nicklaus does better than anyone.

If Jacklin can school his mind to follow that doctrine over four rounds, then he could quite well be the winner next Saturday. He has the game to win and I cannot recall him playing a bad Open, even in his off spell. I just wish that he had achieved this insight into his problems sooner, and had been able to put them into practice earlier. One good round at the Uniroyal, brilliant though it was, is hardly a conclusive road test for a new philosophy.

Having dismissed all the possible candidates, I appear to have argued my way into a semantic cul-de-sac leading to only one conclusion: nobody is going to win the Open. I will stand by that forecast. Turnberry is essentially a course for avoiding errors and, come Saturday evening, I believe that everyone will have lost the Open, except one. We shall acclaim him the winner but in truth he ought to be designated the non-loser.*

Observer, July 1977

---

*It was Tom Watson, of course, after the most brilliant performance of his career.

Survival: Name
of the Game on Tour

Take a thousand young boys and start them playing golf. Maybe one will emerge as a good enough player to think seriously about tournament golf as a career. Now take a thousand of these one-in-a-thousand youngsters and follow their progress on the professional trail. How many will emerge as great champions? Perhaps one.

Those are the bleak statistics of the US tour, the toughest jungle in world golf, possibly in world sport. The tour is a heartbreak trial which destroys all but the most resilient of players. It goes without saying that you have to play well to survive, but skill is the least of the attributes for success. All over America there are men selling balls and tees over golf shop counters who have the skill to be winners.

What, for instance, do the following have in common: Dick Lotz, Tom Shaw, Ken Still, Jim Colbert, Bunky Henry, Dale Douglass, Larry Hinson, Deane Beman, Orville Moody, Monty Kaser, Larry Ziegler, Steve Spray and Jim Wiechers? The answer is that they all won their first tournaments in 1969 and were therefore by definition promising young stars of tomorrow. Where are they ten years later when, according to their goals and aspirations at the time of their triumphs, they should be at the prime of their careers?

Not one of them finished in the top sixty in 1978. By the usual reckoning of what it costs to play the tour, only one – Colbert – can be said to be making a profit. Beman, now the US PGA Tour Commissioner, and two others have left the tour and the rest all earned substantially less than a good caddie, making large losses on their golf and clearly headed for oblivion.

Their stories can be multiplied a hundredfold. The rate of attrition on the tour is horrifying. We golf fans have it all wrong. We tend to measure success in terms of multiple victories. A golfer who has won twice in one season, or who has earned over $100,000, has had a good year in the public estimation. That is an absurdly high standard of judgement. On the tour the name of the game is survival. Anyone who can live by his golf alone, without sponsorship, for five years deserves to be acclaimed as a remarkable player.

What follows is an attempt to put the tour in perspective, and to show what is entailed in being a touring professional and why the casualty list is so great.

After topping the European Order of Merit for four years in succession, Peter Oosterhuis came to America and settled. He is a survivor on the tour but that is about the extent of it.

He has done well for himself in financial terms, but he would not be human if he did not occasionally yearn to return to his native England and reclaim his star status. Apart from contractual obligations, he has ties of natural pride which bind him to the US tour. He would not care to follow the example of others who have returned as failures – and the list of overseas golfers who have been broken on the cruel American circuit is a long one.

Peter Townsend, of England, after a lengthy and disillusioning campaign in America, is only just now blossoming into the player he so long promised to become. Bobby Cole, of South Africa, is now playing his twelfth year on the US tour without ever having made it into the top sixty. Even Tony Jacklin, who succeeded gloriously in America, was finally broken by it.

Graham Marsh, of Australia, a player of international stature if ever there was one, is now finding life grim on the US tour after his initial success. He, too, faces the dilemma of wanting to go out on a high note, and return to the more congenial pastures of world golf. But the longer he remains, the more difficult it becomes to recapture his form.

Soon it will be the turn of Severiano Ballesteros. Will the tour break him? As a Spaniard in an alien land, his chances of bucking the system must be even more remote than those for English-speaking invaders. Of course, he has the game to beat the world, but on the American tour that is not the half of it.

The American tour really is not America. The tour is a distortion of America. The golf club where a tournament is being held is not the same golf club which exists the other fifty-one weeks of the year. The card room is a scorers' office; the women's lounge is a bank; tents and scoreboards and TV towers transform the course.

The people are not the people you find in the club the rest of the year. That man holding up a 'Quiet Please' board may be a professor or a mechanic or a bank manager or an actor in real life. But in this artificial life of tournament week he is just the man who holds up a 'Quiet Please' board, taking a week's vacation and in all probability wearing a special uniform for the occasion which he himself has paid for. It is impossible to enjoy normal human contact with him because he's all too absorbed in the tournament, and he's not himself that week, anyway. He is a Conquistador or a Thunderbird, and acting a part.

In the bar he will buy you, the touring pro, a drink and laugh rather too loudly at your jokes, but the meeting will be at the superficial level of strangers exchanging pleasantries at a party. Come back next week when he is himself again, and you might discover a fascinating man and even make a friend of him. But, of course, there is no next week. Next week you are at another tournament, in the whirl of another artificial environment.

Apart from the club, what else is there in the life of the itinerant golfer? The answer is precious little – the motel, the freeway and the airport – and once again you are in an artificial environment, the world of the transient. The purpose of travel is to arrive, but for the golfer there is no arrival; the purpose is travel. In a very short while it can become soul-destroying to travel without a destination.

The process itself is slick and efficient. Motel standards are uniformly high, but the sting in that judgement lies in the word 'uniformly'. They are all much the same. Of course, there are differences – different coloured curtains and different bathroom appointments – but they are differences without distinctions. You wake up and strain to remember whether you are in Denver or Dallas. The coffee shops and dining rooms strive for original decor and seductive adjectives for the menus, but the food is standardized. Ingenuity and imagination, which is so evident in motel planning, stops short of the menu.

There is a reason why this should be so. Motels are designed for brief stopovers, and are excellent for anyone who is detained overnight on a journey. They are not supposed to be a way of life, yet for the golfers that is exactly what they represent.

The players who grind out one tournament after another, often in a desperate and self-defeating attempt to win exemption from pre-qualifying, face the greatest risk from this sterile lifestyle. It takes enormous self-discipline to plug away week after week in the face of growing physical and mental exhaustion. The greatest luxury a player can enjoy is the ability to take frequent breaks from the tour and return to the world of normality. But for overseas players, and for golfers of limited means, frequent breaks are virtually impossible.

The life cycle of a tournament professional is beset by crises which have nothing to do with his play. Typically, he starts on this rocky road as a good amateur, probably after some years at a college where he has become thoroughly indoctrinated in the philosophy that his success as

123

a person equates with his success as a golfer.

His first crisis is the process of gaining his PGA tour card. No golfer can guarantee to play his best golf any particular week and, while the qualifying system has been greatly reformed in this respect, a strong element of chance still remains. The odds against success at the first attempt for a tour card are about twenty to one, which means that the probability of a severe psychological bruising is equally high.

The destruction of his soul has started, and now it faces another battering from the torture of Monday qualifying. Again the odds are formidable, with 300 players trying for thirty places as a common challenge. If the qualifying school is the equivalent of the entry examination to West Point, then the Monday qualifying is the combat course where many are rejected and returned to the ranks. Now, for the survivors, comes real action with live bullets.

There is statistical evidence to support my long-held belief that it is actually harder to qualify on Monday than to succeed in a tournament. Such a system may be intrinsically unfair, but at least it is as fair as human ingenuity can devise.

Assuming that the recruit manages to qualify for a few tournaments, and that he has the financial backing of a sponsor, he must now win $8000 during his rookie season and $12,000 a year in subsequent ones to retain his card. It sounds modest enough, given the generous level of prize money each week, but the rule claims plenty of casualties each year.

The survivors who establish themselves on the tour now set their individual goals and guidelines, and if we establish $25,000 a year as a reasonable figure for expenses, then anyone confident of topping that amount is secure enough to marry. Often, this decision marks a turning point in a player's career. As in the case of Lon Hinkle, the rootless bachelor days are replaced by the panacea of a perpetual honeymoon. The bride travels with her golfer, and he is transformed on the course because of his settled and happy domestic life.

Now follows the most severe psychological crisis, with the arrival of children. The golfer is torn between his professional ambitions and his natural parental instincts. It is a rare player who is successful enough to take his family on the tour, perhaps with a travelling nurse in attendance, and even that must be a temporary expedient. Schooldays often mean fooling-around days for the absentee father.

Jack Nicklaus is one of the very few golfers who has achieved a domestic stability and an unbroken career, through careful rationing of his time between golf and home. Johnny Miller is certainly wealthy enough to employ any expedient to find a compromise between the calls of his golf and the calls of his family, but he has had trouble finding the necessary golfing motivation. For him, the pull of his family is often too strong, and who can criticize him for being too devoted a husband and father?

Golf is a jealous game, claiming all of a man's dedication and emotional resources. How many wives must have delivered the stark ultimatum: 'It is either me or the tour, you must choose.' The response has eliminated many a good player from competitive play.

A great swing may be a passport to fame and fortune, but it is no guarantee of happiness.

Suppose that the golfer manages to pick his way through the obstacle course of the tour, avoiding the psychiatric wards and bankruptcy and sheer despair, and emerges as a winner, not just once but frequently. Surely then he inherits the earth with never a care to trouble him?

Alas, no. The old saying about familiarity breeding contempt applies with due force to the winning of tournaments. Nicklaus has won sixty-six tournaments in the USA (up to 1979) and his ambitions in that direction are totally sated. Only the great classics, and the desire to add to his unprecedented collection of them, can stir his competitive embers into flame. It is often said that his motivation palled because of his interests outside of tournament play. I suspect that the point should be reversed: that he sought outside interests because of his waning ambitions for tournament golf.

By going in for course design and golf promotion and advertising, he avoided one of the hazards which traps many intelligent golfers. This is the syndrome which causes a golfer to inquire of himself just what the hell he is doing frittering his time away on a silly game while real life passes him by.

Peter Thomson was a victim of such self-doubts. In the middle of a British Open championship his mind would turn to weighty world events – I recall it happened to him during the Vietnam War – and he would be assailed by the overwhelming triviality of professional sport. 'What does it matter?' he asked himself.

Fortunately, he had already won five British Opens, but this destructive feeling can strike anyone at any time. This must be the saddest fate of all: to become that one-in-a-million golfer who makes it to the pinnacle, only to look back and reflect that it wasn't worth it after all.

Golf Digest, July 1979

The President's Putter

Imagine, if you can, a scene of Arctic bleakness. A rampaging wind whines across the tundra, raising eddies and whirls of snow. Underfoot the frosted grass emits a squeaking sound at each pace. Such of the landscape as can be seen during brief pauses in the driving snow is unutterably bleak: a vast expanse of curiously shaped humps and hollows with never a tree in sight.

Two figures appear, marching purposefully and leaning into the gale. They appear to have been dressed by a generous relief agency. One wears two pairs of trousers and a parka whose fur trim is lightly sugared where his breath has frozen. The other is also well swathed, but details of his dress cannot be discerned because his dumpy figure is encased in a combat overcoat.

Both have bags of what appear to be golf clubs slung from their shoulders. Closer inspection reveals that one of these bags contains ten wooden clubs of different lofts, two conventional wedges and a putter.

The other set looks normal. But wait. This figure tears the headcover off his driver and it is revealed as a monster with a face seven inches deep. Yes, seven inches. He shouts above the tempest, 'Shall we give it a go, old boy?' His companion replies, 'Hang on. Better have a snort first.'

So saying, he produces a bottle from the inner recesses of his garments and they both take a pull. The liquid is a mixture of orange juice, vodka and kummel. In turn they put down crimson golf balls, lunge with as much energy as their draperies will permit, and trudge off into the wasteland.

At this point the logical development in the story should be for an ambulance to arrive, disgorging a posse of men in white coats shouting, 'Spread out, chaps, they can't be far away. We'll soon have them back in their padded cells.'

Alas, this is not fiction at all. This is for real. One of those golfers, he of the full set of wooden clubs, is in fact a doctor. His opponent with the jumbo driver, which he uses in conjunction with a tee peg comprising a beer bottle topped by a piece of rubber tubing, is an equally respected

126

member of society, a plastic surgeon. They are playing a golf competition which has been held in an unbroken sequence of absurdities since 1920, save for the war years.

This is the President's Putter, a match-play contest held over four days by members of the Oxford and Cambridge Golfing Society. (For convenience, let us adopt the terminology of the members and refer hereinafter, as the lawyers say, to the Putter and the Society.)

The annual fixture between Oxford and Cambridge universities is the oldest amateur golf competition in the world. It started in 1878 and at one time was a major sporting event. Since most of the young amateurs of any distinction were bound to be at one of the two ancient universities in the days when everyone of good family went to either Oxford or Cambridge, international teams were selected from the university match.

In 1898 the Society was formed, the only qualification being that the members must have won a 'blue' for playing in the university match – dark blue for Oxford; a wishy-washy, diluted, effete light blue for Cambridge. (No prizes for guessing the author's affiliation.)

The Society played a number of matches each year, against the two current university teams, of course, and against notable golf clubs. The Society team even made a tour of the United States just after the turn of the century.

The Putter is generally credited with being the brainchild of John Low, a Scotsman who had a creditable record in the British Amateur Championship. At all events, he presented the Society with its trophy, the putter that Hugh Kirkaldy had used in winning the 1891 British Open championship.

The site for the inaugural event was the Rye Golf Club on the Sussex coast, a links course in the traditional style, which happens to be about as near as you can get to the equator without leaving the British Isles, an important consideration for a tournament to be held during the first week in January.

At this point the question must be squarely faced: why the hell hold a golf tournament in January? You might feel that a society composed of the intellectual elite of the country (in theory, anyway) would command enough savvy to arrange to play in the comfort of high summer.

Well, the official Society rationalization of the date goes something like this: the Putter is a reunion as much as a golf tournament, with conviviality going hand in hand with the competition. It follows, then, that the best time to play the Putter is at a time when the largest possible number of members is available. During the summer the undergraduate members would be in the thick of matches and amateur tournaments, and many of the Old Blues would be tied up with work or scattered about the world – in 1920, remember, Britain had an empire which was administered exclusively by Oxford and Cambridge men. However, everyone made an effort to be home for Christmas, and the first week of January was the obvious moment for a get-together.

It would have been easy for the Putter to become little more than a social gathering, an extension of the festive season with an element of golf to justify the merrymaking. What saved it from this fate was the supremacy in amateur golf of three men at that time. Sir Ernest Holderness, twice British Amateur champion, took the first four Putters and had the honour of attaching his ball with a silver band to the trophy putter's hickory shaft. Even more significant were Roger Wethered and Cyril Tolley, who were dominant figures in amateur golf at this time.

In this period professional golf was not a respectable calling for gentlemen, and good amateurs remained amateur. Both Tolley and Wethered were good, a match for any pro, and so the prospect of a meeting between them represented an exciting golfing confrontation.

The influence of these three players guaranteed a respectability to the Putter as a serious golfing event, and established a tradition which endures to this day. The Putter may have all the trappings of lunacy, and be accompanied by carefree banter (which is the ultimate proof that Englishmen are up to serious business), but at the core of the competition it is a bona fide tournament whose winners count their successes among their most honoured achievements in golf.

Oddly enough, only once has the weather proved altogether too ghastly for the Putter to be played at Rye. In 1963 the snow was too thick to contemplate golf in any form, and the members had to move along the road to the more temperate fairways of Littlestone.

That record has been achieved only by a fortitude and tolerance among the members which is excessive even in the context of golfing fanaticism. David Phiri, who today is the boss of Zambia's vast copper mining industry and probably the most influential man in the country after the President, could not bring himself to venture out into Rye's icy blasts before he had pulled on three pairs of trousers and put six sweaters over his pyjamas, topping off this ensemble with a sheepskin helmet. As he waddled to the first tee with the gait of a constipated penguin, he announced philosophically, 'Well, I have never yet been beaten by a white man in the snow.' Phiri then clamped a piece of chocolate in his mouth – 'It's the only way I can think of to stop my teeth chattering' – and beat his man 8 and 7.

On one snowy occasion, two competitors managed to lose no fewer than six golf balls during the play of one hole.

Darkness is an enemy of the Putter almost as severe as the weather, for an extended match in the afternoon can easily pass the going down of the sun. Almost every member at some time or another has had to putt out the eighteenth green by the light from the clubhouse windows, but when matches go to extra holes ingenuity must contrive other forms of illumination. One trick is to place lighted matches in the cup and then putt for the glow of this miniature bonfire.

The first Putter attracted only a dozen entries, but since then the event has grown steadily, until today more than 100 players compete each year. And the Putter must be unique in the spread of ages, from callow teenage undergraduates to octogenarians.

It is a motley crowd which gathers for this annual ritual of mid-winter. The clubhouse camaraderie is almost as important as the golf. The members pass on tales of previous Putters and memorable characters. Laddie Lucas, former Walker Cup captain and probably the best left-hander that amateur golf has produced in Britain, figures in many of them. Lucas, who went on to become a Member of Parliament, owes his life to golf because, as a young Battle of Britain pilot, it was his knowledge of a certain golf course which enabled him to safely land his ailing Spitfire.

And, of course, there was Bernard Darwin. Everyone has a Darwin story. He was justly famous for his writings on golf and equally notorious for his abominable temper on the course. He would chase after a straying shot with arms waving and oaths pouring forth. Often he tore lumps of turf from the ground with his teeth and, on his knees, would look up and shout, 'Oh, God, *now* are you satisfied?'

During one Putter he was beaten by a Mr Speakman when a beautifully played shot kicked cruelly into an unplayable lie. It was more than Darwin could stand. He threw his club to the ground and yelled, 'Damn this blasted course! Damn this blasted hole! And you, Speakman, damn you!'

It is always said that Darwin was completely unaware afterwards of what he had done or said in these moments of passion, unlikely though that may seem. He must, surely, have known what he was up to when he was playing in a foursomes match in another tournament with an inept partner and he accosted a perfect stranger who happened to be out for a walk on the links. 'It may interest you to know, sir,' said Darwin, through clenched teeth, 'that I am tied to a turd.'

The Putter winds up with the Society's annual dinner and this can be as unpredictable as the golf. One year Sir Harold Gillies, an

129

eminent physician, put together a complicated apparatus of pulleys and levers. As the Society secretary was making his speech, unseen by the victim but in full view of everyone else, the diabolical machine very slowly lowered a chamber pot onto the speaker's head.

The Putter is a peculiarly English occasion, something to be taken seriously but never on any account solemnly.

Golf Digest, January 1978

Tragedy at Augusta

For the first time in the history of major golf tournaments a player has dished his chance through lifting his head while signing his card.

That two people should make foolish errors was a tragic coincidence, but hardly cause for an emergency session of the Rules of Golf Committee or any of the other rather hysterical suggestions which have been so freely bandied about during the past week.

The facts are simple. On the seventeenth hole during the last round of the US Masters tournament last week (April 1968) at Augusta, Georgia, Roberto de Vicenzo sank a putt for a birdie-3 which put him 12 under par for the seventy-one holes. He dropped a shot at the last hole for a round of 65 and a total of 277.

However, his playing partner, Tommy Aaron, inadvertently marked him down for a 4 at the seventeenth, a silly mistake but very easily done as anyone who has ever been in this situation will know. Aaron had quite enough to think about with his own game. It is his usual habit to fill in the card after every third hole, which must fractionally increase the chances of an error. But 999 times out of a 1000 it would be spotted and corrected when the players checked their cards at the end of the round.

Roberto de Vicenzo is a happy-go-lucky character and not given to poring over his card at the best of times. On this of all days he was in no state for accountancy. It was his birthday; he had just played an historic round of golf starting with an eagle on a par-4 and there he was, with Bob Goalby threatening to overhaul him, sweating out the climax of his career. He checked the card four times but in his emotional condition he could have stared at it all day without really seeing it. All that mattered was the total. And with a TV audience of forty million, never has a sporting score been more thoroughly witnessed.

Their evidence was inadmissible. The only material witness was Aaron and he noticed the error too late. By that time de Vicenzo's card was signed, attested and in the hands of the tournament committee. Under the rules of golf, which are quite explicit on this point, they had no choice but to accept that spurious 4 as official.

As everyone now knows, Goalby made it. He 3-putted the seventeenth green to go 11 under par, level with de Vicenzo's *de facto* total, and then had the biggest piece of luck in his career.

His drive up the eighteenth sailed into the trees and rebounded back to the fairway, leaving him a difficult 3-wood shot to be faded into the green. We talked about it later that evening, and he told me his one thought was to avoid the temptation to steer the shot but simply to swing the clubhead through the ball. He played it perfectly, 2-putted, and, as he and we all believed, tied with de Vicenzo.

Goalby was flabbergasted to hear that he was the winner on a technicality. Aaron, meanwhile, had made good his escape. He drove off before the bombshell burst, suffering such miseries as one can only imagine.

It was a frenetic half hour or so when the news became generally known. Goalby factions argued with de Vicenzo fans. Emphatic fists smashed into palms to drive home the point that the darn fool rule ought to be changed.

In their public statements both players were models of tact and sportsmanship. As microphone after microphone was thrust into his face, de Vicenzo bore up bravely. 'I think maybe I make a few friends. That means more than money. What is money, anyway?' But the Pagliacci mask dropped when he was away from the cameras and he revealed his feelings with a heartfelt aside, which for the sake of propriety I will render from his self-styled PGA English as: 'Aah! What a bloody man I am!'

Goalby, too, was deeply upset by it all. We sat talking at a friend's house until after midnight that evening. He was immensely proud, in his new green jacket, of being the Masters champion. He was clearly sincere when he told me, however, that he would much rather have played off and been beaten than be known as the guy who took the title by default. It would, indeed, be a pity if such a reputation should linger around so fine a golfer.

It is only natural for a sensational incident of this nature to arouse strong feelings, but it is important, if the players concerned are not to suffer a severe injustice, that the responses should be appropriate. In my view they should be: acclaim for Goalby as the true champion; commiseration for de Vicenzo on his self-inflicted wound; and, above all, sympathy and understanding for Aaron. In the long run this sensitive and quiet golfer stands to suffer the most from the affair.

Is the rule fair? Is it necessary? In spite of the fact that on this occasion the operation of the rule created an injustice (to Goalby), the answer to both questions must be yes. Golf is one game in which the players themselves must keep their own scores. And the reason for this is that nobody except the players themselves can possibly know what the score is.

Of course, there will always be scoundrels willing to take advantage; plenty of pots have been won by collusion between player and marker in minor golf. So there must be a rule to discourage skullduggery.

The rule is that a player is responsible for attesting the accuracy of the hole-by-hole scores. The total is immaterial. No penalty is exacted if the addition is wrong – that is the duty of the officials.

The purpose of the rule is to impress on players the importance of being meticulous in marking and checking cards. It is extremely unfortunate that two innocent slips, in circumstances of extreme stress, should have been punished in this case under a rule framed to discourage cheating. But there it is. Roberto de Vicenzo is not an honorary joint winner of the Masters; he was beaten just as if he had transgressed by having fifteen clubs in his bag, or had driven a hundredth of an inch out of bounds.

This is not to say that some reform is not necessary. I daresay that in future Masters there will be a system, as in the Open championship, of taking the players off to a quiet room and having an official go quietly through every card, hole by hole, to ensure that such a tragedy could never happen again.*

But this year it happened. And the result must not be clouded. Bob Goalby was the winner, the only winner, and an extremely worthy winner at that.

Observer, April 1968

---

*There has been such a system since the following year.

Ryder Cup Requiem

So the Ryder Cup is dead. It was quietly put down to prevent further suffering and the body was interred in an unmarked grave.

Even though the murderers – or enlightened humanitarians, according to your views on euthanasia – unscrewed the brass nameplate from the coffin and attached it to a new competition in the hope of persuading us that the Ryder Cup lives on in more vigorous form than ever, the fact is that the living spirit of this unique contest exists no more.

The reasons for killing the Ryder Cup were expressed in one of those famous American offers which are impossible to refuse: beef up your team with outsiders and give us a real match or we quit. As a result, next year's (1979) match will be between America and Europe, which may well prove to be a close and exciting encounter, but it will not be a Ryder Cup match.

Of course, the Ryder Cup match was helplessly, if not hopelessly, one-sided. One reason for this was the curious attitude of the British PGA which has long since lost any interest in winning the trophy.

In America the Ryder Cup rates somewhere between the Tennessee Frog Jumping Contest and the Alabama Melon Pip Spitting Championship, although the players themselves have always taken it seriously until Tom Weiskopf declined to play in favour of a week's holiday shooting sheep.

In Britain the Ryder Cup match has always been a cause for national hysteria, born of the hope that one day David might fluke a lucky shot between the eyes of Goliath. That public obsession meant big money, and the PGA has seen the match almost solely as a golden opportunity to dip its bread in the gravy. Team selection was allowed to look after itself. Since defeat was inevitable, it did not really matter who the vanquished might be.

The team was chosen on a points basis, according to performance during the season. The side was, therefore, made up from the half-dozen obvious choices, the good players who could acquire the required number of points from a limited playing programme, and the balance came from among those golfers who slogged away week after week and thereby made the grade as much on good attendance as good golf.

The players themselves wanted it this way, because the system appeared to be fair, and there are considerable perks to be picked up from having a Ryder Cup badge on your blazer pocket, even though you may be an indifferent performer. The result was that never in my experience have I known a British and Irish Ryder Cup team made up from the best match players in these islands. The formula was to gather together the players who had made most money competing in a different game altogether.

No doubt a similar system will be used to nominate the players to represent Europe, with a few selective places to cover individual cases such as Peter Oosterhuis, who lives and competes in America. Whether this team will play with the same fire under the European banner as the Ryder Cup teams did, I take leave to doubt, just as I doubt whether the public interest (and with it the public income) will be as intense.

The theory is that since Spain has won the World Cup for the past two years it follows that Spanish players will be an asset to the enlarged Ryder Cup squad. This view overlooks the undoubted fact that one of the reasons behind Spain's magnificent successes was that Severiano Ballesteros, partnered first by Manuel Pinero and next by Tony Garrido, was playing for Spain. Will they be inspired to rise to such heights by a spirit of European unity?

Likewise, patriotic feelings released in Brian Huggett such determination that he became transformed as a golfer to match the best that America could set against him. Will his successors find the same inspiration in a European team, partnered with men who cannot speak the same language and whose only bond is an envy of American prize rates?

We shall see in due course. I only wish they would provide a new trophy and a new name for this new competition.

Observer, June 1978

I Still Don't Believe It

On reflection, the wonder of Gary Player's winning last round in the US Masters (1978) was not that it was so low but that it was as high as 64, a mere 8 under par. On three holes he left himself the formality of a tap-in putt of less than a foot, and he was therefore entitled to feel slightly aggrieved that the ball had not gone to ground off the previous stroke, even though one was a bunker shot and another a chip (which actually spun out of the hole).

As if that were not fuel enough for a hard-luck story, he also missed putts of eight feet, six feet and five feet, all eminently holable and especially so on a day when his putter was running hot. All in all, he had every reason to rail against the cruel fates which had robbed him of his due 58.

On numerous occasions in the past he has been heard to bemoan his misfortunes over missing three putts of eight feet and under. Now, as he sat at the microphone recounting the details of the day's events, he was unusually philosophical about those lost chances. Maybe at forty-two Player had learned to accept the professional golfer's appointed lot as the plaything of fate? Not at all. He had other targets for his customary sermon on such occasions.

Those who have sat at Player's feet before when he has won a major championship, and there have been eight such times, know the routine by now. Those hooded eyes shine with the fires of fanaticism, the voice takes on an edge of aggression, even truculence. We wait dutifully in the role in which Player has clearly cast us, miserable and ignorant sinners in need of a good blast of hot-gospelling. The only thing which varies from championship to championship is the subject of the harangue.

Over the years Player has preached on many themes – that his latest victory was due to the vital winning properties of practice, or of God, or of practice, or of raisins, or of practice, or of wearing black raiment to absorb the power of the sun, or of practice, or of bananas. One by one most of these doctrines have been discarded. Raisins? They rot your teeth. Practice? When you are tired it ruins your swing. And so on.

So it was with eager anticipation that we waited to discover what the latest secret may have been. Clearly it must be potent indeed to have conjured a 64 from one of the most demanding golf courses in the world.

Exercise and dedication. That is the stuff to give the troops. Player solemnly declared on his word of honour (not that anyone could ever doubt such blazing sincerity) that every night he did something called squats on his bedroom carpet. Further, he hurled weights about. Three hundred and twenty pounds of them. Perhaps it was tons. Just to listen to his description of violent postprandial exertion brings the sweat gushing from his audience, and notes tend to get runny and indecipherable.

'I would like to see Jack Nicklaus go to South Africa five times a year and win tournaments the way I do,' he said. Player is nothing if not nimble in debate. He instantly realized that this line of argument might recoil like a scorpion's tail and sting him in his own neck. One could almost hear the wheels whizzing and the tumblers falling as he mentally reviewed the implications of what he had just said. Gary Player does calisthenics and weight training. Therefore he is super fit. Therefore he wins. Jack Nicklaus does not do calisthenics and weight training. Therefore he is not super fit. Therefore ... wait a minute! I've won eight major championships and Nicklaus has won nearly twice that number. And he wins all over the world. And he turned pro eight years after me. Better hit the abort button.

'Jack Nicklaus is one of my best friends in the world and I am a great admirer of him.' And Jack speaks highly of you too, Gary.

All things considered, it is probably unnecessary to listen to Player's evangelism in order to appreciate his achievements. The miracle at Cana is sufficient without the Sermon on the Mount. On the Augusta National golf course last week he did something which I truly believe that no other golfer could have achieved, or hope to achieve, or even consider capable of achievement. Only Gary Player has the physical and mental toughness, plus the skill, to pull off a trick like that.

No, I am not forgetting Johnny Miller's 63 to win the US Open at Oakmont, which was superficially similar but in essence quite different. The difference was that Miller went out hoping for a low score. Player set off convinced he was going to shoot the lights out. As I watched the round progress I felt the task to be impossible. As a matter of fact, I still think so. But Gary Player is an unbelievable player. Long may he continue to make us believe the unbelievable.

Observer, April 1978

Who's in the Bushes?

During the 1980 European Open a number of players were interviewed for television while walking between shots. It was the first time that this technique has been tried on British TV so far as I am aware – yet another example of a bad American idea being imported without due thought for the consequences.

For years American viewers have seen Ken Venturi and Bob Goalby exchanging pleasantries and chitchat about the progress of play with golfers on the course during tournaments. There is a strict rule that a player must not be approached in this way unless he had indicated his willingness to be interviewed.

More recently the experiment was tried of wiring players for sound so that their every word could be broadcast to the nation, a device which would produce some electrifying dialogue if used on certain voluble players of the European circuit.

The idea of this electronic eavesdropping is to introduce the golfers to the watching public as flesh-and-blood human beings who suffer and rejoice just like the rest of us. The TV planners reasoned, rightly enough, that one of the reasons for golf's falling ratings was that the public did not know the players and could not relate to them.

Week after week some unknown young former college boy would emerge as the winner, and the emotional impact on the viewers was zero because they had no idea who he was, what kind of person he might be, or even what he looked like, since his face had been obscured in deep shadow all week under one of those fashionable and hideous visors.

Get them talking and revealing their innermost hopes and fears, reasoned the planners, and the audiences would be able to associate with them and love them, just as they love Arnold Palmer. The interviews did not help much.

'How's it going, Randy?'

'Waaal, Kenny, any time you drive the ball in the fairway, hit the greens and make a bunch of putts like I did on the front side, you have to be in good shape to shoot some low numbers.'

'And how are you going to play it from here in?'
'I sure hope I can keep hitting it good through the back nine.'
'Well, good luck.'
'Thank you, Kenny.'
Such riveting revelations failed to halt the plunging ratings. The real contribution to telecasts made by Venturi, Goalby and our own Clive Clark is when they give their expert observations from places hidden to the cameras.

'Oh dear. Player has hooked his drive badly into the rhododendrons. Are you there, Clive? How is the ball lying?'
'Yes, I'm here, Peter, and I'm afraid the situation is not very promising. The ball is right behind a tree trunk, lying among a tangle of roots. Not a shot I would fancy.'
'Do you think he has any chance of getting a club to the ball and banging it through the woods to the fairway?'
'It may come to that, but for the moment Gary is addressing the ball with his driver, holding it at full arm's stretch and pointing out to the referee that his left heel is touching what may or may not be a rabbit scrape. Gary is explaining to the referee that a free drop of one club's length would then put him slap in line of an advertisement hoarding.'
'Is there an advertisement in those bushes, then?'
'That is a matter of interpretation. Player's caddie has suffered a sudden attack of total paralysis, and since he has the sponsor's name printed on his jacket Gary is claiming that his status has changed to an immovable advertisement from which he is due line-of-sight relief. He is pointing out the relevant tournament rule and quoting from the Afrikaans version of the book of Decisions. If the referee accepts Gary's interpretation then he will get a free drop on the fairway.'
'What does the referee say about all this, Clive?'
'It is hard to make out, since Gary has both hands round the poor man's throat, but from the expression in his popping eyes I suspect that the referee will defer to the vast experience of the plucky South African champion.'

Dialogue like that, against a picture of dense foliage which shakes violently from time to time, is compulsive television and amply justifies the role of the roving commentator. The objections arise when the commentator intrudes directly into the play by addressing the golfer.

At the European Open eventual winner Tom Kite justified the practice by saying that TV was an immediate medium which could not wait until after the round was over to hear what the player thought about his play. My friends among the ranks of evening newspaper writers immediately responded by seeking the same privileges, since their medium is every bit as immediate. Can you imagine it – hordes of reporters swarming over the fairways? 'That's a dodgy lie you've got in the bunker there, Mr Nicklaus. How about a quick quote for my two-thirty edition?'

No, no. It won't do. No matter how carefully and tastefully and acceptably it may be done, interviewing sportsmen during play must not be allowed. At the very best, it gives a publicity advantage to those golfers who are willing to participate in the scheme. At worst, it could well affect the outcome of play.

Observer, September 1980

Return to Cherry Hills ⚐1

In 1960 Arnold Palmer won the United States Open Championship at Cherry Hills Country Club in Denver, Colorado. Since he was about the most popular man on earth at the time, the tidal wave of euphoria which engulfed this victory obscured everything else that happened that week, including the fact that the runner-up was an overweight, crew-cut amateur by the name of Jack Nicklaus, aged twenty.

The following year this Nicklaus turned professional, and in the seventeen years which followed so many exciting things occurred in his career – such as losing weight, growing his hair and winning more major championships than any man in the history of golf – that the most pertinent fact about him tended to be overlooked. The truth is that Jack Nicklaus is the champion runner-up of all time. Since second place undoubtedly involves losing, we really ought to put his achievements in perspective, hailing him as the champion loser of all time and then adding his secondary accolade of champion winner of all time.

This week (June 1978) the United States Open returns to Cherry Hills and, going by historical precedent, we may forecast the outcome. The most likely result is that Jack Nicklaus will lose. The next most likely possibility is that he will win. We must never overlook the outside chance that he might not figure in the first two places at all, a rare phenomenon which I have actually observed on at least two occasions. For purely selfish reasons, I rather hope that the first eventuality will come to pass.

Nicklaus is a good winner but a superb loser. Anyone who wants a real insight into golf at his level could do no better than sneak into the interview room after Nicklaus has notched up another second place finish in a major championship.

I have known him speak for two hours on such occasions, ranging over subjects from the philosophy of competition to the most esoteric points of technique. Inevitably at some point a buffoon will put a trite question to him, such as, 'Are you disappointed not to have won?' and Nicklaus will shrivel the wretch with a glare from those laser eyes.

These incidents apart, Nicklaus is never more forthcoming and bonhomous than when he has just lost. Two years after finishing second to Palmer at Cherry Hills, Nicklaus reversed their roles in the 1962 US Open, and, ever since then, he has been the man to beat. Many have enjoyed brief successes – Lee Trevino, Johnny Miller, Hubert Green and Tom Watson all achieved temporary ascendancy – but, with one exception, Nicklaus has seen them all off in due course.

The exception, of course, is Watson, and we may be sure that Nicklaus is anxious to put him in his place. It is perhaps too much to hope that Cherry Hills will produce a repeat of their historic duel at Turnberry in the British Open Championship last year, for an encounter of that quality has come along only once in 400 years and is therefore not due again until the year 2377, but if these two should be in contention coming to the final holes I would expect Nicklaus to assert himself over the upstart.

Someone has sagely remarked that the US Open does not guarantee a great winner as surely as our own Open Championship, and while I agree with this contention (as I must, for I was the sage who said it), I am at a loss to explain why this should be. The United States Golf Association goes to inordinate lengths to prepare its championship courses in such manner that only a genius with a complete repertory of shots could hope to get round them at all. Indeed, one of the certainties of this championship is that when I arrive at Denver the locker room will be in uproar as the players come in from their practice rounds, declaring that those USGA sons of bitches have really gone over the top this year. I generally like to be around when Dave Hill finishes his first reconnaissance – it lasted only five holes at Oakmont before he departed in a fusillade of expletives – just to keep my vocabulary up to date.

In theory it is possible to look at a US Open course and draw an accurate specification of the winner. One observes the narrow bands of fairway (mown to three-quarters of an inch), meticulously graded rough, in categories known by the players as 'bloody difficult' and 'bloody impossible', and greens which have been transformed, as far as human ingenuity can contrive, into surfaces resembling polished marble.

Grave men in blue blazers can often be seen testing the greens with a device of extreme scientific complexity which reproduces the action of a putter (don't ask me why they do not use a putter; the USGA spends millions on building steam hammers to crack nuts). If the ball issues from this gadget, rides a crest and rolls on into a bunker – or, even better, a pond – then the grave men slap their thighs and head for the bar shaking with smug amusement.

Clearly the man who can win on such a course must be a master player, with enormous strength of character, patience and intelligence. Someone like Hale Irwin comes to mind. But there is more. Above all he must be the luckiest golfer of the week, which tends to throw the whole thing wide open.

Severiano Ballesteros, honoured by a rare special invitation from the USGA, could theoretically be in for an extra helping of luck, especially as I suspect that he possesses a unique gland which pumps the stuff into his bloodstream, although he would not be my selection this week.

Quite frankly I do not have the foggiest idea who is going to win, which is just as well for otherwise there would be no point in going there to find out.

Observer, June 1978

Foreigners Could Add
a Tonic to the US Tour

Sports administrators have to be political animals, and politics, as we all know, often involves drawing on your reserves of sincerity and passion to express a view in public that is diametrically opposed to your deepest convictions. Our democratically elected representatives justify this practice by explaining blandly that (a) they were misquoted; or (b) their remarks were taken out of context; or (c) if telling a whacking great lie is the only possible way of achieving a desirable result, then a whacking great lie is entirely justified.

Thus, when US PGA tour commissioner Deane Beman remarked that Severiano Ballesteros needed America more than America needed Seve, my mind went back to Baltusrol last June (1980) and I reflected that, but for half a roll of the ball on a single putt, the reigning US Open champion might now be Isao Aoki of Japan. Nobody who watched that historic championship could have denied that Aoki would have been a worthy holder of the title. Indeed, his four-round aggregate would have won any other US Open in history.

If it had happened, then at that moment the world's four major championships would have been held by Spain, Australia and Japan. Jack Nicklaus did more than achieve an astonishing personal triumph at Baltusrol; he saved the face of American professional golf and took some of the heat off Commissioner Beman, who has plenty of problems as it is. Television ratings for the PGA tour events are in decline. Public interest is switching to seniors tournaments, such as the Legends and the Commemorative Pro–Am. The 1981 prize fund represents a pay cut for the pros in real terms when measured against the inflation rate.

By almost every yardstick, the American PGA tour is the finest golf circuit in the world, and by a long way. In its structure, administration, presentation, course preparation and rewards, it is way out in front. Yet it is clearly losing its momentum. It is premature to talk of crisis, for the tour is fundamentally sound, but it certainly needs a tonic to restore it to full health.

The tonic it needs is excitement. The men who gave the tour its

144

massive emotional charge have gone, or are going. Golf became a big spectator sport because of players who dared to be themselves, men like Tommy Bolt who cussed and threw clubs. Men like Arnold Palmer who crackled with emotional static. Men like Gary Player who brought a messianic fervour to the golf course. Men like Dave Hill who had the guts to speak their minds.

These men all evoked a powerful response in those who watched them play. It doesn't really matter what the response is, provided it is powerful. It can be hate, even. The crowds hated Bobby Locke when he sailed to America from South Africa to knock off the heroes of the day and fill his pockets with dollars. But they flocked to watch him. The crowds hated the young Jack Nicklaus when he challenged Palmer's supremacy. But they scrambled to watch him, and sent the TV ratings through the roof.

The only emotion most spectators feel today for the young golfers on the tour is respect for their efficiency. Respect is a prim, low-key emotion and what the tour needs is an injection of emotions to fire the blood – love, hate, joy, contempt, jealousy, rage and happiness. The PGA should strike medals for Lee Trevino and Chi Chi Rodriguez for their services to fermenting emotional responses.

I reject the common complaint that the young players of today are colourless and faceless. They are people, and people are neither faceless nor colourless. They have been conditioned to suppress their personalities. College grooming and harsh disciplinary measures by officialdom have imprisoned their spirits. Take the case of Bobby Clampett. Here we have the reincarnation of Harpo Marx (younger readers ask your parents about the Marx Brothers). Clampett looks like Harpo and has the same sense of impish fun, as he imprudently demonstrated when playing as a marker in the US Open, he improved the shining hour by hitting his drives from a kneeling position. Of course he had to be reprimanded, but the establishment jumped on him so hard I do not believe he has uttered a word since.

Now Clampett is a pro, and I hope he will become himself again. I do not suggest he deliberately set out to clown it up on the course, for the worst sin a golfer can commit is to say or do anything that puts a fellow competitor off his game. All I ask is that he allow his natural personality to show, just as Peter Jacobsen does. Both happen to be terrific players, and they will become better if they do not stifle their ebullience.

Naturally, if a golfer oversteps the bounds of accepted behaviour on the course he must be disciplined. But if I were Commissioner Beman and, say, Bobby Clampett were to express his *joie de vivre* by doing a back flip when he sank a putt, I would admonish him thus: 'That kind of behaviour can damage the greens so you are fined $50. And here is $100 out of the tour publicity fund. Good luck in the next round.'

Golf lacks the emotional involvement that naturally occurs in team sports with partisan hometown involvement, and the emotional response must be generated by the individual players. One way this can be done is by tapping the human instinct for prejudice, chauvinism and good old-fashioned patriotism. On the European circuit there must be at least twenty different nationalities represented in the field, and that in itself creates excitement. The spectators do respond, and strongly, to the clash of their own prejudices. Scots outside the ropes go frantic when Bernard Gallacher makes a charge, and we sophisticated observers of this unseemly fanaticism unconsciously find ourselves pulling for Bernard Langer of Germany. It may be all rather base and shameful thus to betray our cosmopolitan ideals, but it does make for excitement. And I must admit that when there are Americans in the field the old rivalry, fostered so heartily by the Ryder Cup matches, spices the prejudices enormously.

For all these reasons, I am delighted that the American PGA tour has opened the door to overseas golfers. Mind you, the lifting of restrictions has not ushered in the open-house policy, which operates in Europe and which I have long advocated for the United States. It is far from that. But at least today any professional golfer of whatever nationality can tee up his ball and, if he is good enough, can win his card in tournament play without going through that restrictive process of the qualifying school.

Quite a few players are taking a crack at the US tour in 1981, and more will follow, from Europe, South Africa and Australia. Some of them can really play – remember, Ballesteros has not been Europe's No. 1 performer for the past two seasons – and some of them may make the grade. You can never tell. The lifestyles on the world's circuits are so different that some extremely gifted players can never reproduce their form in America, and vice versa.

But the message I would like to convey to Americans is that this overseas invasion is not simply a raid on your treasury. If Sandy Lyle or Nick Faldo or Greg Norman should pick up some tour dollars, it will not be simply a case of reducing the funds available for the American golfers who have loyally supported the domestic sponsors. It will be a two-way traffic. The overseas invaders will be contributing the one element the PGA tour so desperately needs: excitement.

If anyone feels resentment over foreigners arriving to plunder good American dollars then I say: Go ahead and indulge your resentment to the full. Forget your natural politeness to visitors and give vent to your emotions and prejudices. Boo the foreigners, if that is what turns you on. Or cheer them, and whip up some resentments among the people who feel like booing. Throw divots if you must, and carry banners saying 'Limey go home'. Get involved.

One thing I know for sure. If Ken Brown from Britain should happen to fight out a tournament head to head with Doug Black of Atlanta, then by the end of the week young master Black will no longer be one of those faceless, colourless, mass-produced college golfing machines everybody complains about.

It might not cause much of a stir if Doug Black beats Mike White of West Virginia for the Tallahassee Open, but in the case I have mentioned he has only to whip Ken Brown to become a national hero. Then you would get to know him – and I dare say you would like him and would want to go and watch him again. That in essence is what golf needs – in America and everywhere else.

Golf Digest, February 1981

And Then The Justice

Full Of Wise Saws And Modern Instances

Part Four

'On the Tee . . .'

Some characters of golf

A Perplexed 'How?'

Speaking as one who has only to give his family tree a gentle shake to bring down a shower of Black Foot Indians, I was delighted to read that Orville Moody, who is a quarter Choctaw, had won the United States Open championship (1969).

By all accounts it was not a great championship, but the result was as big a surprise as that affair at the Little Big Horn. Where is the elite cavalry now? Last year it was an unknown Mexican, Lee Trevino, who snatched the richest prize in golf. Now Moody has routed the golfing establishment to become a millionaire overnight.

The parodist Miles Bantock anticipated the events at Houston in the lines

Full of zeal, brave Hiawatha
Bought a brassie and a mashie,
Bought a bulger and a niblick,
Bought a baffy and a driver,
Rolled his sleeves up and his trousers,
Paid a quarter to the caddie,
Winked at smiling Minnehaha,
Winked and murmured: 'Minnie, watch me!
Watch me while I wield my brassie,
Or my mashie or my driver!
Watch me hit the ball and knock it
So blamed far they'll never find it –
Watch me knock out Colonel Bogey,
Watch me beat great Auchterlonie –
Auchterlonie, Auchterlonie!'

In the poem, however, Hiawatha did not win the Open. He took a swipe at the ball and when he asked Minnehaha what had happened she replied:

All you hit was terra firma
Merely hit the ground and doubled
Up as if you'd eaten something
That had gripped you in the middle.

151

Moody's victory has astonished all students of golf who can only react with a perplexed 'How?' After serving an engagement as a regular soldier, he joined the golf tour last year, and his record in 1968 gave no hint of coming greatness. He tied for last place in the '500' Festival Open and the Canadian Open, winning respectively $143.33 and $58.09. He made a little money in five other tournaments, without getting higher than twenty-fourth place, and the highlight of his year was to come sixth in the Robinson Open, a feat slightly diminished by the fact that, with the exception of Deane Beman, every big-name golfer on the American circuit took a holiday that week.

In the unofficial world money list, Moody came in at No. 111 having made, I would estimate, a substantial loss on the year's trading figures. This season he has done better, but not spectacularly so, certainly nothing to suggest that he had the remotest chance of winning the Open.

One way and another, there are very few golfers who cannot find encouragement from Moody's example. First there is age. Nowadays, when pimpled prodigies dominate so many sports and puberty marks the beginning of the end rather than the end of the beginning, it is nice to think that a man can start his competitive career at the age of thirty-five.

Then there is the matter of training. Many golfers are given to flights of self-pitying fancy at times, like Peter Cook's character who whined, 'I could have been a judge if only I'd had the Latin.' We imagine that if only we'd been given a sound grounding in golf as boys by expert teachers then we, too, might be piloting our own executive jets from one tournament in the sun to another.

'I never had a lesson in my life,' says Moody, proving that champions are born rather than made. One often hears young players say, 'With a bit of luck I could make it.' To which the answer ought to be, 'If you need a bit of luck you don't deserve to win.'

In fact, champions have just as much good luck and bad luck as anyone else, but the difference is that they ignore the misfortunes. The case of Michael Bonallack playing the third hole at Hoylake against Dale Morey in a British amateur championship was a good example.

Bonallack had the bad luck to have his drive kick left into the rough. He had the good luck of a fairish lie. He fired straight over a wilderness of gorse and rough, and had the bad luck to lose his ball, or so it seemed since the gallery searched in vain for some time.

But he also had the good luck to have among the spectators the captain of Royal Liverpool Golf Club, Mr Selwyn Lloyd. He was well to the right (of course) of the main search party, and, with a politician's instinct for exploring every avenue and leaving no stone unturned, he discovered the ball (good luck) but in a most atrocious lie under a thick tuffet (bad luck).

Bonallack played the shot – about thirty yards and with the flag close behind an intervening bunker – and had the good luck to stop the ball close enough to hole a birdie putt (more good luck, if you ask me, but I'm prejudiced in the matter of holing putts).

There are few golfers who wouldn't have mentally half-conceded that hole at some stage and allowed a whiff of desperation to creep into their game. Bonallack simply ignored the bad luck and so, consequently, did the spectators. They simply said, 'Lucky old Michael to win that hole: a typical bit of Bonallack daylight robbery.'

For club golfers, another ecouraging point about Moody's victory was his statement that he does not believe in too much practice. If he had made that statement publicly at the end of 1968 everyone would have laughed and said, 'And look where it has got you.' Coming from the mouth of the US open champion it has to be treated with respect, but I believe that he is quite exceptional in this respect. Foregoing practice, like being excused polishing boots in the Army, is a dangerously attractive idea and should be allowed on prescription only to genuine cases. The rest of us must soldier away on the practice ground.

But of all the implications of Orville Moody's feat, none is more important, I think, than the fact which he has so triumphantly demonstrated that today's Open championships are wide open. For years the big events have been dominated by a handful of outstanding players against whom the rank and file stood no chance. I don't believe necessarily that the giants are in decline. I prefer the theory that improved standards among the newcomers have had a levelling effect.

Whichever it is, the fact remains that any good player can win fame and a fortune overnight. That is the dream which animates tournament golf, recruits the players and lures the fans. Orville Moody has revitalized the dream.

Observer, June 1969

Will the Real Lee Trevino Please Stand Up

He was scowling as he walked into tournament headquarters. Everything about him was belligerent. The way he walked, the way he thrust a slip of paper at the receptionist, proclaimed him as a man determined to show that he was as good as the next man in order to silence the private inner voice which suggested that he might not be.

I didn't hear what they were saying, but the tone was unmistakable. The voice which I later came to know so well was pitched somewhere between a bark and a whine. Their discussion was brief and soon his squat, paunchy figure was marching out of the room. He was looking straight ahead, still with that thunderstorm frown. The chip on his shoulder was almost visible. What a charming specimen, I thought.

'Who was that?' I asked.

'That gentleman,' said the receptionist with heavy sarcasm, 'was Mr Lee Trevino.'

'I never heard of him,' I said.

'You've just been lucky,' she answered.

Later that day I was at the practice ground and saw Trevino hitting balls. I cast an appraising eye over his swing and was not impressed by that, either. You must understand that we professional golf watchers develop an instinct about these things. Obviously it is not possible to keep tabs on 300 golfers, so when a new one comes along we size him up and decide whether he is one to watch in the future.

I gave Trevino no chance. He was striking the ball well enough, but they all do on the practice ground. Could he be an original, like Doug Sanders, Gay Brewer or Miller Barber, who could repeat with that swing under pressure? (You will gather that I am not a slave to orthodoxy or the classic style. I don't mind how anybody hits the ball so long as he can keep on hitting it that way when the going gets tough.)

Trevino's flat, lungeing style did not fill me with confidence. He gave the impression of a man who was not so much interested in practising his golf as working off some deep grudge against the balls. He was punishing them. Or, more accurately, he was identifying the balls with people and getting his own back.

'Take that, you smart-ass receptionist! Take that, you sneering locker-room attendant!' Trevino was hitting back at the whole world.

Get him out on the course needing to finish 4-4-3 for the tournament, I thought, and that swing will collapse into the biggest hook you ever saw. As a crosscheck on my judgement I looked up his record. He was nearly thirty and had never even threatened to win anything. That figured. There was no need to take any further notice of Lee Trevino.

So much for first impressions. In my own defence I may add that many an experienced professional came to the same conclusions about Trevino and his swing in those days.

Now let us move the story along a bit and introduce a totally different character. By coincidence his name was also Lee Trevino. He had won the US Open championship, and he was sitting in the press tent, relaxed and happy. He was everybody's friend. The jokes – good, bad, clean, vulgar – poured from him like a pro comic trying to do the routines of a lifetime in half an hour. The crowds at the practice ground had been treated to a similar performance. And even on the course, with thousands of dollars at stake, he had gagged with the galleries all the way round.

He may be as shallow as a dirty limerick, we told ourselves, but he is a lovable guy and terrific company away from the course. He knows how to live. The breweries will have to go on overtime while he is in the money, and everybody had better lock up their daughters.

Then, a bit later, I met another Lee Trevino. On this occasion it was a business meeting and I was involved in the production of an instructional series with him. He was all business. Before I could finish a question he was ahead of me, rattling out the answer and directing the photographer to get the correct angles. The nearest he came to a joke was when he was explaining his conception of the two-piece swing.

'I usually tell people I have a two-piece method because, being a Mexican, I'm not smart enough to count up to three.'

He gave a thin, conspiratorial smile. The crowds expect jokes so jokes is what they get. This was a different situation.

It was different in other ways, too. Trevino revealed himself as a profound thinker about the techniques of golf. Everyone knew him to be a canny player by now, plotting his way round a golf course in strict accordance with his prearranged plan.

The refreshing part about Trevino's theorizing was its originality. Nobody ever showed him how to hold a club or make a backswing. That all came as a result of lonely hours of trial and error as a boy. So when he eventually came to pick up a textbook he already knew the answers because he had worked out the proofs. From his own experience he

155

could say 'Rubbish!' to much of the book lore of golf technique.

By the same token he totally rejected most of the concepts of good swings and bad swings.

'Who can dare say I have a bad swing?' he asked. 'The only thing that matters in golf is the scores you put on the board. You don't have to look pretty out there, you have to win. Look at my record and tell me who has a better swing than mine.'

There could be no arguing with the logic of his view. Since 1968 he had scored lower and earned higher than any golfer save, in some respects, Jack Nicklaus. And in direct confrontation with Nicklaus, as in the play-off for the 1971 US Open at Merion, Trevino came out best.

There is even another Trevino, the family man who wants nothing more than to watch his children grow up. But that can be left out of the present discussion. Three Lee Trevinos are enough to be going on with. And the central question to be resolved is quite simple. Which is the real one?

Is it that surly fellow with the crashing inferiority complex? Is it the knock-about comic? Is it the down-to-earth student of golf?

The first thing to remember is that Trevino was a shanty-poor, fatherless Mexican during his Texas childhood, which is one way of saying that the world regarded him as a second-class citizen. Trevino resented the poverty and the prejudice, as all of his kind must. We should not be surprised that people everywhere, who are denied all privileges, react against the system and sometimes fall into crime. Society ought to be gaoled but, of course, it is society which has the impertinence to do the gaoling.

Trevino did not fall into crime, but he deeply wanted to find an identity. What could be more natural than for such a boy to seek the group identity of that rip-roaring, two-fisted body, the US Marines?

As a Marine Trevino found self-respect and the respect of society. From a nobody he became one of the elite, and soon enough his prowess as a golfer made him an elite member of the elite group. With security came confidence and with confidence his golf became even better.

Serving in the Far East helped. At home there had been daily reminders that he was regarded as an inferior. But now he found himself as an American in countries where Americans were acknowledged, especially by themselves, as superiors. At a stroke Trevino had gone from about four down to at least two up.

In this environment his natural talents, notably a quick intelligence and a ready wit, could flourish and develop. And it soon came to Trevino that if he could be a big fish in the small pond of the Marines, why couldn't he be an even bigger fish in the pond of professional golf?

What he forgot – or thought he could lick – was that as soon as he took off his uniform and came home he would revert to being a *chicano* so far as society was concerned.

Once again life was tough for him. But now he was better equipped to handle the tensions. The game of golf had mushroomed to such a degree that an ability to break par was potentially the passport which would break down all barriers. Talking would get him only so far – after that his clubs would have to take over the conversation.

Compared with the college scholarship golfers, and even the elevated caddies, Trevino started his pro career at a considerable disadvantage. But in another sense his unorthodox apprenticeship was an invaluable experience. He was like a boxer without any coach, or trainer, or fancy gymnasium to practise his moves. He was straight into the fairground booth, knowing that he had to win to eat. He learned all the tricks.

'When you are playing for five bucks and you've got two bucks in your pocket – that's pressure,' he said later when someone complimented him on his composure in sinking his Open championship putts.

'Where's the pressure when you've got a five-footer for the Open? Hole it or miss it, you still wind up with a pocket full of dollars.'

He hustled and bustled his way to a big local reputation in Texas. And then, when he finally made it onto the professional tour, he found that the big boys knew most of the tricks, too. Trevino struggled, and he admits that after a bit he was ready to pack up and return to the minor league golf of local tournaments, keeping shop and accommodating any member or visitor rash enough to put out a challenge. He knew he could make a good living that way. On the tour all he was doing was spending his nest egg of hard-won five-dollar bets

Eventually, as the world knows, his wife used her own savings to enter him for the US Open and he went along to please her. It was to be his last fling at the big time. And he won.

With victory came what seemed to be that remarkable transformation in his character. In reality, all that changed was his bank balance. The exuberant personality had been there all the time but, as he put it, 'You don't feel like kidding around too much when you are living on fish heads and rice.'

That win was the trigger which released all his inhibitions. The preamble to the Constitution of the United States declares that all men are born free and equal. After thirty years Trevino had finally given some kind of validity to that lofty ideal. He was free and equal. Aided and abetted by his then manager, the improbable Bucky Woy, he rode

157

his new image hard. A bit too hard for the taste of some, and rather more than he himself felt to be natural.

He likes to make jokes, which is something very different from having to make jokes because people expect it. And, as he consolidated his success, he grew confident enough to please himself rather than others. If he felt low he could be low. If he felt chipper he could gag it up.

He has still, I think, not quite emancipated himself entirely. After all, the gay caballero image is a valuable trading asset and must be preserved. Trevino contrived a remarkable self-discipline along the lines of that useful American TV accessory, the blab-off. This is a switch on a long flex so the viewer can switch off the advertisements without moving from his chair. On the golf course Trevino's personal blab-off enables him to chatter and gag with the crowd as he walks between shots and then, at a touch of a switch, as it were, give his total concentration to the shot in hand.

Even though security is assured for life, Trevino is still not above pulling a stroke. Jack Nicklaus diplomatically denied that he had been put off when Trevino produced an imitation snake on the first tee at Merion. Indeed, he said, the incident had helped to break his tension. All I know is that it scared the daylights out of me, and I was only watching.

Trevino is also a master of gamesmanship. Put him in a play-off with a young golfer and he openly boasts that he will 'psych' him out of it. And he does, of that there is no doubt.

So, in response to the demand for the real Trevino to stand up, all three of our original nominees rise to their feet. The morose Mexican has mellowed with success, but he can still show that face from time to time. The scars of a background like Trevino's never entirely heal. The brash comic has also become diluted. Trevino has given up drinking entirely, and these days the jokes are not forced. He gags when the spirit moves him and his wit is the sharper for it. As for the thoughtful Trevino, he is coming more and more into his own. He is the one I like best, and I look forward to the day when this Trevino is entirely dominant. I think you will like him – he is a very interesting fellow.

Golf World, July 1973

A Worthy Master

Anyone who is presumptuous enough to try to predict the outcome of golf tournaments must be prepared to ensure a regular diet of his own hats. Speaking as one whose digestive system has long since adjusted to felt and straw, I never thought I would see the day when I would enjoy the process. Yet, having rashly slipped the word 'inevitability' into a sentence involving Jack Nicklaus and the US Masters last week (April 1976), I find myself setting down to attack my hat with a knife and fork with a certain relish for once. Virtue should have its reward, in golf no less than in life, and, as Ray Floyd followed one great round with another, the feeling grew with mounting intensity that justice could only be served by victory for him.

Indeed, when he opened up an eight-stroke lead after three rounds it would have been no less than tragic if the triumph had slipped from his grasp. It could have happened. Nicklaus could have opened up with a birdie and an eagle. Floyd could have dropped strokes on the two opening holes. At Augusta particularly these things can happen. That eight-stroke lead could wither to three strokes in two holes easily enough.

Floyd knew it. So did Nicklaus. Equally they knew that such an eventuality, a dramatic reverse on the first few holes of the last round, was the only way that Floyd could be robbed of his deserts. Had such a thing happened, what would have been the effect on Floyd? The outcome is horrible to contemplate. It might have destroyed him, or at least crushed his spirit for months. Walter Hagen was about the only golfer who could shrug off a humiliating reverse with a light laugh and flush the gall from his system with a magnum.

When Archie Compston defeated Hagen by a devastating fourteen holes in a thirty-six-hole challenge match, the experience should have been enough to put the whammies on Hagen in every subsequent encounter with his tormentor. Hagen responded by smearing Compston all over the golf course a week later, the victory touching him as lightly as the defeat. But Hagen was exceptional. Floyd simply had to win, especially as he was conscious that his previous classic victory, the 1969 PGA championship, had been slightly handed to him on a plate by the shennanigans of the Civil Rights demonstrators upsetting his main rivals.

In the evening after that third round, when darkness finally drove Nicklaus from the practice putting green, I ran into him in the locker room. 'I guess I need another Muirfield tomorrow,' he said, referring to his famous British Open charge when he was inspired to produce golf of magical power and accuracy. As we all know now, it did not happen. Three years ago at Augusta, before play began, I asked Nicklaus why he did not set out with the intention of winning by twenty strokes or more. He accepted the implied rebuke to his normally defensive tactics with a wry grin. 'I would like to but I cannot make the important shots until I'm under the gun. It just does not happen for me.'

This time he attacked from the start, successfully for a while, but then, as Floyd produced a crisis of growing intensity for him, Nicklaus found he could not respond. Nobody could mount a telling counter-attack, and so Floyd found himself with that massive lead. To his eternal credit Floyd went out with a noble ambition. In those circumstances most golfers would have been content to play safe and draw on that bank account of accumulated strokes by laying up short of the water hazards and steering clear of trouble.

Floyd would have none of that. His main concern was not with winning. He had already accepted that the green jacket was his for the taking. Now he determined that he would win in worthy style, like a true champion with the flourish of a good last round.

For that the spectators should be duly grateful, because within the space of a few holes all possibility of a contest vanished. At least the fans had the satisfaction of watching a superb exhibition of attacking stroke-making. The question now arises whether Floyd, at the age of thirty-three, can be admitted to the exclusive club of golfers who start as one of the favourites every time he plays. His own pronouncement, 'I am sick of being a mediocre player,' suggests that the transformation from playboy to serious golfer is complete. No one has ever questioned his talent for striking a golf ball, but for years his ambition was channelled into such esoteric pursuits as buying shares in a girls' topless band. Now, while the band may have gone on swinging, he has rededicated himself to golf, and it would be rash to set a limit to his potential.

Golf is not embarrassed with a surfeit of heroes at this time – and some of the established giants are past their prime – and if the Masters of 1976 must be recorded as lacking in competitive thrills, it may well have marked the rising of a bright new star. Not a great Masters, but a Great Master.

Observer, April 1976

The Pirate from Spain

Golf instruction books can be immensely valuable to the novice. Used properly, as I am wont to advise, a book is all you need to become a champion. What you do is balance it on top of your head and then swing a club as hard as you can. Once you have mastered the art of taking a full, vicious swing without dislodging the book, you can play golf. If you should succumb to the temptation of reading it, then all is lost. It might easily take you twenty years to rinse those damaging thoughts out of your mind.

Severiano Ballesteros was immensely lucky when he started playing golf. There wasn't a golf instruction book within miles of his home in northern Spain. True, he was in some jeopardy from his elder brother Manuel, who was a tournament pro, but some native instinct saved Seve from seeking advice or listening to any hints which were volunteered in his direction. The youngster learned how to hit the ball by subconsciously absorbing the example of good players and translating these images into violent action on a trial-and-error basis.

Ballesteros also had a very good appreciation of the value of a peseta, both figuratively and literally. He used to spend hours chipping those Spanish coins into a hole, thereby acquiring an uninhibited swing and a deft touch for the delicate stroke-saving shots. With these two assets he has been chipping pesetas into his own pocket by the sackful ever since, winning a dozen tournaments on five continents before reaching the age of twenty-two.

It would be a gross oversimplification to ascribe Ballesteros's success to his ability as a striker alone. That is probably the lesser part of his talent. What sets him apart, in a way we have not seen since Arnold Palmer took professional golf into his massive hands and moulded it into a major spectator sport, is his buccaneering attitude.

Ballesteros is in the tradition of the pirates who sailed the Spanish Main. His instinctive impulse is to pile on all sail and run out the guns. 'I play for an eagle or a seven,' he says, and his willingness to pay the price for his swashbuckling tactics is one of his main strengths. He is out for rich plunder, and accepts risks which Jack Nicklaus would never contemplate.

161

'On the Tee...'

As Ballesteros returns for another raid on America this spring (1979), how appropriate is it to mention his name in the same breath as that of Nicklaus? Is the handsome young Spaniard a worthy challenger for the title of world's greatest golfer?

As for the long term, I have reservations about Ballesteros's ability to approach Nicklaus's record, unless he can adjust his motives. Money is his inspiration. He refused to play for Spain in the World Cup (although he had won the contest the previous two years with different partners) because there was not enough money in it. He declined the chance to play fulltime on the US tour because there was more money, in the form of guarantees, bribes and appearance fees, on the other world circuits.

Presumably the time will come – and soon at his present rate of acquisition – when his appetite for lucre is sated. That will be the critical moment. Tony Jacklin lost his inner drive as soon as he had achieved his material objectives, and the same could happen to Ballesteros. But if the Spaniard could acquire a fresh motivation, and aspire to smash all the records for the sake of the achievement and not for any thought of reward, then I would not care to put a limit on his potential.

For the moment, we must be content to relish the sight of the most exciting golfer of his generation. He does not know the meaning of playing the percentages; he scorns dangers and once announced, 'The rough is my friend.' On the tee his one idea is to smash the ball straight at the flag; if the green is out of range, even for his inordinate length, he smashes one at the flag anyway.

Often enough some natural feature such as a mountain, a forest or a lake intervenes. Ballesteros then seeks to blast his way forward. In four years as a touring pro he must have made more birdies and eagles without touching a fairway than any other player in history. He has his accurate days, but his scores on such occasions are not necessarily better than when he is in a wild mood, because his chipping and pitching are uncanny. I have seen him play shots which 300 years ago would have condemned him to death by burning for sorcery.

He is still at some risk from fire, because his golfing style and his punishing programme must put him at risk of burning himself out. He has already damaged his back through excessive practice. He is certainly destined to join the US Tour before long, but I would advise connoisseurs to catch him on one of his limited appearances this year. It is possible there will not be too many opportunities in the future, and Ballesteros in full flight is an experience which should not be missed.

Golf Digest, May 1979

Way of a Champion

Dedication, application and hard work are virtues. Right? These are qualities essential to any sportsman who has ambitions to become a world-beater. Absolutely. It is a cardinal rule of sport, and, indeed, of life, that there is no substitute for sheer hard graft.

Blood, tears and sweat are the lubricants of success. Nowhere do they flow more freely than at a golf driving range. You watch them standing in their stalls, pounding ball after ball for hour after hour. And if our original proposition is valid, all these golfers should reap the reward of their dedication and industry by becoming good players. What they are actually doing is practising faults, and ensuring that, say, a tendency to slice is ingrained as a lifelong habit.

The attendant professional will point out plenty of players who effectively destroy any chance of hitting a good shot before they begin, simply because they do not stand correctly to the ball. By the same token, that professional may well kill himself in tournaments before the first shot is hit.

For the bigger events some of the pros make a point of getting to the course a week early, and may play as many as ten practice rounds before the tournament begins. Which of these methods is the most effective? In the opinion of Peter Thomson they are all harmful, and, since he has won more tournaments than most golfers, it is worth taking a close look at the way he prepares himself. To the onlooker it all looks very casual. He strolls to the practice ground, hits three or four shots, and then seems to lose interest.

He then goes to the first tee, and it comes as no surprise to those of puritan mind who worship at the shrine of hard work when he fires his drive into the rough. As the round progresses, those sporting citizens who have dignified their hunches to the extent of laying out hard cash on Thomson with the bookies become concerned. He finds bunker after bunker, and when he does have a clear shot at the green he seems to be aiming wide of the flag. And he does not care, that is obvious from the look of him.

'You must go into an event with a clear mind free of fears, openly expectant and not committed to any preconceived pattern of play,' he told me. 'And everything you do must be directed towards achieving that frame of mind. Take practice. If you haven't got it by the time you get to a tournament you certainly won't find it on the practice range. You know, we have these champions of the practice range who go out and hit hundreds of shots. But it's stupid to rely on the mechanical theory that what you did on the practice ground will repeat automatically on the course. The circumstances are entirely different. The view from the tee must affect you. Suddenly there are bunkers and out-of-bounds to think about. Anyway, suppose I did hit a couple of drives on the practice ground and they both hooked off to the left.

'When I got to the first tee it would be impossible to erase the memory, and I would automatically make some experimental adjustment. Since I play by feel, all I do on the practice ground is to find that feeling of hitting the ball well, and once I've got it I stop.'

Then what about those off-line shots in the practice round? 'My purpose in the practice round is to learn where the serious trouble is and to get the pace of the course, how the ball is bouncing. I start off by deliberately overshooting everything. This gives you the confidence that you have the length to tackle the course, and when the serious competition begins you don't hit flat out.

'Another important point is to drive into a position from which you can set up a winning shot to the flag and that sometimes means choking down on a driver or taking a three-wood.'

Finally, how many practice rounds are necessary? 'One or two only. Playing two rounds a day for a week before a big event is a mistake. You are bound to get into trouble at times, and it's impossible to forget those mistakes. They must influence you later and destroy that vital open-mindedness.

'Afterwards, when you've won, is the time to savour your accomplishment. But beforehand, any feelings of "Wouldn't it be wonderful?" are distractions, just what you need to avoid.'

Thomson's philosophy of don't try too hard, don't work too hard, could easily be corrupted into a doctrine of indolence. But the way he plays it, it is a winning mixture.

Observer, August 1971

The Day Joe Ezar Called
His Shots for a Remarkable 64

The last time I heard of Joe Ezar he was working on the roads down in Florida. He was a nobody. And yet if Joe had been a different kind of person, a fraction more stable and just a touch less fond of the bottle, he might today be enshrined in golf's Hall of Fame. Maybe not. For perhaps it was just that maverick streak in Joe which made possible the most extraordinary round of golf ever played.

The hands which today embrace a shovel were gifted with a golfing talent of rare quality. This is an appropriate moment to recall Joe's finest hour, which took place forty years ago – in July 1936 – during one of his trips to Europe. And if it does not qualify him for the Hall of Fame it does at least deserve a footnote in the history of golf.

Joe, a swarthy Armenian-American, was a colourful character in those days. He won a lot of money, not in prizes so much as in fanciful side bets. He needed cash because he was a man with a very expensive thirst indeed.

Europe in 1936 was boiling up for war, and Joe fitted in perfectly with the mood of those who wanted to squeeze the last drop of carefree enjoyment out of a life which could not last. In Germany he won some cash, and when he found that he could not take it out of the country Joe invested the lot in the current status symbol of wealth, a flashy camel-hair coat. Joe loved that coat and lived in it. He refused even to leave it in the locker room when he played golf and draped it over his shoulders on the course, like a cape.

The precious camel-hair was never out of his sight, and he had it with him for the Italian Open of 1936 at Sestriere, up in the mountains near Turin. Henry Cotton, who had won the British Open in 1934 and was to win it again in 1937 and 1948, was the king of European golf, and on this occasion he had turned the Italian Open into a procession with two hot rounds, including a course-record 68.

That evening he and Ezar were entertaining the crowd with an exhibition of golfing virtuosity, Cotton hitting the orthodox shots and Ezar producing an impressive repertoire of trick shots. Joe's final stunt was to drop three balls on the green thirty-five feet from the hole and invite bets that he could not hole one of them. Considering the rough state of the green, it was a fair bet and several people accepted the challenge. Joe holed the first two balls and laughingly collected his winnings.

The prime objective of the exercise had succeeded, to sort out those in the gallery with a taste for some action. One of them happened to be the president of the Fiat motor company. 'What do you bet I can't equal the course record tomorrow?' asked Joe. The sporting tycoon smiled. 'I'll tell you what I'll do. I will give you five thousand lire for a sixty-six, and ten thousand for a sixty-five.'

'What about a sixty-four?' asked Joe.

'In that case,' said the president expansively, 'I'll make it forty thousand.'

'Very generous of you,' said Joe. 'Now I'll tell you what I will do. I will put down the score I'll make on each of the eighteen holes for my sixty-four.'

He took a card and wrote down his target figures for every hole, finishing with a birdie-3 at the last. Cotton looked at the card and remarked, 'You're mad.' Joe headed for the bar.

In the morning Joe was in no mood for golf. His caddie pulled him out of bed and propped him under a cold shower. Joe protested that he was too drunk to play. 'Oh, no, you're not,' said the caddie, who also had a wager going on the round.

Joe made it to the first tee and wanted to play in his camel-hair coat, to keep out the bitter morning air of the mountains. His caddie persuaded him to compromise; he could wear the coat between shots.

Cotton, his playing partner, advised him to forget the whole thing. 'Nobody could do it. You're asking for eighteen successive miracles.' Joe proceeded to rip off eight successive miracles. 'You could call that round the biggest fluke of all time,' recalls Cotton, 'but the fact is that he did it. He had all the luck in the world, chipping in and holing impossible putts, but the figures came out just as Joe had predicted. Right up to the ninth. He had marked it down for a three but a poor tee shot cost him a four.'

However, he made the unlikeliest of 3s at the next hole where he had predicted a 4. And for the rest of the round Joe's luck stayed with him. Through the bedlam of the crowd Joe reeled off his predicted figures, all the while complaining to Cotton that he was too sick and nervous to hold a club. Still, he did it. He had his 64.

Like all golfers who specialize in trick shots, Ezar had a style which exaggerated hand-and-arm action and rather reduced leg-and-body movement. He played from a wide, flat-footed style and delivered a

166

tremendous lash at the ball with those powerful arms. Cotton described his method as being composed of good points taken to excess. Ezar's right shoulder looked to be too much under his chin at impact; his head too far behind the ball; his eye fixed too firmly on his divot scrape long after the ball had departed; his clubface held square to the shot for too long after impact.

Yet Joe made it work, and never better than on the final drive across the chasm of a dogleg – not unlike the layout of the famous sixteenth at Cypress Point – to hit the flagstick all of 290 yards away.

If he was almost sober by this time, he did not remain that way for long. Within weeks Joe was broke again, and he faced the problem of getting back to America. Here was a real challenge for the man who had once bet he could get his entry accepted for the British Open after the closing date, and, what's more, that he would lead after two rounds. He did exactly that, collected his $2000 winnings and did not even turn up for the third round.

Joe had been present when Trevor Wignall, a columnist for the London *Daily Express*, was interviewing Cotton. Wignall mentioned that he was to sail on the maiden voyage of the *Queen Mary* to New York. Here was Joe's chance to get safely home. At Cherbourg he tagged his golf bag 'Trevor Wignall' and saw it taken aboard. Joe followed, along with all the other well-wishers making their *bon voyages*, and hid in a closet in Wignall's stateroom. Twelve hours later, after the liner had safely cleared Southampton water, Joe emerged and told Wignall what he had done.

The writer asked Joe what he had done with the rest of his baggage. 'This is all I've got,' said Joe, indicating his precious camel-hair coat. Joe wanted to remain a stowaway, but Wignall fixed it with the purser for Joe to work for his passage by giving exhibitions of golf on deck. So Joe came home in style.

If you happen to be driving through Florida and come across an old man in a threadbare camel-hair coat shovelling gravel by the roadside, stop and shake his hand. And if you should have a spare fifth in the car he would certainly appreciate it. But do not, whatever you do, take him up on any bets.

Golf Digest, November 1976

Motivation Is the Key ⟁

If you were asked to nominate the six greatest golfers of the last fifty years it is likely that your selection would be drawn from a list including Ben Hogan, Jack Nicklaus, Walter Hagen, Bobby Jones, Sam Snead, Peter Thomson, Bobby Locke, Henry Cotton, Arnold Palmer, Gary Player, Byron Nelson and Lee Trevino. Permutate any six from twelve and you have a powerful team, assuming that all are playing at their prime.

I will now nominate a six-man team of golfers who did not win a major championship between them and I will bet my immortal soul, given that I can set the conditions of the match, that my lot would win. The conditions are: no spectators, no prizes, no publicity – just six singles playing like club golfers on a Sunday afternoon. My team: Neil Coles, Joe Ezar, Charlie Whitcombe, Moe Norman, Christy O'Connor and Percy Alliss.

Many golfers haven't even heard of Ezar and Norman. And perhaps the point is that they couldn't be made to care whether anyone has heard of them or not. As motivation goes, theirs was always pretty esoteric.

Moe Norman is a genius of the same stamp as Joe Ezar (see the previous chapter – 'The Day Joe Ezar Called His Shots . . .'). Norman lives like a hermit near Toronto in one room without a telephone. As a young man he was a successful amateur, then less successful as a tournament pro because he hated the life on the circuit. Now he drives down to Florida each winter with a friend to follow his trade of playing challenge golf – any challenge provided the odds are right.

His pal does the deals, Norman plays the golf. On one occasion he had a bundle riding on a bet that he could beat a course record on his first try. He was playing with the local pro, and eventually needed a 4 for his winning record. 'What's this hole?' he asked. 'Oh, it's just a drive and a nine-iron,' said the pro.

Norman dropped the ball on the tee and hit his 9-iron up the fairway. Then he took out his driver, spanked the ball on to the green six feet from the flag, holed the putt, pocketed the loot, and drove off.

The common denominator in my six golfers is that while they were all superb players, they were not particularly anxious (or fitted, in some cases) to become great champions. I have never managed to get Coles or O'Connor to admit as much, and I doubt whether they even admit it to themselves, but I do not believe they wanted to become champions in the mould of Palmer and Nicklaus.

Alliss and Whitcombe were likewise content to pursue fame at a jogtrot. Contemporaries may argue that both were poor pressure putters, showing them to be temperamentally unsuited to tournament golf. That argument is surely fallacious. If any one of these six had been driven by the demon of ambition, like those twelve supreme champions, he could have made it.

After all, Jones was temperamentally unsuited to tournament golf. He could barely eat during a competition and on occasion his tie (standard dress for golfers of his era) became so soaked in nervous perspiration that he had to cut the knot after a round.

Byron Nelson was even worse. The so-called 'Iron Byron' suffered from agonizing stomach cramps, threw up before a round, and, not long after his greatest season, playing golf such as no man has equalled before or since, he chose to call a halt to competitive play because his nervous system could take no more.

In discussing the motivation which inspires champions we tend to talk of dedication, application and single-minded purpose as virtues. Taken to the extremes necessary for a champion, these characteristics more often loom as character defects, as all obsessions must.

Without getting too bogged down in the swampy ground of psychology, it is clear that motivation in golf springs from two sources. There is the lure of reward — Tony Jacklin fighting his way out of the Scunthorpe mills towards the dream of a mansion and a Rolls (and losing his inner thrust once he achieved them). And there is the sharper spur of fulfilment, a striving towards the unattainable goal of golfing perfection.

In this second category we find, above all, Ben Hogan, whose pursuit of technical mastery approached the extremes of irrationality normally associated with religious fanaticism such as fire dancing and self-flagellation. Gary Player followed Hogan through the pain barrier, driving himself to super fitness and golfing skill with a brutal regime of finger-tip press-ups and practising until his hands bled.

Jack Nicklaus was also possessed by the devil of achievement. His ambition was reinforced by a competitive nature which dominated his personality like a narcotic drug. Over the years his craving for competition demanded ever stronger doses, until today he simply cannot give his all in a run-of-the-mill tournament.

In order to get the best out of Nicklaus the syringe has to be loaded with a highly refined formula: three holes to play in one of the majors, needing a birdie to win.

In looking for the champions of tomorrow it is necessary to recognize two qualities. A basic talent for golf (the swing may be dodgy but that can be adjusted, *vide* Gary Player) and a rich vein of that magnificent paranoia. Greed can take a golfer so far, but the summit of the game is reserved for those to whom money is an irrelevance. Of course, they make the biggest fortunes, but that is incidental.

Observer, November 1979

The Sound of Nancy

The best way to watch women's golf is to keep your eyes closed. Perhaps I had better come up with a swift clarification of that statement before we get our wires completely crossed. Absolutely, item No.1 on the agenda of explanatory footnotes is that I do not, repeat *not*, mean that women golfers are not worth looking at.

Far from it. When it comes to bird-watching I count myself a connoisseur. The effects some of those lissom girls achieve when they swing a golf club really ought to be forbidden by law. I still break out in a hot sweat when I recall playing in a pro–am with Jan Stephenson on a hot day in Spain when she was dressed for comfort. As for Laura Baugh, I am almost persuaded that it does not matter whether she can break 90.

And when Renee Powell is playing in a northerly direction, and I am observing from the south, if any member of the constabulary in the vicinity happened to be a mind-reader I could go to gaol for my thoughts. No, I have no complaints about the appearance of women golfers. For the moment my mind is strictly on the quality of the golf they play.

With the benefit of hindsight – or hindsound I had better call it, although the word frankly troubles me – I first became aware of the value of closing one's eyes at golf tournaments when I went to watch the late and great Babe Zaharias.

Tramping cross-country through the woods to catch up with her I knew I was on track when I heard that characteristic sound of a golf ball being struck. Something troubled me about the noise, but I pressed forward and was soon engrossed by the sight of that magnificent athlete, combining grace and power in a way that seemed more appropriate to a member of the cat family than a human being.

After a few more holes I was still faintly disturbed because, with all her highly developed skills, there was an element which was not right. The clue hit me when she walked back to a tee and, because of the press of the crowd, I could not see her hit the drive. I fixed my gaze down the fairway to pick up the flight of the ball and listened for the

171

shot. That was it. The sound was not that of a woman hitting a golf ball; it was the noise made at impact when the club is wielded by a good man player.

After that, I repeated the experiment, deliberately closing my eyes so that I could concentrate on the sound without distraction. There was no doubt about it. When a woman swings the club it sounds 'who-ooooosh, plop!' A good man player sounds 'whizz, tok!' If you take a hard-boiled egg, remove the shell and hurl it against a wall, you approximate the sound of a woman golfer's shot. A man's impact is harsher, crisper – more like a .22-calibre pistol being discharged in the next room.

That crispness of impact, caused by the clubhead accelerating (and descending) into the ball, brings immense benefits to the shot in addition to extra length. This is where refinements of control originate – through backspin.

Women sweep the ball away. They may hit it long enough. The good ones hit it straighter than their male counterparts. And they undoubtedly make good scores like this. But what they do not achieve is that virtuoso shot-making ability, moving the ball this way and that and checking it sharply on landing, which is the essence of a genius such as Hale Irwin.

Many years later, having formed the habit of watching women's golf with my eyes shut, I heard that Zaharias sound again. It came from the clubs of Catherine Lacoste, of France, who, when barely out of her teens and an amateur, went to America and stood the world of women's golf on its ear by beating the professionals to win the US Women's Open.

Incidentally, Mlle Lacoste was given the full treatment by some of the girl professionals and cried herself to sleep every night over their bitchy hostility. All these years later, as the mother of a growing family and therefore an infrequent, although still formidable player, she does not care to recall some of the unpleasantness of the greatest week of her sporting life.

Anyway, my point is that I do wish that women golfers would give some attention to the quality of their striking and seek to reproduce the characteristic snapping-twig note at impact. I am not saying, of course, that the noise is a benefit in itself. It is simply an audible proof that the strike is a good one.

The women pros are eminently capable of working out their other problems, such as swing planes and directional control, for themselves. But until they get that snap into the shot, everything else will be in a minor key and that, let me assure them, is not going to be good enough in the future. Women's golf is moving into a new era and if the professionals are to survive they must work and analyse and copy.

For I have heard that sound again. There is absolutely no mistaking it. It comes from the clubs of Nancy Lopez.

Golf Digest, November 1978

Down Goes a Barrier

When Lee Elder sank a long birdie putt at the fourth extra hole of a sudden-death play-off with Peter Oosterhuis in the Monsanto Open (1974), he won the first American PGA tournament of his career and thus became the first black golfer to qualify for an automatic invitation to compete in the Masters. I know only too well what relief that fact will bring to the tournament organizers at Augusta.

For years the Masters has been reviled in certain quarters, notably among opportunist politicians looking to pick up black votes, as a bastion of southern bigotry. The tournament committee has answered these smears with long-suffering grace.

In the case of American golfers, invitations to play in the Masters are given in accordance with a set of fixed conditions, one of which is the winning of a PGA tour event during the previous year. The Masters has always stood out against tokenism, believing that if a special case were made to include a black golfer in the field, outside the limits of the qualifying standards, this would be seen as a patronizing act and would actually harm race relations.

For as long as I have been going to the Masters, the chairman, Clifford Roberts, whose word has been law for the forty years since the tournament began, has been questioned on this subject and he has always insisted, 'As soon as a black golfer becomes eligible for an invitation under the qualifying system he will be welcome at Augusta just like anyone else.'

American professional golf has been integrated (by PGA rule) for many years, and this has been accepted by everyone in the game as fully as in baseball, football or jazz music, for a lesser period of time. If black golfers have been slow to come to the top, the reasons must be sought in the wider American society rather than within the game.

It was a pity that the last ritual of integration should not fall to one of the men whose example over many years was mainly responsible for dissolving prejudice. Ted Rhodes, reputedly good enough to beat any white golfer of his day if only he had been allowed to compete, and also Charlie Sifford, were both born too early to claim the honour of this

174

last act of emancipation, although Sifford still plays fine golf on occasions.

But Elder himself has borne a fair share of the pioneers' burden. He will be forty in a few months, yet he did not join the PGA circuit until 1968. Before then he competed on the (black) United Golf Association tour, contemptuously known as the peanut circuit for its £1000 prizes. In that league he was king, once winning twenty-one out of the season's twenty-three events, and earning enough to put by a nest egg which would see him over the transition to the PGA big-time.

He is deeply committed to civil rights, not in the crusading Arthur Ashe manner but as a visitor to underprivileged areas where he encourages the children to remain in school and elevate themselves educationally.

He himself dropped out, added a couple of years to his age to comply with UGA regulations, and started playing pro golf at fourteen.

Like many youngsters, Elder gripped his clubs cross-handed until he went to work with Lloyd Mangrum, but he did not really become serious about golf until he finished his stint in the army. Mangrum helped him find a job as an assistant and Elder, whose truck-driver father died when he was young, supplemented the meager family finances with a series of hustling side bets. Elder would take on challenges to play on one leg, on his knees, and once in 95° heat in a zipped-up rain suit.

Elder did not go into these matches unprepared. Having made the bet, he would go to a floodlit driving range to practise, sometimes working away all night and going straight to the match with no sleep.

Ted Rhodes virtually adopted Elder for three years, taking him into his home and teaching him all he could about the game of golf. In 1968 Elder was ready, financially and in experience, to join the PGA tour. In that first season he tied with Jack Nicklaus and Frank Beard in the American Golf Classic at Akron, Ohio.

Television covered the play-off. Beard was eliminated at the first extra hole. Nicklaus sank sixteen- and thirty-footers to hold off Elder's challenge and then, on the fourth of the sudden-death holes, Nicklaus made a birdie for outright victory. Elder had to be content with other satisfactions, not least the remark by PGA president Maxwell Stanford: 'Elder did more for Negro golf in forty-five minutes than everybody else had done in forty-five years.'

It was a pardonable overstatement, but there is no doubt that Elder's composure, and his sporting acceptance of those cruel thrusts from Nicklaus's putter, won him enormous personal popularity and respect. If Rhodes and Sifford had largely won the legalistic battle for

175

integration in golf, Elder had won a considerable victory in the campaign for what liberals like to call the hearts and minds of men.

As a player Elder is not spectacular. He is short (5 feet 8 inches) and his forte is accuracy rather than power, especially with the driver.

When Lee Elder walks out of the Augusta National clubhouse next April and steps up to the first tee, I am sure he will be given an enormous ovation. His appearance on that occasion, as I have said, will be purely symbolic in the struggle long since won but none the less welcome for that.

Observer, April 1974

The Two Gary Players

The veteran American golf writer was holding forth on Gary Player. 'Remember when he was on his health-food kick and he had a contract to endorse raisins? He used to go around with a pocketful of raisins, and when he came to the press tent he'd chew them all through the interview, telling us how they made him strong because they had absorbed so much strength from the sun. Then the next year he had a new craze, for bananas. I asked him if he still ate raisins. "No," he said, "they rot your teeth".'

The world of golf is full of such stories about Player. There was a variation on the raisin theme when he dressed himself all in black so that he could absorb the sun's strength. More recently Player went through a phase of declining to shake hands because, he explained, it meant he transmitted some of his power to somebody else.

All of Player's eccentric theories and statements are expressed with those wide eyes blazing their sincerity like P-100 headlamps. Any averagely cynical listener quickly forms the view that the South African is the most gullible human being who ever drew breath, blown like a thistledown this way and that by every passing puff of fashion. Totally cynical listeners get the feeling when Player switches to a religious theme that he must have signed a fat endorsement contract to promote Christianity (although he is, in fact, a devout Christian). Nobody could be that sincere if he were really sincere.

Now Player would have us believe that his British Open win at Royal Lytham and St Anne's (1977) was due to self-hypnosis. We may react by thinking he is kidding himself or that he is trying to kid us.

Player does not mind what we think. I believe it is important to distinguish Player the golfer from Player the superstar. In the phoney world of star-making, Player understands better than most that to be outrageous, and extravagant with opinions, and a good deal larger than life, is good for the Gary Player business. He is never less than honest and it does not really matter if people think him gullible, or inconsistent, just so long as they go on thinking and talking and writing about him.

Once he takes a golf club in his hand, however, he must be done with artificiality. This is real and there is the real Gary Player coping with it. It s! ould be remembered that Player not only played Lytham better than anyone else, but he also thought his way around the course more astutely than his rivals. He does not exaggerate when he hits a golf ball. He is not inconsistent, one day pitching with his wedge and then the next day switching to a mid-iron, and blandly explaining that wedges are hopeless.

Not many people are privileged to penetrate the show-biz veneer and get to know this real Player. I have only once known him to drop his guard publicly and reveal himself. That was in 1969 on a sweltering day at Dayton, Ohio, during the American PGA championship. He was paired with Jack Nicklaus and they were singled out for an assault by demonstrators, one of whom dashed a cup of soft drink into his face. Missiles were being thrown and one demonstrator made a rush onto the green, making Nicklaus raise his putter defensively.

Player stood his ground until the commotion had been subdued by the security men, and then coldly holed a difficult birdie putt. No one knew if fresh violence would break out, possibly in more serious form, but Player continued the round without showing the slightest hint of nerves.

On his usual form, this situation might have seemed ripe for Player to use his interview as a platform for one of his well-known dissertations on politics, or sentimental monologues on the subject of brotherly love. But he declined to talk about the incident publicly, and when we later sat down over a cup of coffee he discussed it calmly and rationally. Real life had broken into the golf theatre, and the real Player responded. For me, that was the day that Player blew his cover.

Observer, July 1977

Keep Playing It Again, Sam

It was a coup for Benson and Hedges to attract Sam Snead to their golf festival at York (1974), and he was one of the major attractions, making this the best-attended golf tournament, save the Open Championship, in Britain this year.

Opponents of appearance money often argue that importing Americans of less than Nicklaus–Palmer calibre does not attract one extra spectator, and frequently the size of the crowds tends to support that view.

At the Benson and Hedges the take at the turnstiles must have approached £20,000 and it was obvious from his personal gallery that a good proportion of that money was spent to see Snead.

He did not disappoint the fans. Snead is one of a handful of golfers (Sarazen is another) who inspire the club player with the conviction that golf is easy. I always get a strong feeling when I see Snead that if someone gave me a club there and then I, too, could hit the ball like he does. Unfortunately that flash of revelation is ephemeral. By the time the tournament is over, and there is an opportunity to put Snead's example to the test, the vision of his swing has faded.

At sixty-two Snead is as supple as a teenager. Leaving the press tent he casually kicked the lintel, which I measured at 6 feet 6 inches. With the advantage of a few years and several inches in leg length, I tried the same trick with indescribable results.

Before leaving, Snead had been in spell-binding form with reminiscences about the old-timers. Ben Hogan's swing was kind of flat, he recalled, adding a barely adequate tribute to his record, and Bobby Jones was not a good iron player. 'Jones was a great driver and fairway wood player and a fine putter, but he wasn't real good with the irons.'

Not like Tommy Armour, the legendary iron player, suggested someone. 'Hell! That was all a mistake,' said Snead. 'What happened was that some reporter saw Armour hit a hell of a shot and dubbed him a great iron player. But actually Armour hit that shot with a wood, only the reporter didn't see what club he used. That's how the legend started.'

Interviewing Snead is a fascinating but professionally frustrating business for two reasons. In the first place one needs a good working knowledge of the rich but racy slang of rural West Virginia. He used the expression 'I got a touch of the old red-ass' three times before I managed to divine from the context that it meant to lose one's temper. Then there is the other difficulty: that 90 per cent of his hilarious stories are totally unsuitable for publication, either because of their extreme vulgarity or their libellous nature.

But he did make one point which all golfers should find of interest, namely his scorn of the modern obsession with using the legs in golf. Golf is played with the arms, he said flatly, with the authority of a man who has seen fads come and go and has outlasted all his contemporaries by twenty years or so.

Just as he has an endless fund of anecdotes about players, so there is a rich treasury of stories about Snead. One of my favourites is of the 1956 Canada Cup at Wentworth. Snead was teamed with Hogan for the United States, and on the flight from America Hogan was anxious to learn everything he could about the course. Hogan wanted a complete analysis of the fairway grass, the texture and speed of the greens, topography, tightness of the driving, and any other available morsel of information. Snead had played at Wentworth and so Hogan asked him what the course was like. Snead reflected at some length and then replied, 'That Wentworth is a sonofabitch.'

Obviously, the question everyone wants to ask Snead is the secret of his staying power. At York it was to put to him that he did not smoke, and drank only the occasional beer. Snead agreed, but with no hint of evangelical fervour. As a failed comedy writer, it was more than I could do to resist the traditional crack, 'Two out of three isn't bad, Sam.'

At this his face lit up with a huge grin. 'That's right!' He added a pithy West Virginian comment which I cannot trust myself to translate accurately. I think I will give up smoking, stick to the occasional beer, and take it from there.

Observer, June 1974

Turning Point for Nicklaus ⚑ 1

What sort of a professional golfer is it who has four goes in consecutive days at a simple par-4 hole of 377 yards and winds up with a total of seventeen strokes and never a sniff at a birdie? What sort of a professional golfer is it who allows the play of another competitor to rattle him so badly that he misses a straightforward three-foot putt? What sort of a professional golfer is it who duffs a 4-iron shot from a perfect lie (off a tee peg, no less) and makes a 5 at a par-3 of 193 yards?

The answer, if you had not guessed already, is that this is a breed of professional golfer such as the world has never seen before, by the name of Jack Nicklaus, who did all of these things in winning the eightieth United States Open championship, setting scoring records with each succeeding round.

The surprising thing was that Nicklaus should have produced the performance of his life at the age of forty after he had gone for eighteen months without a victory and had apparently passed his peak. All through those arid months of slump, Nicklaus insisted that he was still playing well but just not scoring well. He became tetchy at constant inquiries about whether he planned to retire.

In America there are no national newspapers, so at every tournament there is a different group of golf correspondents who, naturally enough, ask the same questions that the golfers have answered the week before in another part of the country. Nicklaus became so frustrated that when he was brought into the press room for his ritual grilling at the Masters in April he announced firmly that he would not respond to questions about retirement. He had made a new commitment of golf, he was practising harder and had revised his usual tournament programme to play more competitive golf.

It all sounded very positive and businesslike, just the kind of things you would expect to hear from a player who is going through a bad patch, as they all do. Nevertheless he failed to dispel the doubts of those who listened to him, and he also failed, as he admitted last week, to dispel the doubts which had begun to assail him. Perhaps he was, indeed, allowing his course-designing interests and business

181

commitments to deflect him from his playing career. Perhaps his desire was on the wane: after all, seventeen victories in the major championships was surely a record which could not be challenged. Perhaps his competitive edge had become blunted.

Nicklaus kept his own counsel but there is no doubt that he indulged in some serious soul-searching after the Masters. He had got into the habit of going to his office first thing in the morning, a practice which his employees deplored. Those with enough seniority and gall begged him to go out and practise and leave them to run the Nicklaus empire.

During the process of personal stocktaking, it had surely occurred to Nicklaus that by the age of twenty-three he had won two US amateur championships, one US Open and one PGA tournament. By the same age Severiano Ballesteros had won one British Open, one Masters, one American PGA tournament, seven Spanish domestic tournaments, and twenty-one major international events, including the World Cup (twice) and the national championships of Holland, Japan, France, Switzerland, Kenya, Germany and Scandinavia. At the age of thirty, it was highly unlikely that Tom Watson could challenge those seventeen classic victories and no other American player loomed as a threat to this record, either. But this young Spaniard was well on course to surpass that record, and Nicklaus has absolutely no intention of being remembered as the second-best golfer who ever lived.

The result was that his ambition was restored to maximum revs, although his play did not immediately reflect the change in attitude. In regular PGA tournaments he prospered only modestly, even failing to make much of a show in his own Memorial tournament at Muirfield Village, the course he designed and built to reflect his personal philosophy of golf. Those comparative failures did not greatly bother Nicklaus because he has long since lost the ability to give of his best in everyday events. He has won sixty-six of them in the USA alone and has nothing to prove in that direction. His objective was purely to work up for the next big one, the US Open at Baltusrol.

He was not a whit dismayed to miss the qualifying cut in the Atlanta Classic the week before the Open, because he found there the one element which was still missing from his game: an effective putting stroke. All he needed now was the stimulus of fear. Tom Weiskopf provided it in the first round by playing like a man possessed three groups ahead. Every time a Weiskopf birdie was posted on the leader board, Angelo Argea, Nicklaus's caddie for the past eighteen years, said: 'Answer him.' Nicklaus duly responded with that 63 on his own account, and was disappointed to miss the three-footer on the eighteenth green which would have given him a 62.

For the rest of the championship Nicklaus needed no sharper spur than the golf of his playing companion, Isao Aoki. Much of the credit for Nicklaus's victory must go to the skill and grit of the Japanese whose influence can be compared with the part played by Christopher Brasher and Chris Chataway in Roger Bannister's four-minute mile.

Observer, June 1980

Henry Longhurst: A Style and Wit that Bridged Two Continents

Looking back on his brief foray into parliamentary life, Henry Longhurst wrote: 'It was on the assumption of an electorate consisting of reasonable men that I ventured into politics. Oh, dear. Oh, dear.'

Anyone who loves golf,' and that must add up to a worldwide constituency of at least thirty million people, must be grateful that the voters of Acton gave Henry the heave-ho in Britain's postwar Socialist landslide.

Not that Longhurst was a bad MP. On the contrary, he was a dedicated and effective guardian of the rights of the people of Acton. In due course he would surely have been promoted, and he would have made a disastrous Minister since his political views were those of a feudal baron. Besides, and this is the point, the world would have lost a sublime writer and broadcaster on the game of golf.

From the moment I was appointed as golf correspondent to a newspaper in direct opposition to his, Henry always addressed me jocularly as Hated Rival, and the first words he spoke to me were typical of the man. A pushy public relations officer had been pestering us to go and look at a Caribbean golf development and Henry said, 'I would not presume to offer you any advice on how to go about this job of golf writing except in this one respect. By all means screw their women and drink their booze, but never, never, on any account, write one word about their bloody awful golf courses.'

The formative influences on Longhurst are all too easy to trace. From his comfortable middle-class home in Bedford, where his family had a retail house-furnishing business, Henry was sent to a prep school at Eastbourne which was to become the subject of some of the most vitriolic prose in the English language by his literary contemporaries.

Henry recalled the morning dish of cold breakfast porridge, into which he once actually threw up. He was then forced to stand in the corner until he had consumed the vile mess – despite which, in his autobiography, *My Life and Soft Times*, he remembered the place with

184

affection, quoting with approval a letter he received many years later: 'My brother attributes the fact that he emerged absolutely sane and fit from five years as a prisoner of war solely to having been at St Cyprians.'

Charterhouse, with its private slang and individual rituals (including a peculiarly barbarous form of corporal punishment) common to all English public schools, gave Longhurst its unmistakable imprint and passed him on to Clare College, Cambridge, where he remained spiritually for the rest of his life.

It is a curious aspect of British university life that while Oxford men emerge with no permanent taint, Cambridge imparts a certain hauteur and plummy smugness, evident in attitude and speech, which brands its alumni for life. That, at least, was the case when the universities were concerned to prepare undergraduates for life, and Longhurst was recognizable as a Cambridge man at a hundred yards until the day he died.

He studied golf, and dabbled in economics in odd moments of his spare time with no great distinction. Golf opened up a whole world for Longhurst. Travelling about the country with the Cambridge team for matches against different clubs, he gained an entrée into the golfing branch of the Old Boy network which opened the door for his career.

The golfing Mafia spoke the right words into the right ears, and Longhurst was invited to join the *Sunday Times* and the *Tatler*, and then the *Evening Standard*.

If Longhurst received a helpful push in the right direction, he quickly proved that he was the right man for the job. He always claimed the status of gifted amateur, since he knew nothing and cared less about the nuts and bolts of journalism, but really he was the most painstaking of professionals. Bernard Darwin had emancipated the golf writer, and Longhurst extended the process. He studied the prose styles of Winston Churchill and P. G. Wodehouse, learning from both the value of economy and simplicity. In twenty-one years he never missed his weekly column and for thousands of us that essay was an essential ingredient of Sunday breakfast.

Writers who choose to specialize in sport can seldom hope to receive due recognition from the literary fraternity, mainly because the limp-wristed coterie of critics who arbitrate on such matters does not approve of the subject. In fact, one of Longhurst's secrets was that he did not write very much about golf. He took golf as a text and then frequently digressed into some subject which had taken his interest, and he was a man with an insatiable curiosity.

His motto might well have been 'Try Anything Once', and this thirst for new experiences led him to try his hand at motor racing on the old Brooklands track, bob-sledding down the Cresta run, going up in a glider, sinking deep into the sea in a diver's suit, and riding on the footplate of a locomotive.

Golf enabled him to travel widely and he made the most of his opportunities, always anxious to divert from the beaten path and see new things, do new things. It was a rich life, and vastly enriching for his readers, and Longhurst accumulated a huge repertory of anecdotes, many of them of a disreputable nature, which made him the most wonderful talker I have ever met. I once sat up all night while Longhurst and Alistair Cooke swapped stories. It was like a tennis match as they capped each other's offerings for hour after hour while I poured the gin and listened.

This gift of story-telling lay at the heart of Longhurst's success as a broadcaster. He pioneered golf commentating on radio and television, and set a standard no one has remotely approached since. He seemed to have an instinct for knowing when not to speak on TV and letting the pictures tell their own story. And when he did comment, dismissing a missed putt with an urbane growl of, 'Ah, well, *there* we are, then,' it was twenty times more effective than the effusions of hysterical and misinformed rubbish most commentators inflict on the viewer.

Longhurst cheerfully admitted to being a bit of a snob. He rationalized his preference for dukes to dustmen by saying that they were invariably more interesting, and it was this element of snobbery, I believe, which made him slightly uneasy at being branded a journalist, a profession which carries a powerful social stigma in certain quarters, notably in the world of golf.

He was fond of telling the story of attending a championship at a Yorkshire club in his early days when a potting shed was considered quite adequate as working quarters for the despised press. A senior writer had protested at these arrangements, and Longhurst happened to be busily writing in the shed when the secretary and a committeeman passed by and he heard one of them say, 'There's one of them in there now.'

That disdainful remark has passed into the vocabulary of golf writers and is used to this day whenever the press is disparaged. Longhurst delighted in deflating that kind of pomposity, but at the same time he kept himself slightly aloof from the journalistic pack.

In many ways Longhurst led the most enviable of lives, and he knew it. He lost no opportunity to gloat to his readers about being in some exotic place, lazing, with only the clink of ice against glass to disturb the perfect peace. As I know all too well, following the golf trail is not all beer and skittles, and Longhurst also suffered private tragedies which must have made the cheerful tone of his writing excessively difficult to sustain.

Both his son and son-in-law were killed in wasteful accidents. He himself suffered horribly with illness, and was brought to the brink of suicide. He wrote in his column about that incident, revealing that he overdid the job of fortifying his nerves and fell asleep before he could swallow the tablets.

Later, after a good recovery, I asked him about his health. 'I have to go back every three months for a check-up,' he said. 'I alway ask for the last appointment of the day so that if the prognosis is unfavourable the pubs will be open.'

Finally the prognosis was unfavourable. I do hope Henry's glass was full. He would not like to go out on a wave of sentiment and sorrow. Let us remember his zest and wit, and what better way than with a snatch of Longhurst prose, written in his beloved windmill home on the Sussex downs for his autobiography:

Bobby [his bull terrier] had a wooden pole, five feet long and the best part of three inches thick, which must have weighed several pounds. It was his great delight to get this pole by the point of balance in his massive jaws and run flat out with it, straight at an opening in the wall about three feet wide. The collision was frightful to behold and sometimes he would somersault clean over the pale at impact. With blood coming from his back teeth he would then collect the pole, retire and charge again.

Henry Longhurst was a bit like that with some of his opinions. The world is a poorer, duller place without him.

Golf World, September 1978

The Lean Pantaloon ... His Youthful Hose Well Saved
A World Too Wide For His Shrunk Shank .

Part Five

Tomorrow It Will Be Better

A forlorn search for golfing salvation

Bang that Tyre ⚑

This article sprang from an earlier reference in a column to a
favourite training and teaching drill of Henry Cotton's,
the great British professional, who believes the hands
are the key to golf

First the equipment. You need an old tyre, as bald as possible. Service stations and tyre centres will give them away, happily. Then you will have to get an old golf club and a stick.

You can perfectly well use a club from your own set, but you may be inhibited by a fear of breaking one of your favourites. Much better have a special exercise club so you can bash away with abandon. I suggest a 3-iron, or something close, so that daily familiarity will eliminate the common phobia against using long irons. Just walk into any golf professional's shop and wave a pound note under his nose. He will find an odd club for you and be delighted to be rid of it. Most likely he will also throw in the stick, in the form of a golf shaft complete with grip.

Five minutes' work will restore the comforting tackiness of the grip. If it is a shiny leather grip, smear it with a thin coating of castor oil. If it is rubber, scrub it with scouring powder and it will come up like new.

Now for the drill. Site the tyre flat on the floor, in an area where you can take a full smack at it without demolishing your Waterford crystal chandelier on the backswing. It is best to have the tyre up against a solid object such as a wall, for once you get into the swing of it, the tyre will jump about. I have mine up against a bookcase, and when I am in really vicious mood I dislodge the complete works of William Shakespeare.

Start with the stick, or shaft. The first exercise is to tap out a drum roll against the tyre gripping the stick with the left hand only. Just gentle backhand taps, taking the stick back no more than a foot, but as fast as you can. The temptation will be to flick at the tyre with the side of your hand leading. Wrong. Hopeless. Imagine the stick is an extension of your arm, and you are tapping the tyre with the *back* of the hand, thumb on top of the stick and gripping with pinkie and ring finger only. If it feels awkward and feeble and clumsy at first, that is a good sign. It means you have a vast potential for dramatic improvement in your golf.

Most people believe bad golf is caused by the stronger right hand dominating the swing. Nonsense! The left hand is much more likely to

191

be the culprit. Once you have that left hand under control with a correct grip, then you can safely let fly with all the power you can muster in your right hand.

Beat out a tattoo of twenty-five taps like this, as fast as you can. At first you'll probably use a wristy stroke, but as you progress you should seek to reduce wrist action, and be able to complete this exercise keeping the stick and arm straight, as one unit.

Cotton insists that contra-exercises are essential, so now do twenty-five forehand taps on the other side of the tyre, still retaining your grip with the thumb on top, as if slapping with the palm of your left hand. Switch the stick to the right hand and repeat both exercises, again with the thumb on top of the stick and gripping mostly with those last two fingers.

The next exercise is a larger version of the first. This time take the stick back farther, about waist high, and cane the tyre, exerting real force and venom. Still do it as fast as possible, making that stick swish and whistle as it cuts through the air.

Remember when you are doing these exercises you should stand as tall as possible, with a nice straight back. Do twenty-five each of these intermediate smacks. On the first day, if you have applied yourself with gusto, you should be almost fit to drop. Grit your teeth and proceed to stage three. Take the club and grasp it with both thumbs on top of the shaft. Get the left hand well under. If you can see three knuckles as you address the tyre you are cheating yourself. Two is the maximum.

Take the club back halfway, about waist high, and belt the tyre as hard as you can. No, really *belt* it! Make it jump. Lash it. Crunch into it. Kill the thing. Forget any notions of correct golfing style. Concentrate on unbridled, primitive, animal power. You are a wild stallion kicking down a stable door. Smash into that tyre with every atom of strength in your body. Twenty-five is enough to start, followed by twenty-five backhanders to prevent your body growing lopsided.

Finally, repeat the process with a full swing, giving it everything you've got. Now you can collapse. Within half an hour your pulse should return to normal, and that vermilion hue around your neck will have disappeared. If you wake up next morning feeling as if a band of steel has been placed around your upper chest and is getting tighter and tighter every second, you may be reassured that the exercises are working! Repeat the routine morning and night until it becomes easy. Then work up to fifty bangs on each exercise, then 100.

Do not rush this process. Remember that with your awful swing you've been using the wrong muscles. They are the ones in tone, and it will take time for them to become dormant while the new sets of muscles get into fighting trim. In a month or so you should find that even with increased workload morning and evening, the exercises are child's play. And on the golf course you will hit the ball much farther and with a much crisper contact. If the direction is not everything you might wish, we can introduce a further exercise of my own fiendish devising, designed to improve your style.

Add some weight to your practice club – some lead wire wound around the hosel is ideal. Add it progressively, week by week, at the same time introducing into your routine a further exercise of hitting the tyre with the club using the left arm only. Take the club back without bending the wrist, thus ensuring that you make that vital turn with the shoulders and body, and then whip the clubhead into the tyre with all your might.

Those of you who have been unwise enough to read golf instruction books may ask how to produce proper leg action, or wrist pronation, or weight transfer. Forget all irrelevant nonsense. If you belt that tyre as hard as you can your legs will automatically operate just like Arnold Palmer's, and the same goes for all the other esoteric points of style.

The only thought to keep in mind, both during the exercises and on the golf course, is 'sting that tyre (or ball)'. The effect to aim for is not a heavy blow. Cotton uses the image of caning a boy. You need a stinging whip-crack action to raise a weal – bring a touch of sadism to your golf, and make that old tyre yelp and jump with pain.

There is also a valuable psychotherapeutic spin-off to the exercises. Imagine that the tyre is someone you dislike, and the daily pounding can provide a splendid release for that excess poisonous bile. I myself put twenty yards on my drive simply by seeing the tyre as various people whose contribution to my welfare has been sadly lacking.

A final word for golf widows who are contemplating giving the exercise equipment to the old man for Christmas and who may be feeling ever so slightly guilty at making him a present of what appears to be a pound's worth of rubbish. Just remember that this collection of rubbish represents the source of undreamed pleasure and satisfaction, a whole new world of heady achievements such as carrying across bunkers which have long been out of range. For once the thought really is more important than the gift.

Observer, November 1979

Time to Fight Back

In the beginning, so we are told, when a lightning bolt chanced to galvanize a stray morsel of nucleic acid (or whatever) and life was formed as a simple self-reproducing cell, a process of evolution began which might well have been designed for the express purpose of creating the game of golf.

Theologists may dispute this theory of destiny. Anthropologists can curl their lips in scorn. Let them wallow in their ignorance, for the facts are beyond refute. Consider how those first living cells adapted to conditions on the cooling surface of this planet. They went their different ways, and in a matter of a mere zillion years or so they developed into complicated organisms, as plants, fish, fowl and mammals.

Some of these evolutionary processes ran into pretty much a dead end. One lot became the ant and another strain became the anteater, and it is difficult to see evolution taking that trick much further.

It was, and still is, highly competitive stuff, essentially the same as match-play golf with survival going to the fittest and the smartest. Take the apes. Some of them grew tails and took to the trees; others went in for huge teeth. Both strains guessed wrong in the evolutionary race. The winners were the ones who gambled on brain size and fingers for their survival kit.

Those became *Homo sapiens* (that's us), and any paleontologist studying fossil remains and wondering if he has found the missing link need ask himself only one question: could this creature have played golf? Did he, in short, have a large enough cranial space to enclose a brain capable of reading a tricky sidehill putt? Did he have fingers capable of forming a Vardon grip? And were his legs strong enough to support him in an upright position for a full pivot? If so, then that was our ancestor.

The temptation is to assume that since plant life and man have achieved a kind of perfection, represented by Jack Nicklaus knocking the pins down at Augusta National, the evolutionary process is complete, destiny has been fulfilled, and golf will continue forever and

194

ever, golf without end, amen.

Not by a long shot. That same magical process which produced golf from the primeval slime can also destroy it. Evolution is a continuing process, and, unless we watch it carefully, we are likely to condemn our great-grandchildren to a life without golf. Mainly what we have to watch is the golf car, for therein lies the seeds of our destruction.

Twentieth-century man is fast evolving a style of life which makes legs superfluous. Elevators, escalators and the ubiquitous automobile supply man's mobility. When you think that in five years the fashion of the miniskirt began to change the shape of women, giving them an extra protective layer of fat on the thighs, imagine how quickly our male legs will wither from lack of use. In a couple of generations, the left leg will have disappeared altogether and the right leg will have degenerated into one enormous, prehensile toe for depressing brake and accelerator pedals.

Golf can save mankind, but only if we banish golf cars from the face of the earth and get out there on our own two legs, marching five to seven miles across the fairways. Cars are an abomination anyway. They are ruinous to golf courses and add greatly to the expense of a game that is becoming absurdly costly as it is. Cars slow the pace of golf, diminish the pleasure and eliminate the physical benefits of healthy exercise.

Where cars are compulsory, and this seems to be a growing practice at resort courses, the golfer is doubly abused, first by being ripped off and secondly by being denied a substantial part of the benefits and enjoyments of the game. Furthermore, the player who always rides a car is doomed never to improve his game, only to suffer a decline in skill in direct proportion to the atrophy of his calf muscles.

Golf cars should be reserved exclusively for the infirm and should then be permitted only after a most rigorous medical examination. The rest of us should get out and walk. We owe it to ourselves and to mankind. Get those pulses pumping with honest exertion. Drag fresh air down into that murky sump at the bottom of the lungs where the old cigarette smoke normally lies undisturbed. The feeling of dizziness at the unaccustomed strain of walking up a gentle slope will soon disappear; muscle tone will reappear in these flabby frames; the joy of living will spring up within us just as soon as we get those red corpuscles chasing around inside us.

Now there is work to be done. Take a 54-pound hammer and grasp it lightly with an overlapping grip. Swing slowly, keeping that left arm as straight as possible and making a full turn with the upper body. Wait for it at the top and then smash that hammer head into the guts of the nearest golf car. The moment has arrived for man to start fighting back against the machine.

Golf Digest, August 1978

The Prodigy from Spain

By now, we are all prepared for Severiano Ballesteros to rewrite the record books. First, however, I suspect that he will rewrite the instruction books. Just as Bjorn Borg does nót know how to hold a tennis racquet, according to the most informed punditry, so Ballesteros is under a tremendous disadvantage in having a bad swing.

Really, it is a terrible action to judge by the teachings of the experts. Bob Toski, the guru of American golf, solemnly proclaims that it is pretty well impossible to stand too close to the ball at address. Johnny Miller says the same thing. Yet look at this poor, unenlightened Ballesteros positively stretching to reach the ball, with his hands well clear of the body. With such a bad address it is surprising that Ballesteros manages to hit the ball both better and farther than any other class player.

As if that were not enough, he then commits another cardinal sin when he takes the club back. Read any instruction book and it will tell you to keep that right elbow pointing at the ball during the backswing. Why, there was once a vogue among instructors to get their pupils to clasp a handkerchief under their right armpits and make sure that it was not dislodged on the backswing.

Since instruction books are not normally published in Spanish, I doubt whether Ballesteros has ever been aware of the absolute necessity to keep his right elbow tucked in to the body. Even so, surely one of the Spanish professionals would have pointed this out to him at some stage? Well, no. Ballesteros has never taken a lesson in his life, not even from his brother Manuel.

Many golfers have sought to point out the error of his ways, but he stubbornly refuses to listen to them. He simply carries on in his ignorant way, allowing that right elbow to fly as wide as it likes on the backswing. Jack Nicklaus, another inordinately long and accurate player, makes the same basic mistake of technique. Jimmy Bruen, a legendary long hitter from Ireland had his right elbow practically pointing at the sky. Ballesteros has won more tournaments in more places than any other twenty-one-year-old in the history of golf, and

197

on that flimsy evidence he has the temerity to claim that he is right and the textbooks are wrong.

He learned how to hit the ball by the hopelessly inadequate method of 'monkey see, monkey do', watching good players and copying the things he felt were right. In particular, it felt right to him to push his hands as far as possible away from his body throughout the swing, and to get his hands as high as he could at the top of the backswing. That, he insists, is all there is to hitting long distances. And that is the key thought he keeps in mind when he is playing, plus the supplementary idea of making a strong thrust with his legs. That is the beginning and the end of his golf philosophy.

Of course, with those two points uppermost in his mind, certain other advantages occur naturally. For instance, he gets a full turn of the body on the backswing. And when he wants to get a little bit extra out of a shot – such as when he needs to carry some trees 300 yards away with his driver – he makes no attempt to put any extra oomph into the shot with his arms, or body. All he does is snap his wrists with a bit more zip as he comes into the impact zone, like cracking a whip when you want to make a louder bang.

He is, of course, extremely fit and strong, although he does no special exercises to strengthen his legs or arms. His only concession to the athletic disciplines is when he has a complete layoff from golf. During those periods he exercises his hands by stretching them aloft and clasping and unclasping his fingers fifty times. One daily session of this exercise is all he needs to keep his golfing muscles in trim.

As with all the great players, the hands are the key to his game. He grips his clubs extremely gently, with just enough pressure to prevent the club from flapping about. I offered him my forefinger and asked him to take his normal grip. The pressure would not have squeezed toothpaste from the tube.

It is a conventional form of grip in every other respect and, of course, it will tighten involuntarily as he reaches the impact zone. This subconscious application of pressure on the grip is necessary to withstand the considerable forces which pull straight down the shaft during the business part of the swing and, with that knowledge, we can devise a simple experiment to test the efficiency of the grip.

Address the ball with a light grip on the club. Now, without doing anything else, tighten the grip and watch the clubhead. If it twists by the smallest fraction, so it will twist during a full swing, with dire consequences to the shot. Until a player can perform this grip-tightening experiment without effecting any change in the position of the clubhead he might as well not try to play golf. Indeed, it is one of

198

several good reasons why I ought to give the game up entirely, in addition to the powerful lobby among professional golfers who have had the misfortune to draw me in pro–ams.

Back to Ballesteros. How good is he? The former British Amateur Champion Guy Wolstenholme has been around long enough to have played many times with the young Nicklaus, as well as all the contemporary greats. He believes that Ballesteros is a much better player than Nicklaus was at twenty-one and that the quality of his striking is equal to Sam Snead at his best. Ballesteros has the skill to play all the shots, moving the ball either way with equal facility, and he has the cheek to use all his shot-making in the tightest situations.

The exciting prospect is that he is getting better every week he plays. What a pity he does not know how to play the game properly.

Observer, August 1978

A Martyr to the Waggles

Breathes there a man with soul so dead who never to himself has said, 'If only my clubs were exactly right, I'd belt the ball right out of sight.'

Sitting in my study I can count 140 golf clubs displayed around the room or stacked in a corner. Most of them are, to a greater or lesser degree, antiques. But more than thirty are modern and still in regular use. When the fancy takes me I can select, say, a splendid old rut-iron and hit a few shots with a bramble pattern guttie in the garden. Or I might compare the feel of a McEwan long spoon with a carbon-fibre shafted driver by whacking plastic balls.

None of this makes me an expert on golf equipment. But I defer to no man in my experience as a victim of the neglected golfing disease known as Waggle. Twitch, or yips, is the fashionable golfing ailment. Waggle, let me tell you, is much more virulent and painfully expensive.

Wagglers, as sufferers from this complaint are known, are basically obsessed by the thought expressed in those lines of doggerel at the top of the page. They devote their lives to a search for the perfect golf clubs. They believe – and often enough they are quite right – that their present clubs are costing them several shots a round.

And so they mope around pro's shops, waggling away at the display sets. When playing with strangers they suddenly remark, 'Those clubs look nice – mind if I have a bash with one of them?' In extreme cases they resort to do-it-yourself experiments with their clubs, grinding the irons, altering the lofts, lengthening the shafts and goose-necking the hosels.

Whenever I look up, my eye catches a spoon fitted with a pistol grip, which seems to mock me. It is a silent witness to the folly of the waggler (who, in turn, can testify that this experiment, designed to cure an overstrong left-hand position, was an abject failure).

Waggle is incurable. But eventually the disease enters a stage when it can be contained. The victim finally comes to realize that his own shortcomings as a golfer are to blame for his scores, rather than deficiencies in his equipment. This climacteric can go either way. The waggler may fall into a deep melancholy and go quietly mad. Or, as I like to believe in my own case, he can murmur '*Mea culpa*' and accept his fate bravely.

He then rationalizes his situation. What is a scratch golfer, anyway? He is doing no more than the riveter in a shipyard who smacks the rivet with his hammer right on the head every time. So what sort of big deal is that? Furthermore, I enjoy my bad golf enormously, while it is a matter of simple observation to conclude that the good players are desperately unhappy.

With the addictive phase safely past, the waggler is now free to develop his interest in clubs for its own sake. The other day I was playing with a 3-handicap golfer who was turning on some impressive stuff with his irons. I forebore to ask if I might try one of his clubs, since that stage is safely under control nowadays, but I was interested in the flighting of his shots, and asked what shafts he had. To my amazement, he had to inspect the label and then said: 'R, whatever that means.'

The man is content – but I feel, nevertheless, that he is missing quite a lot through his complete disinterest in the form and development of clubs. I would not wish him a dose of the waggles, but there is a happy and rewarding medium.

In some ways golf must have been a much better game 200 years ago when the first clubs were being formed. With their peacock uniforms and gargantuan club suppers, from which no member retired with less than a gallon of claret in his belly, the golfers of Edinburgh were indeed favoured. Their actual golf, I imagine, was not up to much. Their clubs, of course, were all wood at that time, carried higgledy-piggledy under the arm of a ruffianly (and frequently drunk) caddie.

And the ball they played was what we refer to as the featherie, although many were stuffed with hemp, flax or straw. By all accounts, the featherie could be a very good ball, but it was a lottery whether you got a round one, and in wet weather featheries soon lost whatever shape they had. As for the techniques of golf, we know from the inordinate length of those clubs that you had to swing very flat with a pronounced sway at the knees.

I don't suppose the players minded much. After all, in their terms the equipment was a vast improvement on the even longer and heavier clubs, and boxwood balls, which had been the golfer's lot for 200 years.

In the earliest days the making of clubs and balls was the domain of the bowmaker. These craftsmen had a long tradition in working with beech and split-ash shafts, and they turned naturally to these woods for making the implements for this frivolous sport.

But the waggle virus was already in the air, and men dreamed of having such clubs as would transform them into the finest players the world had known. On reflection, perhaps the middle of the nineteenth century was the golden age of golf. It was at this time that the game made a significant advance. The guttie ball was introduced, and at once the wooden clubs had to undergo changes to accommodate the unyielding impact of the new ball. Beech was too hard for the guttie and the new generation of clubmakers turned to woods like apple and pear.

Some golfers tried to modify their clubs by facing them with patches of leather to soften the shock of impact, but this was merely a temporary palliative.

Men like Hugh Philp, whose skill as a clubmaker was never surpassed, fashioned beautiful clubs which are recognized today as works of art. A gentleman golfer would go to Philp (or to Douglas McEwan, James Wilson or Robert Forgan) in the same spirit as he might visit his tailor, to be 'fitted'.

We can imagine Philp selecting blackthorn heads (specially planted on a bank so that the stem would bend naturally to make the 'scare'), and then the two of them discussing which were the pick of the latest consignment of hickory shafts.

Everyone specified Tennessee hickory, but the real cognoscenti insisted on shafts from the central strip of Tennessee. Lowland hickory was too soft; that from the high ground was brittle.

Philp would then get to work with saw, spokeshave, plane, rasp, file and chisel to fashion the heads and then gouge them out into delicate shells to be filled with lead. With the heads spliced to the shafts and finished with a hare's foot dipped in a mixture of oil and varnish, the customer would return to waggle and pronounce verdict.

'Perhaps this one's a fraction stiffer than the others?'

'Certainly, sir.'

Philp would then shave a micromillimetre off the shaft, or pretend to, and the customer would depart with a set of clubs which were – and I choose my words with due deliberation – better matched than anything you can buy today.

What is more, and here I voice a purely personal opinion, the grips of untanned hide over a layer of felt-like cloth were also better than anything available today.

Apart from the need for a more robust form of head, and a softer one, in the woods, the guttie stimulated development of iron-headed clubs. The iron, previously used mainly as a specialist club for recovering from cart tracks, followed a similar process of sophistication, with a few lunatic aberrations along the way.

They were an inventive race, those clubmakers, and whenever I read modern advertisements with all their pseudo-scientific mumbo-jumbo about reducing the weight of the hosel and putting it where it counts, I take down a number of early irons which have had holes bored in the hosel for that very purpose. There really is very little new in golf clubs. Somewhere, sometime, somebody has tried it before – and that goes for speed slots, and aerodynamic-shaped heads, and all the modern gobbledygook not excluding heel-and-toe weighting.

Golf World, March 1974

Secrets of the Black Art

Mirror, mirror on the wall, who is the greatest putter of them all? There have been times when Bob Charles might have allowed a smug smile to form under the shaving foam in anticipation of the response. Most of us would not bother even to ask the question; the mirror is sure to come up with Willie Park Junior, Bobby Locke, or Locke's own nominee, Walter Hagen.

Magic looking-glasses should try to get hold of a copy of *Putting Made Easy*, published in 1935, or, better still, have a private showing of Paramount's Pictorial Golf Chat number P-O-11 shot on 27 June 1931.

That film stars the undoubted number one putter of all time, a retired American businessman named Mark G. Harris. But before exhuming the remarkable deeds of the late Mr Harris, let us first look at putting standards at the highest level of the game.

The American penchant for statistical analysis provides the evidence. In the US Open the winner will roll his 75-footers up to $4\frac{1}{2}$ feet and get his 30-footers to within 1 foot 9 inches of the hole. He will sink one putt in seven from 20 feet and hole 50 per cent of his 7-footers. He will produce the same level of accuracy when chipping from the fringe.

Those figures may not sound too impressive, but it must be remembered that the player will be under the intense pressures of championship golf. I would say that Mr Harris was playing in comparably tense conditions when he performed for Paramount's cameras, with absolutely no funny business about retakes.

He played fifteen strokes as follows: he holed one chip from 35 feet and left two others within 12 inches of the cup; he holed one chip from 45 feet and left two others within 14 inches; he holed all three of his putts from 8 feet; all three from 14 feet; and hit a tee peg three times in succession with 7-foot putts. Phenomenal!

My reason for hauling Mr Harris out of the archives is that we are now entering the season of carpet-putting and that, according to the master, is how to learn the black art. It is interesting to compare his

204

method with that of Locke and see if any points emerge which can be taken to be fundamentals of good putting:

Stance

Harris: Feet about 9 inches apart, weight evenly distributed, left foot exactly at right angles to the line of the putt, toes in line, knees slightly bent. (Harris said that a man with an inherent tendency to putt to the left of target could correct his aim by slightly withdrawing his right foot to a closed position, and vice versa for the reverse tendency.) The trunk is well bent over the ball so that a glass of beer could happily be balanced between the shoulder blades.

Locke: Very similar, except his feet are only 4 inches apart, with the right foot slightly withdrawn.

Grip

Harris: Basically the same as for all other shots but with the club held more in the fingers. Pressure is firm but not tense.

Locke: Agreed, but the club is gripped lightly.

Ball Position

Harris: Just inside the left toe.

Locke: Opposite left toe. Harris addressed the ball with the centre of the clubface; Locke with the toe of the club, although he made contact with the centre.

Backswing

Harris: The golf swing in miniature. Thus the forearms and club go slowly back in one piece, keeping the clubhead low in a gentle sweeping movement and with a slight rocking of the shoulders. The clubhead takes a natural arc inside the line.

Locke: Again a low backswing, almost touching the turf. The clubhead comes back inside the line but the blade is kept square throughout.

205

Forward Swing

Harris: In its own good time, like the pendulum of a clock, the clubhead swings through the ball with a low finish. Length of backswing governs length of putt. Blade absolutely square at impact. Fingers impart 'touch' with a slight breaking of wrists through impact. Follow-through is along the line of the putt for at least 6 inches.

Locke: Left wrist kept firm in relation to forearm through the ball. (Photography shows a slight hingeing through impact, however.) Low follow-through. Position of ball opposite left toe means clubhead meets ball slightly on upswing. Head is kept absolutely still and the whole action is slow and smooth. Above all, the grip is kept loose.

And good luck. If we really are in for a long, hard winter, some good may come out of it if we all emerge in the spring with the skill of Mark C. Harris. It would be worth wearing out a carpet for that.

Observer, November 1976

How Far Is Far? 1

Back in the days when Britain used to have winters this was the time of year when hardy souls used to go to the golf club and spend the morning looking out of the window.

In any given four-ball there are always three optimists who tell each other, 'I think it's easing up a bit,' while the fourth member stoutly insists, 'It's set in for the day.'

Usually, it is this pessimist who turns away in despair and flops down in a chair, reaching for the nearest golf magazine. Nothing in golf is ever certain, but it is a pretty safe bet that the magazine will feature an article on 'How to Make the Best of Winter Golf', or 'How to Tune Up for The Spring'.

Having perpetrated a fair volume of such drivel myself, in a ghostly capacity, I can reveal that, with the exception of Gary Player, I have yet to meet a tournament pro who practises what he preaches in the sphere of calisthenics, beyond the exercise of tearing up his scorecard and heel-and-toeing briskly to the bar.

In private, the pros argue that their muscles are conditioned for golf and they keep them in trim well enough by playing, which is small comfort for a snowbound reader.

Yet there is something which can be done to improve your golf when the course is closed, and it is all the more attractive because the exercise can be performed while slumped in a deep chair with an appropriate beverage gripped firmly in the right hand.

Lee Trevino (who else?) is the high priest of the art, which we might call Fruitful Meditation. He expounded principles of FM in slightly painful circumstances during a practice round. We had been chatting lightly of this and that, and with particular emphasis on the other, when his caddie, Neal, handed me the bag and asked if I would tote it for a hole or so while he nipped off for a hot dog.

Trevino drove, and when we reached the ball his mood changed to brisk seriousness. 'What is it?' he asked. I suggested the 7-iron. For a moment it was touch and go whether he killed me with his bare hands, but his innate good nature prevailed. He caressed the ball with a 5-iron (about seven feet left of the flag), and lectured me in tones of a magistrate binding over a criminal to keep the peace.

'Never tell a pro what club to hit. Don't even put your hand on the club you think he will choose. You don't know how I feel about the shot. You don't know if I fancy floating it, or nailing it, or cutting it or hooking it into the flag. That can make a difference of forty yards or more with any one club.

'That's the biggest difference between a pro and an amateur. You think in clubs, we think in distances. What's the length of the fourth hole at your home club? Is there a feature round about the driving length?'

I confessed, in some confusion, having played my home course for only twenty years, that I could not recall the exact yardage but that there was, indeed, a pond on the right of the fairway to catch a sliced drive.

'How far is the front of the pond to the front of the green?' Trevino asked.

Again I had to admit my ignorance but insisted that in normal conditions, in stillish air, an 8-iron was about right. Trevino withered me with a look. 'If I didn't know my distances to a yard I wouldn't be able to break eighty on this or any other golf course,' he said.

I put it to him that many great players had never used yardages.

'They might not have reckoned in yards, but they used distances. They checked and calculated, and if they thought in terms of clubs that was OK because they knew exactly how far they hit the ball. You don't. I could save you six shots a round *at least* just by walking round and telling you how to tackle each hole. You could save yourself four shots without me, just by thinking like a pro.'

How?

'Well, the first thing – and it's the toughest part – is to admit to yourself that you are not the best striker of a golf ball who ever lived. Nicklaus wouldn't attempt some of the shots you guys try to pull off. So accept that you're going to hit some clinkers and play for them.'

Fortunately Neal returned to put an end to this painful discussion, and I watched how the professional caddie operated. As he reached the ball he intoned, 'You have a hundred and seventy-two yards to the flag. Sloping lie. Wind left to right. Bad trouble left of the green.' Trevino pulled out a club and hit the ball close to the cup. He has Neal to do most of his meditating for him but there is no doubt that Trevino is right.

We would all do better if we thought better.

Observer, January 1976

An Impossible Game ⚑

Golf does not bear thinking about. Just consider what the player has to achieve. He must accelerate a weight of some 6 to 11 ounces from zero to 100 m.p.h. in less than half a second and deliver it to its target with a precision well within a tolerance of 1 per cent, lateral, vertical, angular and directional.

Just to make the operation interesting, the Rules of Golf specify that this weight must be fitted to the shaft in such a manner that the shaft is both twisting and bending at impact. If the player fails to meet that rigid specification of 1 per cent tolerance in just one of the four impact conditions, then the shot is ruined.

It sounds impossible, and for my own part such a theoretical conclusion has been amply proved by exhaustive practical tests. The game *is* impossible and nobody has ever come remotely near to mastering it, as evidenced by normal scores in the region of 70 by the finest exponents of golf against a theoretical minimum of 36. In other words, the best players make at least thirty-odd errors per round.

In fact the percentage of mistakes is much higher than that. I have asked many great golfers how many perfect shots they hit in a good round, and I have never known anyone claim more than five.

In a whole lifetime of golf I have hit exactly one perfect shot, totally flawless in planning and execution. I had driven into trees, as usual, and took great care in working out my recovery. The clubface connected sweetly, the ball rose sharply and found the gap no bigger than a dustbin lid high in that leafy roof. Now the delicate fade I had imparted on the ball took effect, swinging it back onto the line of the pin which I could just detect in the morning mist. I knew, with utter conviction, that the shot was perfect. And so it proved when I walked forward through the swirling fog and found my ball plugged two inches from a rake which had been stuck in a fairway bunker sixty yards short of the green.

The point of all this is to demonstrate a universal truth which every golfer demonstrates for himself each time he takes club in hand, namely that golf is a game of errors. It follows that those who aspire to play the game well should strive to reduce their mistakes and, even more so, to practise ways of nullifying those inevitable mistakes which cannot be eliminated.

That is the message which has gone out to every amateur golfer in England with serious aspirations, from boys to senior internationals. The dismal decline in playing standards has prompted the English Golf Union to produce a blueprint for golfing revival.

For instance: 'Do you spend too large a part of your practice time on your long game and too little on your short game, including putting? If you could save two strokes a round by getting down in two from off the green twice more than you do now, what a difference it would make.'

For instance: 'Have you got a really sound method of pitching, chipping, bunker play and putting? Consult a professional. There seems to be a reluctance to play a variety of shots with different clubs; too much playing with a wedge, perhaps?'

For instance: 'Do you really think about percentages? How often are you faced with a shot from off the green that would need quite a poor shot with a putter to leave the ball *outside* six feet, and quite a good shot with a wedge to get it *inside* six feet? Try a number of shots with different clubs, including the putter, and compare the results; that is what percentages are about.'

For instance: 'Do you play too much by measurement and not enough by feel? Golf is not a mechanical game, though it is more nearly so if greens are heavily watered, fairways soft and there is little wind. These conditions seldom occur in Britain, so golf by feel when the ground is hard and/or the wind is blowing is still important.'

For instance: 'Have you got a "safe shot" to guarantee getting the ball on the fairway from the tee at a critical moment? It is well worth trying to work one out.'

This circular offers golfers a fine basis for resolutions. If it does no more than make them pause and reflect on the purpose of the game, to get round in as few strokes as possible, it will have served a useful purpose.

Observer, February 1978

Statistics Uncover the Secrets of Golf

Oh, very well then. You've been extremely patient. For something like 500 years you've been waiting to learn the secret of golf, and finally I have decided to reveal it. As a matter of fact, it has been revealed before. Harry Vardon spelled it out. So did Bobby Jones. Ben Hogan realized it late in his career and told the world. Nobody listened, because there was no way to prove that the secret worked.

Now that the US tour is keeping full statistics, and people are paying attention to them, the secret of golf is uncovered for all to see. All you have to do is aim your drive down the left side of the fairway *and hit it with a high fade.*

Why, oh why, you ask, have I waited so long to divulge this information? Well, it all goes back to those far-off days when aeroplanes had propellers and a foolhardy US Navy undertook to teach me to fly. Hatchet-faced instructors would assess the progress of us intrepid birdmen, and grade us in terms of baseball statistics. Knowing nothing of baseball, and loss of baseball statistics, I never knew how I was doing.

Anyway, we won the war and I emerged as a staunch disciple of Winston Churchill's dictum that there are lies, damned lies and statistics. Particularly sports statistics.

This lifelong mistrust of sporting statistics drew me naturally to golf, a game blessedly free of decimal points and performance averages. Until last year. Then the US tour started measuring and analysing the game, and, in the line of duty, I have spent four months with a cold towel wrapped around my spinning head trying to make sense out of the statistics.

The first thing to do is reject the obviously idiotic figures. The money list, for example, is meaningless since it makes no distinction between the golfer who played forty tournaments and the player who teed it up only twelve times. Instead, we must look to the stroke averages for a measure of performance. Likewise, we can dismiss the tables for birdies and eagles, since these simply reflect a summary of golfing skills. And while we are about it, we can toss those putting statistics into the trash basket because they are hopelessly biased in favour of the player who misses greens, chips up to the flag and holes out from eighteen inches. They tell us nothing about putting skill as such.

The revealing tour statistics are those for driving distance, driving accuracy, hitting greens in regulation, sand saves and scoring averages. First, this exciting business of giving the ball a big bash off the tee. Driving distance is revealed as golf's major false god. Anyone who averages 260 yards off the tee must be rated a long hitter, but those who strive for an extra ten yards are simply slugging themselves into oblivion.

Driving accuracy (given a decent quantity of horsepower in the shot) is much, much more important than distance. Jack Nicklaus is the only player who drives the ball both long and straight, and his rank in accuracy off the tee (thirteenth) is somewhat falsified by his tactics of occasionally deliberately firing his ball into light rough for position. It may sound trite, but the art of good golf as shown by the statistics is to put your shot into a position from where you can hit the green in regulation figures.

That conclusion, which can now be backed by statistical proof, leads me to the all-important secret of golf. From personal observation I would say that nine pro golfers out of ten draw their drives, as the result of an obsession for length. They start as kids, striving for every inch of length because of their simplistic reasoning that the shorter the second shot the lower the score. They won't be told. Explain that a faded drive down the left makes the fairway twice as wide, and they reverse the argument, saying that a hooked drive down the right has the same effect. It doesn't. The high faded ball sits where it lands while the hooked ball pitches and runs – into trouble as likely as not. That is the real story of the tour statistics.

Are you still unconvinced? Then I invite you to run your eye down the scoring averages and, if you must, down the money list. In both cases the top ten leaders of 1980 are players who fade the ball. The only incongruity is Andy Bean, whose natural shot is right to left. Three years ago I daresay that Bean would have been the leader in driving distance, for he used to give the ball an almighty smash and hook it back into the fairway. Today he is only just in the top thirty for distance off the tee, for he has seen the light. He is a reformed hooker, and that is vastly encouraging.

I believe it was Arnold Palmer who remarked that all pros are fighting a hook. In his case it was certainly true, but he never got the club into a position at the top to make a sweet pass at the ball, and he had to turn himself inside out on the downswing to avoid a real snapper.

So there's the secret: fight that hook, and, if the ball still goes left, then fight harder – until you have mastered that lovely, money-winning high fade.

Golf Digest, April 1981

Shape of Things to Come, Alas

It's no wonder that oracles went out of business. They were altogether too clever for their own good, forever coming up with smart-ass answers with ambiguous interpretations ('I say, Pyrrhus, that you the Romans can conquer'), thereby hedging all bets. We would not stand still for that kind of verbal trumpery these days.

In the world of golf there is only one oracle still functioning. He survives because he gets right out there at the end of the limb, and then, when the bough is swaying in alarming fashion, he proceeds to stick his neck out. Of course Dr Gary Wiren does not call himself an oracle, North Palm Beach, Florida, being too close to Salem, Mass., to take any chances. He operates under the title of Director of Club and Professional Relations of the PGA of America, but everyone knows that he is an oracle.

Recently American magazine *Golf Digest* consulted Dr Wiren, and asked: 'What will the game of golf be like in the year 2001?' People of a conservative disposition should read no farther.

If you are having trouble with a hook, for example, you will punch up the problem on a computer console attached to your TV set and a suggested remedy will be displayed on the screen. If you then try it and it does not work, you feed in more information and get more answers. If by any chance the program does not cover your unique fault, then you call the acknowledged expert on the videophone. He watches your swing and demonstrates where you are going wrong.

Mental control will become increasingly important. Golfers will be taught how to recognize their own stress symptoms and how to combat them. The practising of psychological exercises will become as important as hitting shots on the practice grounds.

A computerized handicapping service will operate throughout America (and possibly internationally). Wherever you go your handicap, automatically revised each month, and your last ten scores, plus much more information about your game, will be available at the touch of a button.

Instead of buying mass-produced clubs off the shelf, the trend will be increasingly towards made-to-measure clubmaking, with sets balanced and shaped to suit individuals and their personal idiosyncrasies.

The ball with a centre composed of rubber thread wound under tension on a core will be replaced by solid balls of new synthetic materials. Dr Wiren does not promise that they will be cheaper, as they should be, and he does not touch on the subject of specialized balls. I believe that quite soon every brand will be available in high trajectory, low trajectory and regular, not to mention the option of rubber or synthetic cover and a choice of three different degrees of hardness.

As land becomes scarcer, so alternative forms of miniaturized golf will proliferate, using balls which can be driven no farther than 150 yards on courses confined within thirty to forty acres.

To carry our clubs we will employ automated bag-carriers which will follow us around the course like well-trained dogs, while those deluded boobies who prefer to ride between shots will use hovercraft which cannot damage the turf.

Agronomy will perfect methods of controlling weeds without the use of chemical sprays, and the growth of trees will be artificially stimulated. This may not mean instant golf courses, exactly, but at least it will not take fifty years for a new course to mature. While I am delighted to note that Dr Wiren makes no mention of artificial turf in his vision of the future, I am slightly wary of new wonder grasses. While the scientists, particularly at Penn State University, are very good at producing hybrids, I think that God is rather better.

The language of golf will change under metrication. This will put a heavy responsibility on the people who influence such revolutions. It is obvious that our grandchildren will not speak of missing a three-footer, but I dare to hope that they will not adopt the expression 'to miss a meterer'.

The area of the oracle's predictions which gives me the most anticipatory satisfaction, and which arouses my strongest scepticism, is his view of the golf club of the next century. He foresees a return to basics, with clubs cutting back on services such as residential accommodations, dining rooms operating six nights a week, dance bands and social functions.

My own crystal ball shows an extension of such activities. With greenkeeping costs going up, in spite of new grasses which do not need cutting twice a week and synthetic granular substances for bunkers which require no maintenance, I believe that social activities will have to be expanded in order to subsidize the golf. Mind you, it will be done in a businesslike way, and run by experts, but if golf is to survive as a game for Everyman then clubs will have to diversify more and more to generate income.

Nude female mud wrestling every Thursday night at Sunningdale? Regular Sunday evening disco at St George's? I am afraid so, but then I always was a pessimist.

Observer, February 1979

Tear up the Commandments ___1

There is only one assertion I am prepared to make about the origins of golf and that is this: ever since man started knocking a ball about with a club in competition, the loser has reflected, 'There must be some trick to hitting the ball which he knows and I don't.' The myth of a golden key to golf has sent thousands of golfing Jasons off on improbable quests. It has spawned hundreds of books promising to reveal the secret.

There is hardly a part of the body which has not been singled out as golf's vital organ. The big toe of the right foot has been championed as the source of accuracy and power. So, too, has the third finger of the left hand. In the twenties there was a bestseller which advanced the theory that good golf depended upon the tilt of the chin at address. It had to point at the right knee, as I recall. There is a teacher in America at the moment who has achieved guru status among tournament professionals, and he locates the source of great golf in the sternum.

The idea of a key move, or secret, is a comforting one, especially for a husky male who is outdriven by a slip of a girl, because it protects the ego from excessive bruising. You and I could have been great players but for the misfortune of being born with the wrong shape of sternum, or a hammer toe, or just plain ignorant of that secret move.

Stern realists who refuse to believe in fairies may be interested in a poll I conducted among a group of experienced American tournament players. Watching them on the practice ground side by side, all hitting more or less perfect shots but with a bewildering variety of methods, it occurred to me that, since the shots were basically the same, they must all be *doing* something the same. After all, it is a scientific fact, is it not, that an identical result can spring only from an identical cause? So what was the common denominator, the *sin qua non* of good golf?

I put the question to the players. Tom Watson thought that grip and posture, or stance, constituted the foundation of good golf. He is obviously right in the sense that if either is hopelessly unsuitable then the player has no chance of hitting the ball decently. However,

217

since there are considerable variations in both grips and stances among the champions, we have to qualify Watson's universal truth into a wishy-washy generalization such as, 'You must grip the club and stand to the ball in such a way as enables you to hit the ball properly.' That is hardly worth carving on a tablet and lugging down the mountain.

Johnny Miller said, 'Only one golfer in a thousand grips the club lightly enough.' That is much better as a revelation. I think we can pencil in Miller's commandment for starters. 'Thou shalt grip the club lightly.'

Charles Coody rather set back the research programme by saying that there was no absolute truth. 'I believe that through the ball we are all the same. We get the clubhead moving on the target line for the split second of impact, but we have different ways of getting it there.' In a sense his view is encouraging, for it can be interpreted to offer hope to those of us with idiosyncratic methods, but his essential message – 'Do what you like so long as it works' – does nothing to advance the search.

Orville Moody felt that the common factor among good players was their timing and coordination. And how can these essential virtues be acquired? 'The only way you can get it is to keep your head still.' That's better. Ben Crenshaw and Chi Chi Rodriguez are examples of players who allow their heads to move during the swing, but perhaps they would be even better if they did not. We can safely endorse golf's oldest commandment: 'Thou shalt keep thine head still.'

Typically, Lee Trevino grasped the point of my questioning quicker than anyone else and responded more positively than the others. 'Every good golfer keeps his left hand leading the clubhead through the shot and moving towards the target after impact. That is the key move, and if you do that you automatically eliminate some of the common faults. It stops that right shoulder coming round before impact and smothering the shot. The hips slide as you come into the shot and then they turn, but all the while that left hand must be going straight through towards the target.'

Perhaps we can encapsulate that thought into: 'Thou shall lead with thine left.'

I felt we were just beginning to get somewhere when I ran up against the articulate and intelligent Dave Stockton. 'The common factor in all good golf swings is the hand action,' he said. Was he endorsing Trevino's point? No, this was something different. He thought for a bit and then expanded his ideas. He saw hand action as an innate ability to whip the clubhead through the ball at high speed and with absolute

218

accuracy. All good players, he believed, possessed good hand action. That is what enabled them to find the ball with the clubhead and counteract errors in their swings. Practice helped, of course, but having good hands was basically a knack or gift. I then had no choice but to put the dreaded supplementary question which might end my dreams and those of the great legion of hackers.

This same question could condemn all instruction books as nothing but confidence tricks, since the implied promise of such works, and sometimes the explicit guarantee, is that if you follow the simple advice you will be a scratch golfer in a matter of months.

'Are you saying,' I asked, 'that in order to play golf well you have to be born with a special talent for the game?'

Stockton is a kindly man and I could see the compassion in his eye – that same look a doctor employs as he rolls up his stethoscope and steels himself to deliver judgement – when he answered, 'Yes, I guess that is what I am saying.'

Tear up those commandments, brothers, for we are doomed. Rabbits cannot aspire to become tigers. Forget the big toe or the little finger, the chin or the sternum. Man's destiny lies within his genes.

Observer, January 1978

Know Thyself

What sets golf apart from other games? One of the arguments goes like this: tennis is terrific but a novice player could not hope in his wildest dreams to return the serve of Jimmy Connors; basketball is beautiful if you happen to be young, athletic and seven feet tall; fencing is fantastic, but unless you can find an opponent at the same standard of skill you are liable to go home covered in punctures; boxing is butch, but if Muhammad Ali is the only person in the gym looking for a workout you'd better forget it. Take any sport you care to mention. It only works if the two sides are evenly matched.

Except golf. Back in the misty distance of the Middle Ages two anonymous Scots (or possibly Dutchmen) got together one quiet Saturday morning and one said to the other, 'Tell you what, Angus (or possibly Hans), why don't we make some clubs and balls and belt them about the countryside down by the beach? Since I am bigger and stronger than you, I'll give you two up a side for a five shilling (or possibly guilder) nassau, plus skins and automatic presses.' At that moment was born Golf's First Article of Faith, namely, that, thanks to the handicapping system, a hacker can tee it up with Jack Nicklaus with a realistic chance of beating him.

In due course other Articles of Faith were propagated – golf is a left-sided game; the secret of power is the late hit; the rules are simple; luck evens itself out; and many others. All of them bear as much relation to reality as that other medieval notion: that the earth is a flat plate born on the backs of four elephants. None of these fallacies, however, is quite so fatuous as that original concept that we are all equal on the golf course and that we are all playing the same game.

Equal? I will wager my Scottish grouse moors, my chateau on the Loire, my Tudor mansion, all my Rolls-Royces, my private Boeing 747, and, yes, my youngest daughter's hand in marriage, that no genuine 24-handicapper, with his full stroke allowance, could live with Jack Nicklaus.

The same game? Stand by the first tee on any Sunday morning and observe closely. You will recognize that there are at least four different

220

games being played.

1. *Mr Universe Syndrome Golf.* The competitors in this game are easily spotted. They stand with feet spread wide, right hands well under the shaft and knuckles gleaming white. As they take the club back the tendons stand out like hawsers in their vermilion necks, and they frequently emit an audible grunt at impact. Their conversation is dominated by asking each other what club they took. Their satisfaction comes from getting up at a par-5 with a drive and a seven-iron and they make no attempt to conceal their contempt if, as frequently happens, they lose the hole to a player who needs four shots to reach the green and then single-putts . The only cerebral activity involved in this game is a single-minded thought: hit the ball as hard as humanly possible. These are the people who watch the pros and comment scornfully, 'Did you see Tom Weiskopf needed a three-iron at the sixth? Hell, I was pin-high with a five on Saturday.'

2. *Classical Swing Golf.* The exponents of this game see golf almost as a ballet, an exercise of beautiful movements. Notice the player who grips the club by wrapping each finger into place one by one. He then lifts the club to the horizontal and stops, checking the set of his left wrist with ill-concealed admiration. Just like the books say it should be. He then completes the backswing and makes a languid pass through the empty air, flowing through to a high finish which he holds in statuesque pose. Subconsciously, these golfers are hoping to be mistaken for Gene Littler at a distance. Some of them become very skilled at miming the perfect swing, and the only drawback to this form of golf is that when they try it on a ball they usually scuttle it twenty yards along the ground. They put this mishap down to a smidgeon too much pressure with the third finger of the left hand, and on the next shot they try to work this refinement into their act.

3. *Conversational Golf.* This is a game mainly, but not exclusively, preferred by women. It has been cruelly remarked that for these people golf gives them something to think about while they are talking. I believe that is overstating the case, because the essence of this game is that no thought whatever is given to the golf. Indeed, players frequently walk past their balls because they are so engrossed in social exchanges.

4. *Professional Golf.* This is a game in which the player starts off by being ruthlessly honest with himself in recognizing his capabilities and weaknesses. Within the framework of that assessment, he analyses the hole to be played and plots the sensible route for him. Then,

having decided where he wants to put the ball, he proceeds shot by shot, concentrating fully on making a good, clean contact with the club he has selected as the most suitable implement to do the job. Oddly enough, this game is not confined to professionals. Some amateurs play it, mainly elderly men who are content to pop the ball a modest distance straight up the middle of the fairway.

Every golfer, myself included, likes to think he is Category 4.

Golf World, May 1977

Love Thy Putter

Imagine, if you will, the scene in ancient Syracuse about the year 250 BC. Archimedes is lying in his bath, pondering the problem that has engaged his attention for years. Suddenly he has a flash of intuition. He yells 'Eureka!' and dashes naked into the street. He grabs the first passerby by the toga. 'I bet you don't know what the quantity of water removed by any body immersed therein is equal to.'

Now, just suppose that the stranger had answered, 'Sure I do. It equals in bulk the bulk of the body immersed. Everybody knows that, it's common knowledge.'

Archimedes, we can surmise, would have felt pretty sick. Which is exactly how I feel after fifteen years of pretty strenuous research into putting. Last week I unlocked the mystery. And as the secret lay revealed, I realized that it had been lying there fully revealed all the time.

My quest started when I first took up golf. I had a raggle-taggle bunch of old hickory-shafted clubs, and I didn't really expect to do very well with these obsolete cast-offs. But that first Christmas of my golfing life I received a present of a brand-new putter.

It radiated with shiny steel newness. It had a huge head of some composition material, pretty coloured plastic rings on the ferrule and a virile leather grip. Such a club! I couldn't wait to get on the green to use it. And I putted rather well.

In time the rest of my clubs were also steel and shiny, and the putter lost something of its special cachet. Then a child used it to hammer nails and the head broke. The putter was cast aside like a superannuated mistress. Callous youth turned to new delights – putters with fashionable heads, putters with seductively arched necks, and even one empty-headed creature that emitted a noise like a cry of pain as it struck the ball. And my putting got worse and worse.

Then I began collecting antique clubs, and in a street market I picked up a rusty specimen whose tiny head wobbled on the end of the warped shaft. I rubbed it down with emery paper and polished it until the words 'Warranted hand-forged' stood out proudly. The shaft was

223

much too short for anyone but a pigmy, but that putter became the favourite of my collection. Almost everyone who saw it could not resist taking it down from the wall and saying, 'What a little beauty.'

You can guess the rest. I sought out the remains of my first putter and put its shaft into the head of that beautiful antique. And, by all that's wonderful, it worked. It really did! I don't hole everything, although I tell people I do, because nobody holes everything, greens being what they are. But I get them thereabouts, and sometimes there, which is the limit of any sensible person's ambition.

The secret lies, of course, not in any fortuitous accident of balance or shape, or weight, or loft, or lie. I don't suppose it is in reality even a 'good' putter by any accepted standards. The secret is love. I love that putter, therefore it works.

If I ever see a golfer smash his putter into the turf again I shall turn away, knowing that here is a no-hoper. Love makes the putts go in. That is my message for the world.

It is not an original thought. Bobby Jones loved Calamity Jane and would not part with her for a king's ransom. Bobby Locke, the greatest putter of all time, took his putter to bed with him when he toured America for fear she might be stolen. Greater love hath no man.

No wonder you see golfers with their putters all bound up with insulating tape. These are the constant lovers for whom divorce is unthinkable, regardless of the quality of the shaft.

I give you, then, the first commandment of golf: Love Thy Putter. At the present rate of progress it will take me 135 years to reveal the other nine commandments, so don't rush me.

Observer, September 1970

Maybe It's not All
Your Fault

There is not much time. Soon they will arrive to lead me away. Specialists will prod me and lick their fingers and remark, 'Yes, it is true. He *is* turning into marshmallow. Very interesting.'

Knowing the medical profession, there will be a slight conflict of opinion. Somebody will insist that I am turning into Turkish delight. Or jelly. What does it matter? The point is that I must warn you all before it is too late. One of the Gorgons has survived and is at large. All who gaze on her hideous countenance, with twin heads and simulated snakes made of elastic for hair, will instantly be turned into marshmallow.

The name of this monster which has appeared among us from the dark ages of mythology is the Uniroyal Comparative Golf Ball Testing Device, or UCGBTD for short, and pronounced like a death rattle in the back of the throat.

It is a mechanical golfer contrived in the most fiendish fashion so that it can hit two balls at once. The golf club part of the device is similar to a centre-shafted putter, in T-form, and is operated by cranking back the shaft against the tension of powerful springs.

Two balls are loaded on tee pegs side by side, and at the touch of a button the double clubhead swings down and delivers an identical wallop to both balls. The loft and power of the shot is roughly equivalent to a good professional hitting with a 4-iron.

Uniroyal have been taking this vile UCGBTD around Britain for months, although I expect that the public health authorities will eventually realize that it is turning the nation into marshmallow and have it put down.

The keepers buy golf balls of every available make at the local professional's shop, including Uniroyals, so that there can be no suspicion of rigging the evidence. They now invite you and me to nominate which balls we would care to see fired simultaneously so that we may compare their flight characteristics.

So far so good. Nothing to worry about, in theory. For my first selection I chose a Maxfli and a 65, to see what difference, if any, was evident between a balata-cover and a polymer (which Dunlop calls Polydur and everyone else refers to as Surlyn). The Maxfli flew slightly higher but both balls plonked safely into the centre of the net 180 yards away.

The net is fifteen to twenty yards wide to accommodate gusts of side wind. On the very next test the trouble started. An American ball and a Uniroyal were teed up and UCGBTD did her stuff. The Uniroyal flew sweetly into the net but the other one dived sharply left, in that sickening low hook which we all know so well. 'Oh, ho!' said one of the keepers. 'Ah, ha!' said his colleague.

They repeated the test with the same two balls. Same thing again, the nasty swinging hook barely halfway to the net and fifty yards wide of target. For the benefit of cynics who may be harbouring dark suspicions that one side of the clubface might be slightly offset to induce just such unfavourable results with rival balls, I must state that on this second test the balls were switched to opposite tees. There was no hanky-panky.

One of the keepers explained. 'What we have here is a rogue.'

'A rogue?'

'Yes, it happens with all manufacturers. You get the odd ball with an offset centre and it goes all over the place.'

'What do you call the odd ball?' I asked, with the first tremors of disquiet pulsing behind the belt buckle.

'Oh, I'd say about one ball in fifty, on average. Anybody who can play a bit can detect one right off.'

In thirty years I have never detected one, although I have often – all too often – had days on the golf course when the ball went nowhere and in eccentric directions.

There was no time to ponder the awful implications of the odd rogue ball, for worse was to follow. On the very next test the two balls, a Penfold and a Wilson, left the machine nicely enough, crossed in mid air and both missed the net, one to the left and the other to the right. They looked to have been hit with, respectively, a gentle fade and a touch of draw.

'Rogues?'

'Oh, no. You get that with just the slightest imperfection in manufacture. You could get one or two of those in a box of a dozen; it is just about the same as when you have been playing with a ball for a while and knock it out of shape.'

How can you possibly play golf in the knowledge that no matter how purely and accurately you may strike the ball the damned thing is liable to curl away into the pond? Confidence is all in golf. How can you be confident once you have learned that your ball may have a mind of its own.

There was only one further possible horror to be discovered about golf balls, and I hardly dared broach the subject. 'I suppose that we can at least be sure that two balls of the same make will go the same distance? I mean, the professionals pace out their shots pretty well to the inch, so they must be able to rely on one ball going the same distance as another.'

The keeper unwrapped two balls of the same make and loaded them. One carried the net and the other pitched a yard or so short.

'Tell me,' I croaked, 'how much variation in distance do you find between two balls of the same make?'

'On a shot of this power,' he replied breezily, 'you could easily get a spread of thirty yards.

Thirty yards! I staggered away, with the whole edifice of golf collapsing around me and the marshmallow rising fast. Golf is based on the central tenet of faith that if you hit, say, a 7-iron perfectly the ball will fly straight and plop down 150 yards away. Now I had absolute proof that even if I hit the ball perfectly it might pitch anywhere between 135 and 165 yards away, and in goodness knows what direction.

It was small comfort to hear the Uniroyal man cheerfully call out that since they had put UCGBTD on public display all manu-facturers had tightened up on quality control and things were getting better.

I have tried playing golf once since that fearful revelation. My opening drive went deep into the left rough. Was it a rogue or was it too much right hand? I abandoned it and sliced a second. Me or it? Should I point the left shoulder a bit to the right or unwrap another pill? The game has become impossible. The marshmallow has reached the brain.

If, by some miracle, I should recover, I will recount to you the results of my experiments with golf balls and a billiards table, which prove that only one ball in a dozen is spherical and that putting is therefore totally impossible as well.

Observer, October 1977

Lastly The Caddie. Sans Teeth, Sans Eyes, Sans Everything!

Part Six

Deeming, Dropping and Devil Worship

A bemused fumble through the rules

Away with Three-Letter Words

Old Man Par may be a helluva player, good enough to earn $100,000 a year on the American PGA tour and win thirty-three US Open championships, but I would like to get him in a dark alley one night and club him to death with my mashie. I would use a gun except that I know my limitations when it comes to shooting Par.

We are all scared of this vicious old tyrant. He has put the whammy on all of us golfers, from the struggling hacker to the lordly champion. We are slaves to this evil brute, and my call to all golfers today is to rise up against the despot. We have nothing to lose but our chains.

Par works his insidious ways by hypnotic influence, brainwashing us to believe that under Par is good and over Par is bad. That state of mind is the worm in the golfing apple, the ruination of the game as an enjoyable exercise and as a professional sport.

Remember the last time you went out with card and pencil and ran up a 7 early in the round? Disaster! Tragedy!! Cataclysm!!! Right away you realized your chance of scoring well or winning the contest had vanished, and you shredded your card in rage and disappointment. The round was ruined, the day was ruined, and you might even have started an ulcer because of that 7.

The reason for this surge of bile in your vitals, which subsequently caused you to kick the dog, yell at the kids and have a fight with your wife, was that you were in the thrall of Par. You were relating your play of that hole to an arbitrary figure printed on a piece of pasteboard. If you had stopped to reflect that the hole was long and uphill, you were playing into a gale, conditions underfoot were heavy, the green was newly spiked for aeration and you were receiving a handicap stroke anyway, then the catastrophe would have loomed as no more than a rub of the green. Certainly nothing to get overheated about. But you were thinking of that smug old charlatan Par, and you felt inadequate, humiliated and emasculated.

Experienced tournament pros also fall for Par's sordid little scam. Observe them at Augusta, playing the fifth hole into the wind. This is a treacherous hole at the best of times, long enough at 450 yards, and you must run a narrow gauntlet between sand and rough to reach a switchback green that ought to be rated as a par-3 in itself if you are putting from the edge. Even the best of players can take a 6 without playing a poor shot. They do and you can see their knuckles whiten on the sixth tee as they determine a swift and spectacular revenge on Par. Once a golfer starts thinking those dangerous thoughts then Par has got him, sure as sure.

Why do we worship this blackhearted dictator? Who needs him? He performs no useful function in golf. He does not even have the respectability of antiquity. The ancients who shaped our game knew not Par. He is an upstart and his only contribution to the game today is to enable the TV companies to put up illiterate captions such as 'Putting for birdie'.

Once upon a time Par had a useful purpose by providing the basis for handicaps, and he proved so troublesome that he was replaced by the more rational course rating. As an Englishman I am not too well versed in the intricacies of course rating, since it is an American invention, but I have a definite idea how it ought to operate.

The system clearly demands a golf panel representing the entire spectrum of the game, and it might comprise the president of the USGA and one of his hit men, say Frank Hannigan; two wise and experienced players such as Gene Sarazen and Julius Boros; one enlightened layman to represent the noble army of hackers, a position for which I myself would be perfectly suited; plus female equivalents in each category, the candidates being selected for their wisdom, firm bosoms, golf skill, well-turned calves, logic, sculptured hips, intelligence and generous natures.

This panel would visit a different course each day, play a round of golf and then allot a course rating over a long and convivial luncheon. Such is my unselfish devotion to the ideal of public service that I am prepared to drop everything and join such a panel the minute I get my letter of appointment. Sadly, knowing the USGA, I suspect that course ratings are prepared by feeding aerial photographs into a $10-million computer. All the poetry is disappearing from life these days.

Either way, Par is obsolete. He is discredited as a handicapper, and a menace as the arbiter of how many strokes should be needed on an individual hole. Away with him, I say and, while we are at it, let us shoo away that motley collection of feathered freaks we call birdies and eagles and albatrosses. They are all irrelevant; all that matters is the final counting at the end of the round.

The only reason golf needs a hole-by-hole rating is to provide a basis for that most splendid form of golf, the Stableford, in which a net score of one over par earns one point, a net par two points and a net birdie three points. Should we allow Par to retain this last shred of authority? I am against it. Let us instead call back from retirement that fine character, Colonel Bogey, a figure in a First World War soldiers' song who later became the golfer's mythical adversary, i.e. the bogey was the number of strokes in which a good player was expected to play a hole. What we would term a long par-4 today was treated as a 5 by Colonel Bogey, which may have been the origin of the American term 'bogey', which means one over par. The Colonel did not hit the ball all that far ('Arthritis, you know'), but he was deadly straight and never 3-putted. I see him as a bonhomous figure in shapeless tweeds with a powerful bouquet of whisky on his breath.

He is generous and fair. 'Took one more stroke than old Bogey, did you? Give yourself a point with my compliments, laddie. Beat me by a stroke on that hole? Splendid, that's three points.' Bogey is the kind of person we need in golf. We can live with course rating. But as for that three-letter-man Par, the game can well do without him.

Golf Digest, May 1980

What Is a Stroke? _____ 1

Since golf is a game in which the winner is the player who takes the fewest number of strokes, it is important that we all understand exactly what is meant by a stroke.

Smart Alec: For goodness sake! Everybody knows what a stroke is. It's when you hit the ball.
Devil's Advocate: What if you miss the ball?
S.A.: That's a whiff, or air shot, and that's a stroke, too.
D.A.: But a practice swing is not a stroke.
S.A.: No, because in that case you are not trying to hit the ball. There has to be an intention. Let me read you the official definition: 'A stroke is the forward movement of the club made with the intention of fairly striking at and moving the ball.'
D.A.: I see. So the stroke does not begin until the club starts to move forward?
S.A.: Exactly. That's why you can stop and start again if you are disturbed at the top of your backswing.
D.A.: Wait a minute. There are two forward movements of the club during the swing. As you complete the backswing the club is moving forward toward the target. Then it moves backward, away from the target, at the start of the downswing. It does not move forward again until the hands are hip-high on the downswing. So where does the stroke begin?
S.A.: It is generally accepted that the stroke starts with the beginning of the downswing.
D.A.: So when the definition says 'forward' it really means to say 'the precise moment when the club has ceased to move forward and is about to move backward for the second time since the address position?'
S.A.: You're nit-picking, but that's about the size of it. Anyway, what does it matter?
D.A.: Well, it matters for two reasons. First, the USGA insists that in the rules every word means what it says. Now if the USGA means what it says when it says that every word means what it says, then it is

unfortunate that it uses the word 'forward' when it means 'backward', or possibly 'downward'. Second, it is critical to establish exactly when a stroke begins. As you know, if a ball falls off its tee before a stroke is made, it can be reteed without penalty. But if a stroke is made in such circumstances, then that stroke must count.

S.A.: In that case, we must accept that a stroke has been made once the downswing has begun.

D.A.: Right. It would be wildly impractical to try to measure the moment when the club starts moving forward halfway through the downswing. But in a recent case a player saw his ball topple off the tee just as he was starting to move his club backward – or forward as the USGA describes it.

S.A.: So the stroke had to count.

D.A.: Not at all. The player claimed that he aborted his intention to strike the ball as soon as he saw it fall, therefore it was not a stroke within the meaning of the rules. The USGA upheld his claim and published a Decision to that effect.

S.A.: Is that true?

D.A.: Absolutely. I swear it.

S.A.: But even if he moved the club only one-hundredth of an inch forward – or backward if you are going to be pedantic – and then aborted his intention, he still had made a stroke. After all, his intention was there during that hundredth of an inch. We all have that intention right from the instant we start the takeaway.

D.A.: I could not have put it better myself.

S.A.: But that Decision makes nonsense of the definition of a stroke.

D.A.: The definition was nonsensical anyway. We have been through all that.

S.A.: Still, that Decision has all the force of a Rule of Golf. I am beginning to get an idea.

D.A.: Tell me more.

S.A.: Well, like most high-handicap players, I have a pretty good idea that the stroke has gone haywire even before the clubface meets the ball. I get that Oh-my-God-I've-come-across-it feeling.

D.A.: Me too. Indeed, I've incorporated a shout of 'Fore!' in my backswing, plus a yell of 'Oh, Hell!' as an integral part of my follow-through.

S.A.: But according to this Decision, I can abort my stroke as soon as I feel that I'm coming into the ball all wrong.

D.A.: So it would appear.

S.A.: And then, when I snap one into the water hazard, I can claim that I had not made a stroke.

235

D.A.: Always provided that you honestly did abort your intention before the club met the ball.

S.A.: Of course. It must be an honest abortion. Still, in such a case I would be perfectly entitled to play the shot over again.

D.A.: Over and over again until you hit one straight. That is the clear implication of the Decision.

S.A.: And then I could go on aborting my approach shots until I hit one close to the pin.

D.A.: A rule is a rule. You are entitled to use it to your advantage.

S.A.: Do you suppose I could abort the odd putt?

D.A.: Why not? It is a stroke within the definition. In fact, it is the only stroke within the definition, since it does start with a forward movement.

S.A.: If I aborted enough bad shots, I could go around in 65 every time.

D.A.: Only if you were playing in a competition where you could be sure that the officials knew the rules and were prepared to administer them fairly and without prejudice.

Smart Alec: You mean the US Open. You're right. I'll go out and win the Open.

Devil's Advocate: And the best of luck to you, sir

Golf Digest, January 1979

Burn Those Rakes

According to the official definition, a bunker is an area of bare ground, often a depression, which is usually covered with sand. This is rather like describing a nun as a naked woman who is usually covered in voluminous clothing. My point is that nowhere in the official literature of golf is there any explanation of the purpose of a bunker.

Purpose? Surely it is obvious. Bunkers were a natural feature of the land where Scots first started to play the game. Sheep cropping the grassy duneland scraped out depressions into which they could huddle for protection against the icy winds, and thus the main preoccupation of those early golfers, armed with nothing more suitable than shallow-faced wooden clubs, was to avoid these perilous pits.

As other courses were built inland these sandy scrapes were artificially created to copy the original coastal models. Their function, suggested by the official name of hazard, was to punish the player for a shot that strayed from the approved line – and who can doubt that in those early times the cost of recovery was usually one shot at least, often more.

Bunkers were therefore places to strike fear into the heart of the golfer, and for most of us incompetent boobies among the rank and file of golf that purpose survives all too well. Who among us has not lost his half-crown among a tumult of flying sand and expletives when the match seemed safely won?

But not the professionals. Ever since Gene Sarazen invented the broad-soled wedge and perfected the technique of modern sand play, these hazards have lost their terror for the pro. He marches into the trap with composure unruffled, shuffles his feet into position and flips the ball up to the flag stick almost every time. Lee Trevino casually holed a bunker shot to lay the foundations of an Open championship victory. Gary Player prefers his ball to lie in sand rather than in fluffy grass.

The rules of etiquette require us to smooth out holes in bunkers after our frenzied excavations, and nobody is more meticulous in this duty than the professional. By the same token, no one is more distraught on these odd occasions when his ball lies in a heel print. The eyes roll towards heaven in an extravagant pantomime of self-pity. Why me? Why *me*?

It is not unusual for professionals to make representations to tournament organizers if the bunkers are not in pristine condition, or if there is not a rake handily placed beside each trap. At the risk of alienating every professional in the world, I would like to suggest that the time has come for the powers-that-be to restore the original purpose of bunkers and put the fear back into them.

The only club I know which follows such a policy is Oakmont, near Pittsburgh, where they use a specially designed machine to plough the bunkers into nerve-jangling furrows.

Some clubs achieve the same effect by accident, such as Knole Park in Kent, where deer roam through the bunkers and the club officials have not been able to frame a suitable local rule to give relief from their footprints.

Peter Thomson, one of the very few professionals who is passionately concerned to preserve what he considers to be the essence of golf, believes that the rule of etiquette about smoothing bunkers should not only be repealed but reversed. Players should actually be forbidden to repair their footmarks; bunkers should be left as rough as possible so they would once more acquire the power to make the golfer quake with apprehension.

Perhaps some brave tournament sponsor might care to try the experiment. If that happens, I just hope that I am present to hear the wails of anguish.

Observer, June 1968

Count Your Stimps

How fast are the greens at your club? Swiftish? Like greased lino? Like putting on treacle tart? On the slow side? Middling?

Please, please, do not give me these tired old expressions based on fallible human judgements. This is 1978, the era of the silicon chip and the space shot. The day of the decimal is upon us. We must have facts, not opinions. Be precise. Slide rules, OK?

In the face of such a response you may well turn ugly and growl that the speed of a green is ephemeral and personal and highly subjective, with one man's swiftish being another man's middling-slow. As well, you could argue, seek to measure in thermal units the warmth of a baby's smile, or gauge the radiance of a butterfly's wing. Some things, like weighing a sack of potatoes, may well be amenable to scientific measurement, but the speed of a green is within the domain of the poet who scorns calibration even though he may express himself in metric feet.

To all of which I reply quite simply: 'Nerts.' And you for your part assume a tone of scorn in your response: 'All right, smarty, how fast are the greens at *your* club?'

The answer is that at this time of year they putt at 5.92 stimps, and if you will raise your head from your hands and cease that groaning I will explain about those stimps.

Forty years ago a certain Mr Edward S. Stimpson invented a device for measuring the speed of greens. Like Leonardo Da Vinci and Copernicus and many another inventive genius, this Stimpson was ahead of his time. The world of golf took one look at his device and yawned.

Lately the United States Golf Association took another look at the thing, improved it, and, even as I write, Stimpmeters are being dispatched in their hundreds to golf clubs all over the United States. The improved Stimpmeter consists of a yard of V-form aluminium bar one and a half inches wide and has a notch near one end.

To operate the Stimpmeter, you find a fairly level area of green and rest the plain, or non-notched, end of the device on the grass, holding the other end about six inches above the turf. Now you place a ball in the notch and slowly raise the end of the Stimpmeter. At a certain height the ball will roll out of its notch, down the groove and along the grass. You measure the distance it rolls from the end of the Stimpmeter and repeat the process twice more, giving you three readings. Now you switch positions and roll three balls down the Stimpmeter in the opposite direction. The average of these six readings is the stimp measurement.

Many will surely point out that you could obtain exactly the same effect by getting down on all fours and pushing a pea with your nose to and fro across the green, always provided that you enlisted the wonders of microtechnology and fitted a tiny pressure gauge to the tip of your proboscis.

So you could, but I must ask you to keep any such frivolous ideas to yourself because this is a serious scientific study which could well result in lower scores for all of us.

Course superintendents can use the Stimpmeter to eliminate the variation of speeds between one green and another. By adjusting the amount of watering, or the height of his mower blades, he can now produce eighteen greens of uniform speed.

As we all know, the problem in putting is mainly one of judging distance rather than direction, and if every green has the same stimp value then half the battle is won, given that we are smart enough to notice when we have a downhill putt. The USGA uses Stimpmeters in preparing the course for the US Open championship – of course.

You are not convinced, I can tell. Sceptical vibes are flooding in so strongly they are making my coffee cup dance in its saucer. Very well, be like that. Stick with your hit-or-miss methods of guessing how fast a green will putt by looking for grain and feeling the give in the turf under your toes and noticing if the particular green is in perpetual shade and therefore liable to putt slower than the others. Use your instincts. Fly by the seat of your pants. But just don't whine when we scientific golfers beat those pants off you.

For myself, I welcome scientific progress in the game. It would not surprise me to learn that even now men in white coats are fitting minute strain gauges to individual blades of grass in order to produce rough of uniform tenacity.

As for my 5.92 stimps, you may be interested to know that this figure represents what Willie Park would have called 'Slowish'. Bobby Locke would have called 8.5 'Fast' and I hate to imagine how Bob Charles would describe 4.5 stimp-feet. What a pity they did not have our modern advantages; they might have become quite good putters.

Observer, October 1978

Some Innocents Must Suffer _____ ⌐|

The doctrine of the greatest good for the greatest number is rough on minorities. Take the case of the television family's little Jimmy Osmond, who clearly has to be sacrificed for the sake of society. When they slip the pill into his ice-cream soda and he feels the approach of eternal sleep he will doubtless ask, 'Why me? What have I done wrong?'

Hopefully, some humane person will be on hand to explain, 'Nothing, that is the point. Quite the opposite, you are too good, too wholesome, too winning, too cheerful, too cute and your teeth are too damn straight. Worse, it is not an act. Everyone realizes that you are just as cute and wholesome off-stage. We have an idea that Donny and Marie might be secret glue-sniffers so they are getting off with life imprisonment, but you have got to go.

'You see, all over the world people watch you perform and slowly that mawkish wholesomeness pouring in electronic waves from the TV screen turns the viewer's cerebral cortex into marshmallow. Millions upon millions are being transformed into mushy-brained zombies. The human race is in danger. That is why you must be martyred, not because of your guilt but because of your excessive innocence.'

By the same token, some innocent golfers have to be put down for the sake of the greater good. The golfer, by definition, is an honourable man. He is honest, for this self-regulating game can only be played on trust. He is courteous and considerate, since these virtues are demanded by the laws of etiquette. Most likely he is also a good husband and father, kind to animals, a regular churchgoer and given to works of charity.

Such are the men under sentence of martyrdom. They must be eliminated for one reason: because THEY SHOUT ON THE GOLF COURSE.

Shouters are a curse and an abomination. For the purposes of the bill, which United States Golf Association President Sandy Tatum will surely rush through the golfing legislature, the term 'shout' shall be deemed to include whooping, hollering, bellowing, yelling and other audio-disturbances likely to distress players on adjacent fairways.

Often enough, the unseemly din is well intentioned. As an opponent's drive heads inexorably towards the woods, the kindly golfer screams, 'Hook, baby. Hook!' By this means he proclaims his friendly and sporting nature. Unfortunately, he proclaims it with such vehemence that a third party, crouched over a putt half a mile away, is so startled that his tense frame is seized by a violent spasm, causing him to send his ball scooting past the hole and very possibly into a bunker.

No court in any civilized land (i.e. where golf is played) would convict, if this injured party were to descend upon the culprit and beat him repeatedly over the head with his putter. 'In all my years on the bench,' a judge will say, 'I have never come across a clearer case of justifiable homicide. You are free to go.'

However, we cannot have unbridled carnage on our golf courses. The blood would play hell with the greens. Besides, every man has the right to a fair trial. Most nations have it written into the constitution, in effect, that every thoughtless, loud-mouthed fink is innocent until proved to be a thoughtless, loud-mouthed fink.

Every golf club will be empowered to set up a properly constituted kangaroo court in the locker room. Any member who has been fingered for violating the decibel limit shall be called to book and, unless he can actually show the court the hornet sting or similar proof of extreme provocation, he shall be soundly lashed with wet towels and warned as to his future conduct.

On a second conviction he shall be taken from the court, cast into the deepest pot bunker on the course and stoned with 100 compression balls. Humanitarians may raise their eyebrows in alarm at this proposal, knowing that at a club such as Burning Tree on any average Sunday half the Cabinet and many important captains of industry give offence to such a degree as would put their lives at risk.

In practice, once word of the first executions begins to get around, the deterrent effect will be immediate. Habitual whoopers and yellers will quickly find that golf is possible, with no loss of enjoyment, when played at normal conversational volume. As for those occasions which we all experience, when only a timely profanity can save a man's sanity, we will learn that the remedial properties of an oath are not diminished if uttered sotto voce.

Perhaps we could start by making an example of some well-known tournament pros – goodness knows, there are plenty of shouters among them – and have the TV cameras cover the grim punishment.

Of course, women will be exempt from the provisions of this law for the very good reason that, no matter how severe the threat of retribution, no woman could prevent herself from squealing, giggling or caterwauling for the five hours it takes to play a round of golf.

The solution in their case is a compulsory gag, available in pretty pastel shades, to be fitted before they are allowed on the first tee, and so designed that only a special electronic beam will release the device as the wearer passes through the soundproof door of the women's locker room on her return from the course.

Golf Digest, July 1978

The Trick Is not to Bleed

What is sportsmanship, anyway? Good manners (of which I approve) are a part of it. Good form (of which I am suspicious) is another part. Hypocrisy is a major element. As an ethical concept the combination is far from suitable for the players of games and it is interesting that the most successful of all games – soccer, in which fouls are used tactically – has dispensed with it almost entirely.

However, public comment on gamesmanship, rulesmanship, sportsmanship and bloody-minded-manship has dragged golf into the arena of discussion. Writer Anne Scott-James, for instance, in the course of pleading that skills at cheating are too valuable to waste on games and should be reserved for world affairs, quoted some examples from the golf course.

'The killer player,' she wrote, 'can ask his caddie loudly for a six-iron and then take out a five-iron, confusing his opponent. Or say falsely: "This is a hole where you must hit two good shots to get in," so the other man ends up in the next county.'

Really! The only effect of these ploys would be to convince the intended victim that he was playing a halfwit. The gamesmanship of golf is a matter of infinite subtlety and when practised by a master the loser does not even realize he has been conned out of the match.

A certain amount of psychological warfare is permissible. Any experienced professional, when playing against someone who wants to hurry, will automatically take things at a leisurely pace. Equally he will become taciturn when playing a chatterbox. These are legitimate tactics, necessary to preserve a player's tempo and not primarily designed to upset the other man.

Nobody should be disturbed by gambits of this elementary nature. The real dangers of the psyche are more insidious. On the tee, for example, it is important to suppress any hint of satisfaction at having hit a good drive. Faced with the evidence of a grunt of ecstacy, or a smug holding of the follow-through position for a moment too long, the gamesman opponent will know your weakness. He will then risk rupture to outdrive you and, having done so, has as good as won the

244

match with this one shot. Your injured pride will urge you to put everything into your next shot, and he, noting your ball sail away into the trees, will hit a steady one with his five-iron.

A favourite time to impose this sort of pressure is when both balls are just off the fairway and he, the killer-golfer, has to play first. He takes out his 4-wood and walks forward a little way to survey the land. As he walks back he glances down to see how your ball is lying. He then puts the 4-wood back in his bag, selects a wedge and chips his ball out sideways onto the fairway. The subconscious trap is set. 'So he believes I can't hit the green from here,' you think. 'I'll show him.' This is exactly what he intended you to think. In that frame of mind there's an excellent chance of your fluffing your ball farther into the rough while he, nicely on the fairway, has an easy shot.

Possibly the most fruitful area for slipping a grain of irritant into the sensitive mechanism of a golfer's concentration is the matter of asking him to sink a short putt. Until I actually heard it, I would not have thought it possible to speak the words, 'Just pop that one in, old boy,' with such cunning inflexion that it conveyed the message: 'Please, God, help me keep a straight face when he twitches this one past the hole.'

Another method is to say nothing but simply turn away and start strolling towards the next tee. How do you interpret this action? An unspoken concession? Or did he mean you to sink it? In this moment of ambiguity you tap at this tiny, formality of a putt, your putter blade digs into the turf behind the ball and it stops on the brink. 'Oh, what bad luck!' His condolences sound only slightly too sincere to be sincere.

The highest form of psychological by-play has nothing to do with putting your opponent off his stroke; it is a game of concealing all signs of emotional turbulence, of watching for evidence that he is beginning to crack and drawing inspiration from it.

The all-time virtuoso of dead-pan golf was the South African, Bobby Locke. He had the reputation of being entirely devoid of nerves, but this does him less than justice. He suffered the same agonies as anyone else but concealed them beneath a demeanour which has been described as like that of an archbishop's butler and becoming, in the moment of victory, like the archbishop himself.

Locke's majestic progress round a golf course was the result of a lesson he learned early in his career. At the age of seventeen he was playing in the semifinal of the Transvaal amateur championship and stood 4 down with six to play. At the thirteenth hole Locke holed a long putt and noticed that his opponent turned pale and walked much faster to the next tee. The result was a bad drive and Locke ultimately won

245

the match.

In his book, *On Golf*, Locke describes how he turned this incident over in his mind many times and evolved his philosophy of watching his opponent's – and concealing his own – reactions. 'My opponents never know when I am on the defensive. Golf, I can assure you, is not all attack. Tactics enter into it, but only I know what is going on in my mind.'

Every trick has been tried at one time or another to disturb Locke's composure. He has been insulted, needled, flattered, out-driven and out-putted, but nothing has ever succeeded in forcing him to vary his deliberate routine on the course.

This facility for negative reaction is, to my mind, the ultimate in gamesmanship. For if an opponent gets the feeling you just aren't human it is but a short step to convincing him that you are invincible. Everyone gets wounded in a game of golf. The trick is not to bleed.

Observer, September 1967

Foxed by a Rule

The time is June of 1981. The place is Merion Golf Club. Heavy rain, I regret to reveal, has reduced those famous fairways to mush and after several suspensions of play we are at last ready to hail a new US Open Champion. Who is he? I shall not spoil your enjoyment of the championship by revealing his name and will merely say that he is a worthy young man, a fine player who has been a professional for five years, four of them as a college student.

The moment of which I write is after he has hit a superb drive down the eighteenth, needing a 5 to win, and is walking up to his ball. Naturally he is accompanied by a rules official of the United States Golf Association. For convenience we may refer to these two principal characters as Player and Referee.

Player (observing the top of his ball, which has sunk into a deep crater of mud): Plugged ball in fairway. Free drop, OK?
Referee: I presume you mean: ball embedded in its own pitch mark in a closely mown area through the green.
Player: Sure.
Referee: It is a useful habit to cultivate, when talking of rules, to employ the correct nomenclature. The word fairway does not exist in the Rules of Golf.
Player: But this is a closely mown area through the green, isn't it?
Referee: Most certainly.
Player: So I get a free drop?
Referee (wincing visibly): The rules make no mention of the expression 'Free drop.' Under Rule 16-2 your ball may be lifted and dropped without penalty.
Player: Terrific. (*The player lifts his ball and drops it. The ball comes to rest six inches behind the pitch mark.*)
Player: Is that OK by you?
Referee: I must warn you that if you play your ball from there I shall be forced to penalize you two strokes for failing to comply with the procedure of Rule 16.

247

Player: How come?

Referee: You have elected to take relief under Rule 16, which states quite clearly that the ball must be dropped *as near as possible* to the spot where it lay. Your ball is a full six inches from the spot where it lay. Clearly it is *possible* to drop it nearer than that. It is possible to drop it five inches away. Or four inches. Remember that in the Rules of Golf every word means what it says. We have a note in the preamble to the rules to stress that very point, in case anyone had the idea that we intended the words to mean something different from what they say.

Player: You want me to redrop? You know – Rule 22.

Referee: Quite impossible, young man. Allow me to draw your attention to the detailed provisions of Rule 22-2c: If a dropped ball rolls into a hazard, onto a putting green, out of bounds or more than two club-lengths from the point where it first struck the ground, or comes to rest nearer the hole than its original position, it shall be redropped without penalty. Your ball did none of those things. It simply fell plop in the mud and stayed there. There is no provision in 22-2c for a redrop for a ball that plops in the mud.

Player: So what do you want me to do?

Referee: Let me see if I can resolve your dilemma by consulting with my colleagues. *(He speaks into his walkie-talkie and men in blue blazers converge in droves, waving rule books. They huddle in deep consultation. The referee turns back to the player and continues.)* You're in luck. Since you did not drop your ball as near as possible to the place where it lay it has been ruled that you dropped in a wrong place. Therefore you may have another drop under Rule 22-5a. *(The player lifts his ball and redrops. This time it comes to rest two inches from the pitch mark.)*

Player: How's that. That's as close as humanly practicable to drop it.

Referee: If the legislators meant that you must drop the ball as near as humanly practicable to the place where it lay then they would have framed the rule in those terms. They are precise men with precise legal minds and if they say as near as *possible* that is exactly what they mean.

Player: Are you saying that I still can't play the ball?

Referee: Of course you cannot. That was a really splendid effort, to drop within two inches of the spot where your ball originally lay, but it is not as near as *possible*. You must see that.

Player: I have to drop again?

Referee: Dear me, no. That would never do. You have had two drops and both times you have dropped in a wrong place. Now you have to *place* the ball.

Player: Will you tell me exactly where I must place the ball?
Referee: Of course. You must place it as near as possible to the spot where it lay. *(The player picks up his ball and gingerly balances it on the edge of his pitch mark.)*
Player: How's that?
Referee: That is not as near as possible. Don't forget that the ball lay right in that pitch mark.
Player: Are you telling me that I've got to put it back in its plug mark?
Referee: I am not telling you; that is what the rule is telling you. *(The player places the ball in the plug mark.)*
Player: Now are you satisfied?
Referee: It originally lay right down deep in that plug mark. You could only just see the top of the ball. To get it back as near as possible to where it lay you must press it down harder. After all, you don't want to win the championship by bending the rules, by giving yourself a better lie than the rules entitle you to, do you?
Player: Very well. How's *this*? (He stuffs the ball deep into its original plug mark.)
Referee: Perfect. You have now followed the procedure of Rule 16-2 to the letter and are free to continue play without penalty.

The end of this story is almost too harrowing to relate. The player blasted his plugged ball clear with a mighty smash of his sand-iron. The ball rose high in the air and buried up to its waist on the fairway some thirty-five yards nearer the hole. Not daring to risk another ruling, he tried to force the ball forward with his 3-iron but he dug too deeply into the squelching turf and the shot was smothered. He finally holed out for a 7 and was seen late that night reeling through the quiet streets of Ardmore, Pa, clutching a bottle of Ol' Red-Eye, finest Kentucky knee-walking bourbon, and muttering, 'Don't talk to me about Catch-22. It's a cinch compared to 16-2.'

Golf Digest, October 1980

Legitimate at Last

Be it known that from this day henceforth I am available for selection to play in the Walker Cup match.

All my adult life I have been haunted by a recurring nightmare. The two teams are parading for the flag-raising ceremony. The pipe band of the Sheboygan (Local 517) Teamsters Union is waiting, elbows aquiver, to launch into *God Save the Queen*. Suddenly a member of the British team clasps his stomach and subsides to the ground with a groan.

Then another goes down. Three, four ... five! Some dread epidemic is decimating the ranks of the British linksmen, probably coffee narcosis. Consternation. Hurried conference. The British captain announces that of course the match must go on. He strolls over to me and smiles urbanely. 'I say, old boy, do you think you could borrow a pair of spikes and some sticks from the pro shop – you're playing top for Britain in ten minutes.'

Something much like this actually happened to Bernard Darwin, the golf correspondent of *The Times*, and he went out and duly won his match in true *Boy's Own Paper* tradition. Darwin was a good player, though.

For five years, just in case, I immersed myself in a thorough study of the Rules of Golf, and at the end of that time I could guarantee to win six holes in a match. I perfected, for instance, a square cut in which the toe of the driver just shaved the ball, propelling it violently at a tangent against the shin of my opponent (loss of hole, Rule 26-2b), and a range of innocent remarks such as: 'Extraordinary how a dip in the ground foreshortens the view,' designed to provoke the response: 'Do you think a five-iron is too much?' (Seeking advice, loss of hole, Rule 9-1a).

By now I had worked my way through to Rule 41 and had armed myself with a micro-gauge ('Mind if I just take a peep at the grooves on your wedge, my friend?') and was well into the Appendices.

Then I discovered the Rules of Amateur status and my plan collapsed. Being of an essentially honest and sporting character, I realized instantly that I was not eligible for the Walker Cup team. Accepting golf equipment without payment ... permitting my likeness (a moot point, that) to be used publicly ... receiving expenses ... giving golf instruction. I would just have to tell the captain: 'Sorry, skipper, I am disqualified as an amateur; you will have to settle for Donald Steel of the *Sunday Telegraph*.'

Now, as from 1 April (1978), (the choice of that date could hardly be more appropriate for announcements from the Amateur Status Committee), all is changed. An amateur may now be employed in the sale of golf merchandize. An amateur may also receive free equipment provided no advertising is involved. The United States Golf Association has declined to go along with this amendment all the way.

The American legislators have thrust their heads deep into the sand and issued an edict to the effect that, if you are the type of player to whom manufacturers would like to give free equipment (i.e. an accomplished golfer who needs clubs, balls, etc., in order to compete), then such gifts are forbidden. However, if you are a hopeless golfer, such as no manufacturer in his right mind would dream of assisting, then you can take all the freebies you can get.

Under the revised regulations it will be much easier for a young golfer from a humble background to play his way to the top of amateur golf without cheating on the rules of amateur status. It is a pity about the Americans, though. Now, more than ever, the Walker Cup match will be contested between teams of golfers who are not eligible to play, according to the lights of the other side. It is rather like organizing a horse race and then having half the riders appear on camels while their opponents are mounted on giraffes.

As for myself, it is a relief to be legitimized after all these years as a golfing pariah and shunned as an outcast by amateurs and professionals alike. If the call comes I shall be ready to play for Britain, certain to go six up.

In the meantime, equipment manufacturers should note that they are perfectly entitled and with free conscience to shower me with clubs, bags, balls, cashmeres (no pastel shades, please, I am a primary colour man). Nor are American manufacturers banned from indulging in such munificence, for in no way could they be accused of jeopardizing my amateur status 'because of golf skill or reputation'. In an uncertain world that, alas, becomes surer every day.

Observer, April 1978

Deemed to Be Amateur

How often do you deem? Disregarding the example of lawyers (always a good principle) of throwing in the odd deem in order to sound as if they were providing value for their exorbitant fees, when did deeming fall from public favour? The word reeks of the 'Upstairs, Downstairs' world before the First World War. 'The master deemed his breakfast egg to be a few moments overdone, cook.' 'Oh, did 'e indeed, Mr 'Udson? Well, I deem the Master to be an old fusspot.'

Yet the official literature of golf still teems with deems. What other group of sportsmen would stand by having their balls deemed unplayable? Or deemed to have been struck by a club while moving a loose impediment? Or deemed to be out of bounds?

Now, after a lingering and painful obsolescence, another favourite golfing word has been overtaken by the pace of life. 'Amateur' has been dropped by cricket, tennis and soccer. It used to be a good word, as pure and unsullied as the condition it described. Then the International Olympic Committee robbed the fair amateur of her semantic virtue, leaving her a raddled slag of a word. Now no one has a good word for the good word, except golfers.

Amateur has long since lost its meaning. When John Ball, winner of eight British Amateurs and one Open, strode the fairways of Hoylake, amateur was at the height of her state of grace. Amateur was excellence; professional was a crass and inferior condition, not to be allowed into the clubhouse.

Today amateur means second-rate. We no longer have to qualify the word in such ways as 'thoroughly amateur' or 'amateurish' to imply a botched job. Amateur by itself will do. But the rulers of golf, who in no other respect resemble social workers rescuing fallen women, loyally support amateur and everything it used to imply. At a rate averaging better than one a week, failed professionals apply to the Royal and Ancient's amateur status committee for reinstatement as amateurs. (The number is much higher in America.)

Most of these people were an embarrassment to pro golf, goodness knows, but surely bankruptcy and shattered ambitions are punishment enough for regularly failing to break 80. Not at all. The governing bodies deem that these misfits be cast into limbo. During this probationary period they must not enter competitions as amateurs, or play on amateur teams, and they must get permission from their clubs to compete in purely club events. Finally, if they satisfy the Inquisition that they have not transgressed in the matter of playing for money, accepting prizes above a retail value of £50, lending their names for advertisements, making personal appearances, writing golf instructional articles, selling golf equipment, accepting gifts of equipment, or expenses, or free transport, or scholarships, or indulging in activities detrimental to the best interests of the game, or gambling heavily, they may be re-admitted to the kingdom of amateurism.

Now you may find all this highly admirable. It is certainly refreshing that *somebody* is really concerned these days to maintain standards, rather than undermine them. The vision of the R and A as a kind of latter-day Canute defying the oncoming waves of commercialism and moral laxity is not unattractive.

At least, it would be attractive if it were not for the ludicrous fact that its partner in the battle to preserve amateurism, the United States Golf Association, is working to a different set of Commandments. For the Walker Cup match it would be quite possible to produce two teams of amateurs who are patently not amateurs according to the rules of the other side.

For example, an American golf scholarship student wearing a $200 prize watch would be ineligible as an amateur under British rules on two counts. A British schoolmaster who taught golf to pupils for more than 10 per cent of his working life would not qualify under American regulations.

Now the Americans have widened the gulf even further. The Tournament Players' Division of the American PGA is to hold a qualifying school for embryo tournament players in June and the USGA has agreed that amateurs may enter, without risk to their status. Both sides pay token lip service to the rule that an amateur must not 'take any action for the purpose of becoming a professional golfer'. That rule, which used to read 'any action which clearly indicates *the intention* of becoming a professional golfer', still frightens British amateurs who are hoping for selection to international teams.

Yet in America a boy can get a university scholarship and take what is virtually a degree course in pro golf. And now he can sit the PGA's entrance examination without risk to his amateur status. Any reasonable man would deem such behaviour to make a mockery of the ban on 'any action for the purpose of becoming a professional golfer'.

253

So two sets of rules flourish. They are expressed in words which have either lost their meaning or whose meaning, although clear, is distorted to express something quite different. While the amateurs, shamateurs and semi professionals are competing for the Walker Cup, the rulers will be talking rules. The rest of us are at liberty to deem the impossible deem that they will abandon the untenable concept of amateurism entirely.

Golf World, May 1975

Commandments of Golf ⚑1

Picture, if you will, the children of Israel gathered at the foot of a mountain. The lone figure of Moses descends. He has an uneasy look about him. As he reaches his people, he lays down his burden of stone tablets and wipes his brow. One of the elders greets him. 'Is that all there is? Just ten rules?'

Moses shakes his head sadly. 'You've got to be kidding. This is just the index. I couldn't carry all those commandments, no way. You'd better yoke up fifty teams of oxen and fetch the rest down from the peak. Would you believe, there's a foreword; there's a twelve-paragraph section on etiquette; there are thirty-six definitions and forty-one rules; there's an appendix on local rules; there's an appendix on the design of clubs, with diagrams yet; there's an appendix on markings of clubs; there's an appendix on handicaps; there are forty-seven paragraphs on something called amateur status; and there's a policy statement on gambling. And you see that big mountain over there? Well, I've got news for you – that isn't a mountain at all; it's a pile of tablets on something called Decisions.'

The elder sighs deeply. 'But, Moses, our people will never be able to learn and follow such a mass of legislation.'

Moses, by this time in no mood for discussion, snaps back, 'Listen, you can't expect a simple code to cover all the complexities of life. You might get away with ten commandments to regulate a simple game, such as the one those herdsmen are playing over yonder with their crooks and balls of camel hide stuffed with feathers. But these are for all of life – and that is no game.'

Now, we cannot expect divine wisdom from the rulers of golf, but I do believe that we can reasonably ask for a vastly simplified set of rules. That view is reinforced by the latest batch of revisions, which were announced as an expression of the policy to make the rules as simple and concise as possible, but which actually complicate the game for those of us who have to learn them all over again.

Whenever the cry goes up for simpler rules of golf, the answer comes back that it is necessary to have a comprehensive set of regulations to

255

cover all the myriad situations that can arise on a golf course. After all, say the legislators, golfers are playing for important titles, and vast amounts of money, and therefore it is vital to have rules to cover every contingency.

That argument overlooks two pertinent facts: (1) ninety-nine out of 100 golfers are not playing for titles or money – they're playing for fun; (2) most of the complexities in the rules are needed because the aim is to provide a specific prohibition against every possibility that human ingenuity can devise to cheat. If you start with a rule that says, 'Thou shalt not cheat,' then the task of producing a simple set of rules becomes entirely possible.

Let us have a go at drafting Rule 1. 'Golf is a self-regulating game and can therefore be played only in a spirit of trust, honesty, sportsmanship and honour. Every rule must therefore be obeyed in the letter and the spirit, without seeking advantage from loopholes in the fine print. Anyone seeking to pull a fast one, or attempting to interpret the rules by the moral standards used by a secondhand car salesman in filling out his or her income tax return shall be disqualified.'

I admit that such a rule could be improved by polishing, but you get the general idea. Having established that preamble, rules such as 'You must play the ball as it lies' become simple. There is no need for reams of clauses and subclauses prohibiting improvements to the lie, or the line, or the stance. Everyone knows that such shenanigans are cheating and they would not try them.

Once the principle has been firmly established, the way is clear for immense carnage among the proliferating verbiage of the laws. And if the opportunity is taken to eliminate most of the esoteric rules, then by my reckoning you get down to, say, a dozen rules of golf.

Anyone ought to be able to grasp and remember ten or twelve simple rules. And because it is common experience that most breaches of law are through ignorance rather than evil intent, then the game would be instantly improved because there would be no ignorance.

There remains, of course, the odd 1 per cent of professionals and hot-shot amateurs who are engaged in life-and-death struggles for fame and fortune. They will claim that they must have every possibility covered in black and white in the rule book. Very well, let there be a comprehensive set of competition regulations, to be adopted as local rules for important events. Let them have their petty regulations defining what does or does not constitute damage to a golf ball to the extent that it may or may not be declared unfit for play. (You and I, in our basic code, will not change a ball during the play of a hole in any circumstances, unless possibly the thing shatters into pieces. We will know well enough when the spirit of golf demands that a ball be replaced.)

Am I chasing an impossible ideal? No matter how clear and concise the basic rules might be, there will always be borderline cases needing adjudication. Yes, indeed. In that event, I commend the policy of one club I know that has a winter rule allowing preferred lies on the fairway. Often enough a player will not be entirely sure whether his ball is on the fairway or a closely cropped area of semi-rough. The convention at this club is that if you are in doubt and ask your opponent whether you may improve the lie, then the answer has to be: 'No.'

Golf Digest, January 1980